How Firm a Foundation?

How Firm a Foundation?
*An Exegetical and Historical Critique of the
"Ethical Perspective of [Christian] Reconstructionism"
Presented in* Theonomy in Christian Ethics

TIMOTHY R. CUNNINGHAM

WIPF & STOCK · Eugene, Oregon

HOW FIRM A FOUNDATION?
An Exegetical and Historical Critique of the "Ethical Perspective of [Christian] Reconstructionism" Presented in *Theonomy in Christian Ethics*

Copyright © 2012 Timothy R. Cunningham. All rights reserved. Except for brief quotations in critical publications or reviews, no part of this book may be reproduced in any manner without prior written permission from the publisher. Write: Permissions, Wipf and Stock Publishers, 199 W. 8th Ave., Suite 3, Eugene, OR 97401.

Wipf and Stock
An Imprint of Wipf and Stock Publishers
199 W. 8th Ave., Suite 3
Eugene, OR 97401

www.wipfandstock.com

ISBN 13: 978-1-60899-461-8

Scripture quotations taken from the New American Standard Bible®, Copyright © 1960, 1962, 1963, 1968, 1971, 1972, 1973, 1975, 1977, 1995 by The Lockman Foundation. Used by permission. www.lockman.org

Scriptures taken from the Holy Bible, New International Version®, NIV®. Copyright © 1973, 1978, 1984, 2011 by Biblica, Inc.™ Used by permission. All rights reserved worldwide.

Material taken from *Theonomy*, by WILLIAM S. BARKER; W. ROBERT GODFREY. Copyright © 1990 by William S. Barker and W. Robert Godfrey. Used by permission of Zondervan. www.zondervan.com.

Material taken from *Theonomy in Christian Ethics*, by Greg L. Bahnsen. Copyright © 2002 The Bahnsen Family Trust used by permission of the publishers, Covenant Media Foundation.

Think not that I am come to destroy the law, or the prophets: I am not come to destroy, but to fulfill. For verily I say unto you, Till heaven and earth pass, one jot or one tittle shall in no wise pass from the law, till all be fulfilled. Whosoever therefore shall break one of these least commandments, and shall teach men so, he shall be called the least in the kingdom of heaven: but whosoever shall do and teach them, the same shall be called great in the kingdom of heaven.
—Matthew 5:17–19 KJV

In all of its minute detail, (every jot and tittle) the law of God down to its least significant provision should be reckoned to have an abiding validity—until and unless the Lawgiver reveals otherwise.
—*Greg L. Bahnsen*

We conceive, the whole bulk of the judicial law, as judicial, and as it concerned the Republic of the Jews only, is abolished, though the moral equity of all those be not abolished . . . [but that] a judicial, not a ceremonial law . . . should be perpetual because Christ in particular hath not abolished it, to me seems most unjust.
—*Samuel Rutherford*

Contents

Preface • ix

1 The "Theonomy Debate" and Why It Matters • 1
2 The Scriptural Foundation for the Theonomic Hermeneutic • 28
3 Is Christ "Confirming" or "Completing" the Law? Matthew 5:17 • 42
4 When Will the Law Disappear? Matthew 5:18 • 105
5 Christ Applies His Teaching: Matthew 5:19–20 • 129
6 Reformed History and Theonomy • 133
7 Theonomy and Legal Practice: One Practical Problem • 183

Bibliography • 187
General Index • 195
Names Index • 197
Scripture Index • 199

Preface

The psalmist cries "O how I love Thy law!" (Ps 119:97a). In the more than thirty years since coming to Christ while a high school student, I have echoed that cry many times. Converted in a church where the pastor taught us to read the entire Bible systematically, I was soon attracted by the simple justice and sheer *rightness* of the civil stipulations God laid down for Israel. From these laws I learned many things about my heavenly Father: what he takes joy in and what he detests. Often, as I contemplated yet another injustice of this evil age, I have rejoiced in prayer that "righteousness and justice are the foundation of [Your] throne" (Ps 97:2). This love for God's judicial laws led to an eagerness to see them rightly applied in modern states—an eagerness that was only strengthened when, in the late 1990s, Canada saw three notorious murder convictions (the Marshall, Morin, and Milgaard cases) rightly reversed–and the reversals in two of these cases were significantly affected by the difference between Canadian and Mosaic laws at one key point. More recently the reversal in the equally notorious Steven Truscott case effectively drew attention to the same point.

It was just before the turn of the millennium when I first encountered the late Greg Bahnsen's remarkable book *Theonomy in Christian Ethics*. As I studied this lengthy book, I recognized the tremendous amount of research and background reading Bahnsen had done to support his thesis. I also appreciated the forethought that he put into countering objections, and the thoroughness with which he had worked through the implications of his thesis. Most important, I agreed with Bahnsen then, and I agree with him now, about the importance of his subject. God's civil laws, although first given to regulate a covenant relationship between God and Israel that no longer exists, are *righteous* responses to evil in the world, and as such, they still have much to teach us. Both Bahnsen and I agree that the world will be greatly blessed wherever its magistrates rightly apply the blessings of God's civil stipulations to the judicial practices of modern states, a blessing that comes into particularly sharp relief when one considers the injustices too often perpetrated when laws are not informed by the Sinaitic statutes.

As I read *Theonomy*, I realized that the heart of Bahnsen's thesis was a rationale for applying the Mosaic judicial laws today. With that realization, I began to wonder whether *Theonomy*'s teaching on the contemporary applicability of the Mosaic civil laws might be the blueprint evangelical Christians needed to guide their return to political involvement. Only two steps remained: I needed to check Bahnsen's work against Scripture and against the testimony of church history. For even though rightly applying God's civil stipulations in modern states is an important blessing, I knew that we must give careful consideration to the rationale we propose for so doing. If our rationale is biblical, we can expect God to bless it; if it is confessional, we may safely reintroduce the idea that the Mosaic judicial laws have a role to play in the contemporary political process without starting a civil war in the churches. But if our rationale is not biblical, God will not bless it, for "let us do evil that good may come" is not a methodology that Scripture favors. And if Bahnsen's rationale for Theonomic ethics is unconfessional, introducing it will divide Christians and weaken our testimony to the world until the dispute is resolved. Only if our rationale for instituting the Mosaic judicials is both biblical and confessional would such a division be justified.

As I tested Bahnsen's proposed Theonomic justification for instituting God's civil stipulations today against Scripture and Christian history, I discovered significant problems with his thesis. In particular, I discovered that Bahnsen's analysis of the crucial passage Matthew 5:17–19 is simply untenable: in that passage Christ does not teach what Bahnsen thinks he does. When I turned to study how Protestants have historically justified the Mosaic judicial laws' applicability in New Covenant–era states, it became apparent that Bahnsen's reading of the Westminster Confession of Faith on this point (as well as his understanding of many of its authors' views) was also incorrect. Since his justification for instituting the Mosaic stipulations is neither scriptural nor confessional, it should be rejected by Christians in favor of a biblical and confessional approach. But when I also discovered that comprehensive refutations of Bahnsen's errors were not widely known and that many of his admirers were using the Internet to spread his views unchallenged, it became clear that this book needed to be written.

Some of Bahnsen's early critics clearly misunderstood him at a number of points. In an attempt to avoid falling into similar errors, I engaged in extended debate with some students of Bahnsen's approach. I am particularly grateful to Matt Doyle, to whom I owe my introduction to Bahnsen's work, and to Glenn Peoples, whose comments led to a major reorganization in the flow of the argument. I thank Colin Tayler, Mike Warren, Hermonta Goodwin, Jacob Aitken, and Martin Foulner: our interactions over the last ten years have made this a better book. In addition, I invited three of Bahnsen's very close followers to act as pre-publication reviewers of this book and I deeply regret that they were unable to accept my invitation. The assistance of Bahnsen students Dr. Kenneth Gentry and Rev. Christopher Strevel and Bahnsen's publisher, Dr. Gary North would have been invaluable in finding any errors that may have survived my attempt to read Bahnsen's work with an unbiased eye.

There are many others who deserve thanks for influencing this project, but only a few can be mentioned. High school teacher Shirley Sage gave a thirsty high school student "a cup of cold water" and introduced me to the Reverend James McAllister, through whom God implanted three rock-solid convictions: that all Scripture is God's Word; that all of it must be read, understood, and lived out; and that Christians must test everything they learn in the realm of theology against Scripture. Dr. J. I. Packer's *Knowing God* introduced me to reformation theology, helped me hold on to Christ while passing through a very dark time, and led to my studies at Regent College. At Regent, Dr. Gordon Fee's exemplary teaching of Biblical exegesis gave me the tools to undertake the project; some years later Dr. Don Lewis confirmed my then-uninformed hunch that the debate over Bahnsen's Theonomic vision was an important issue, even if the topic was unknown to our immediate ecclesiastical circles. His offer to publish an article on the topic in *Crux*, the Regent theological journal, was the final push I needed to start writing. At Vancouver's First Baptist Church, the late Dr. Stanley Grenz, fellow brass player, theologian, and friend, generously took time from his impossibly busy schedule to read the rough draft and told me that my years away from the academy had not dulled whatever writing skills I may possess. I am grateful for the memory of his encouragement to complete the project.

It is hard to find fitting words to thank Margaret, my treasure of a wife, who has shared the first decade of our marriage with the writing of this book. While simultaneously working full time as a teacher of nursing, writing her master's thesis, and coping with serious health challenges, Margaret frequently reminded her too-often preoccupied husband that correct doctrine is useless unless it leads to that godly and joyous living in God's grace that she so often exemplifies. I have tried to take her example to heart as the work progressed.

All the thanks in the universe will not suffice to thank the Lord Jesus Christ, who loved us and released us from our sins by his blood— to him be the glory and dominion forever. As I send this book forth, I pray that it will encourage its readers to rightly apply his ways to the political questions that challenge us as citizens and voters.

1

The Theonomy Debate and Why It Matters

THE WORD *THEONOMY* DERIVES from the Greek words *theos* (God) and *nomos* (law). Until recently, it has been used to categorize various views that see God as the source of ethics: using *theonomy* in this sense, Cornelius Van Til recognized that there "is no alternative but that of theonomy or autonomy."[1]

Individual views within the category differ, however, in a number of ways, one of which is their conceptions of exactly how the Bible is meant to function as the source of civil ethics today. At one end of the theonomy spectrum is Tillich's existential encounter between an individual and a moral principle, an encounter that cannot be generalized to serve as the basis for state law. Next in line is the Dispensationalist argument that all of the Old Testament Mosaic law (Genesis to Deuteronomy) is irrelevant today unless particular stipulations stated there are reiterated in the New Testament. After that, we find the view put forward by Calvin and followed by the Westminster Confession of Faith (WCF), which posits that particular Mosaic civil laws may or may not apply today depending on whether the specific principle of justice underlying them may be justly applied the same way in the New Covenant era as it was in the Old. (Although the "intrusionist" ethic of Meredith Kline is popular among many Reformed preachers and teachers today, it seems to rest on a somewhat different foundation than the one the Divines employed).[2]

---

1. Van Til, *Christian Theistic Ethics*, 121. Since Van Til made his remark eighteen years before *Theonomy in Christian Ethics* was published, it is clear that Van Til meant theonomy in the sense of the category label rather than the specific ethical perspective later popularized by that book.

2. Kline, *Structure of Biblical Authority*, 158–59. Kline did not claim that the Mosaic judicial laws are entirely without relevance for present-day states. If any of his followers has made such a move, that view is clearly non-Confessional. For although the

Finally, one comes to the view that starts with the Calvin-Westminster continuity of the Mosaic judicial principles and adds to it the additional postulate that all Mosaic civil laws and punishments are also presumed to apply today, except where biblically amended by the Lawgiver. This view, "the ethical perspective of [Christian] 'Reconstructionism,'"[3] was best described and advocated by Greg Bahnsen, and over time it has also become known as Theonomy.[4]

From the Reformation to the present day, the Calvin-Westminster view has been the dominant Reformed perspective on how to apply the biblical civil laws to post-Sinai contexts, and some less formalized derivatives of it seem to undergird a great deal of contemporary evangelical political activism.

The last thirty years, however, have seen an ongoing debate between Christian Reconstructionists and those holding to the Calvin-Westminster view—a debate with implications that reach far beyond Reformed and Presbyterian circles. If Christian Reconstruction's ethical perspective is correct, it is not only Congregationalists and Baptists whose confessions follow the WCF at this point,[5] who must repent of their erroneous understanding of civil ethics and embrace the Reconstructionist ethical perspective. Since almost all Evangelical Christians—from Jim Wallace and *Sojourners* on the left to Christian

---

Westminster Divines held that the Mosaic laws expired with the Jewish state and no longer applied as a unified legal system, they recognized that some laws remain valid in the new era as far as their underlying general equity thereof "may require" and formulated their view as WCF 19:4. When Kline later claimed that WCF 19:4 was marked by "inadequacies and obscurities that mar the analysis of the law" (Kline, "Comments on an Old-New Error," n. 4), he failed to realize that way the Divines employed the term "general equity" in this clause enables believers to distinguish between the typological, non-permanent aspects and laws of the Mosaic covenant, which have expired with that covenant, and those aspects and laws that remain just today.

3. Bahnsen, *Theonomy*, xxiii.

4. While Bahnsen correctly denied that the "ethical perspective of Reconstructionism" was the only meaning carried by the term *theonomy* (Bahnsen, *Theonomy*, xxiii), it is unfortunate that neither he nor his critics coined another term for the Reconstructionist perspective. The ommission has often led to equivocation and misunderstanding in later discussions. In an attempt to minimize that problem, this book will capitalize *Theonomy* when referring to the ethical perspective of Christian Reconstructionism and will leave the first letter in lower case when referring to the category label. Quotations, however, will follow the spelling of the original writers.

5. These confessions are the Baptist Old London Confession and the Congregationalist Savoy Declaration of Faith.

"Tea Party" members on the right—use variants of the WCF principle to bring a biblical perspective to political activism, almost the entire American evangelical movement will find their views challenged, if not transformed, if the Reconstructionist ethical perspective is proven to be biblical. On the other hand, if the Calvin-Westminster view is correct, "the ethical perspective of Reconstructionism" must be abandoned.

There is no doubt that the Theonomy debate has been good for North American Christians; one writer has rightly said that if Theonomy "did not exist, someone would have to invent it."[6] When the debate began, many evangelical Christians were beginning to abandon their forefathers' unbiblical withdrawal from politics, and they needed a Christian perspective to guide their reentry into the political arena.[7] The debate that followed the appearance of Bahnsen's *Theonomy in Christian Ethics* focused much-needed attention on considerations of how and where the Mosaic laws should be applied today.[8] In addition, the Reconstructionist ethical perspective was and remains a timely reminder that the Mosaic civil laws must always be the starting point for Christian political thinking, even if some of them are no longer applicable.

While Christians should be grateful for these positive outcomes of the Theonomy debate, it also created serious adverse consequences, including an acrimonious tone in discussions within the American Reformed community[9] and a real increase in opposition to the gospel by outsiders.[10]

---

6. Davis, "A Challenge to Theonomy," 389.

7. In 1983, Christopher H. J. Wright observed that there "had been a long dearth of ethical engagement with the Old Testament. Cyril Rodd . . . in 1956 . . . was discouraged from any interest in the subject of Old Testament ethics on the ground that there was no future in it. In 1970 . . . nobody had written anything on it in English for fifty years. In 1973 . . . a distinguished German professor told me . . . 'the subject doesn't exist.'" Wright, *Old Testament Ethics*, 13.

8. "Such is the increased interest in the field [of Old Testament ethics] that, of the approximately four hundred titles in the bibliography of this revised and updated edition, almost 75% are dated between 1983 and the present" (Wright, *Old Testament Ethics*, 13–14). An examination of Wright's bibliography reveals that Bahnsen's *Theonomy* played a significant role in stimulating this discussion: many of the cited works react to *Theonomy*, some in considerable detail.

9. An infamous example is Gary North's likening of Bahnsen critic Meredith Kline to Bambi encountering Godzilla in his "Prologue" to *By This Standard*, xvii–xviii.

10. See, for example, Olson, "Invitation to a Stoning."

To avoid misunderstandings, it is best to begin by clarifying the key issue at the heart of the Theonomy debate. The debate is not about whether the entire Mosaic law continues to be valid today, unaffected by Christ's coming. Theonomists recognize that detailed obedience to the ceremonial laws of the Old Testament—laws pertaining to Jewish ritual sacrifices, the festal year, and some other items—is no longer required.[11] Neither does the debate concern questions of whether "*Localized Imperatives* [given to the Jews]—commands for specified use in one concrete situation"[12] continue to be binding today, for Theonomists recognize that these directives are "not principles with continuing force of law from generation to generation."[13] The disagreement is also not about whether the Ten Commandments still govern Divine-human and interpersonal relationships in the New Testament, since "all Ten Commandments from Exodus 20 and Deuteronomy 5 are repeated or are alluded to in the New Testament,"[14] in contexts that clearly show that the Ten Commandments are intended as moral axioms of the New Testament. Most important of all, Theonomists are not exchanging justification by faith in Jesus Christ for justification by the works of the law. They do not see obedience to divinely unamended civil laws as part of our justification,[15] but as the "Christian's pattern of sanctification . . .

---

11. Bahnsen, *Theonomy*, xxvi, thesis 5.
12. Bahnsen, *By This Standard*, 5.
13. Ibid.
14. North and DeMar, *Christian Reconstruction*, 85.

15. Bahnsen, *Theonomy*, xxvi, thesis 1. Recently, however, some Theonomists have followed Norman Shepherd's attempt to redefine the relationship between justification and sanctification in a way that many believe does compromise justification by faith alone. Bahnsen died before this controversy reemerged, and his full view of the matter is not yet publicly available. But one thing is certain: Even though Bahnsen agreed with part of Shepherd's controversial understanding of James 2, his published writings contradict Shepherd's denial that justification by faith was achieved on the basis of the imputation of Christ's active as well as his passive obedience. Since this denial is a fundamental consequence of Shepherd's position, Bahnsen's Theonomy should not be confused with Shepherd's teaching, as the former is clearly not a necessary consequence of the latter. Whether Bahnsen would have broken with his former teacher over the imputation question is impossible to say.

Even if Bahnsen supported the remainder of Shepherd's view apart from the difference over imputation of Christ's active obedience, critics of the Reconstructionist ethical principle must not overreact to any errors Bahnsen may have made concerning justification by faith and jump to the conclusion that, because he was wrong on justification by faith alone (JBFA), his argument justifying present-day use of the Mosaic

continual growth into conformity with the stature of Christ,"[16] a growth in which "the power of the Holy Spirit frees [believers] from the power of sin unto death."[17]

The real subject of the debate is the Mosaic judicial laws, and the disagreement is not about whether *any* Mosaic civil stipulations should ever be applied in modern states. Both sides affirm that the Mosaic civil laws are "inspired by God and [are] profitable for teaching, for reproof, for correction, for training in righteousness" (2 Tim 3:16). Many of Bahnsen's critics see no contradiction between rejecting the Reconstructionist justification for Mosaic civil ethics while simultaneously maintaining and promoting the view that modern societies would be well served if more, if not most, of the Mosaic civil laws and punishments were to be rightly applied as the laws of our lands.[18]

The real issue is this: which of the different hermeneutical principles employed by the two sides to resolve questions of how and to what extent God intends the civil laws of the Old Covenant to apply to New Covenant–era states is correct?[19] Does God want Christian citizens to promote and have their magistrates enforce all Mosaic civil laws, that is, those stipulations in the Pentateuch governing Divine-human or interpersonal relationships coupled with sanctions to be enforced by the Israelite community (excepting those implicitly or explicitly amended by the Lawgiver in the New Testament)? Or does God require something else from us? Theonomists believe that promoting the institution of all scripturally unmodified Mosaic civil laws remains a New Covenant duty

---

civil stipulations is therefore unscriptural. The two doctrines are taught in different Scriptures, and to conflate them is the slippery slope fallacy. If Bahnsen did, in fact, go so far in his defense of Shepherd as to land in error on JBFA, one cannot say that his error on this doctrine necessarily invalidates the Reconstructionist ethical perspective; the most one can say is that any (hypothetical) error in his stance on JBFA only illustrates afresh the point that Christians should thoroughly test what he says against Scripture—something all of us should be doing at all times in any case.

16. Bahnsen, *Theonomy*, 37.

17. Ibid., 136.

18. Vern Poythress is one Reformed writer discussing the matter, and his book *The Shadow of Christ in the Law of Moses* not only criticizes some elements of Bahnsen's thesis, but goes on to attempt to describe what differences a realized Calvin-Westminster perspective would bring to the current American political and legal systems.

19. Hermeneutics is the art of applying principles of interpretation to biblical teachings to first derive their meaning and then to apply those teachings to significantly different contexts from those to which they were originally given.

for Christians today. Those who take the Calvin-Westminster approach hold that today's civil authorities are not bound to the Theonomic position, believing instead that the Bible teaches a different approach, an approach summarized in chapter 19, section 4, of the Westminster Confession.

What makes the matter more complicated is that both camps often agree that particular Mosaic civil stipulations remain just today. Theonomists repeatedly suggest that this unity of conclusions means that there is no difference in the hermeneutics by which these conclusions are reached. Yet critics have noted that while differences in reasoning used by the two groups seem irrelevant when both sides come to the same conclusions, the differences become problematic when the two camps arrive at different results. When this happens, Christians need to know whether the truly biblical approach is Reconstructionism's "abiding validity of the law in exhaustive detail"[20] (except, of course, where the Lawgiver amends it), or whether God intends his people to follow the Calvinist-Westminster appeal to applicable general equity underlying a given civil law.[21] This objection Theonomists have largely ignored.[22]

The Reconstructionist perspective has not been generally accepted by American Reformed or Presbyterian ministers and laypeople, nor has it made significant inroads into the broader Evangelical community. Theologian John Frame recently remarked that while it "continues to be much discussed in classrooms of Christian colleges and seminaries [more] moderate positions . . . seem to be winning the day."[23] Yet

---

20. This phrase is Bahnsen's title for chapter 2 of *Theonomy*, in which he discusses what he believes Christ was teaching in Matt 5:17–20.

21. See Barker and Godfrey, "Preface," 10; Ferguson, "An Assembly of Theonomists?" 327, 333, 343.

22. As far as the present writer is aware, to date only one Theonomist has attempted to address this objection. In his article "Theonomic Precedent in the Theology of John Calvin," 323, Strevel adduced a number of Scriptures that, he believes, discredit the view that the debate is about the hermeneutical difference between the camps: it will be shown below that this attempt was not successful. Despite citing Ferguson's prefatory remark that the issue "is one of fundamental hermeneutical perspective" in his "Theonomy and Confession," 164, n.14, Gentry did not address Ferguson's observation that "whatever similarities may arise because of the Confession's qualifying clause it would be absurd to suggest that the [hermeneutical perspectives of Theonomists and non-Theonomists] are identical" (Ferguson, "Assembly," 327).

23. Frame, "Machen's Warrior Children."

Theonomy continues to find a number of advocates championing it as Reformed orthodoxy, most notably through various internet sites.

Some Reconstructionists believe that the rejection of Theonomy in theological seminaries is due to scholarly cowardice. Bahnsen's publisher claimed that when dealing with a challenge as comprehensive as Bahnsen provided in *Theonomy in Christian Ethics* and *By This Standard*, "Christian academics have adopted a policy of prudent silence."[24]

This claim, however, is incorrect: Christian academics have long noted cogent reasons to reject Bahnsen's views, but a full critique of the key portions of his work has never been undertaken by a Reformed writer. Consequently, lay Christians encountering Theonomy often are ignorant of the true case against it, and give the perspective more credibility than it deserves.

This book critiques Bahnsen's understanding of the most critical biblical text in the debate and attempts to demonstrate that he has significantly misunderstood the positions of Calvin, other Reformed teachers and the Westminster Confession concerning the relationship between the Sinai covenant's ethical stipulations and the Christian obligation to the Mosaic judicial laws today.

CALVIN AND THE WCF ON THE MOSAIC JUDICIAL LAWS

Most Theonomists believe that their view of how the civil laws should apply today is essentially that of Calvin and the WCF.[25] In order to determine the issue at the heart of the Theonomy debate, we must first ascertain whether this claim is correct. We will do so by reviewing exactly how Calvin and the Westminster Divines applied the Mosaic civil laws in the New Covenant,[26] and then we will examine where Theonomists take their stand.

Calvin's *Institutes of the Christian Religion* was the first major Protestant theology to address the New Covenant role of the Mosaic civil laws. To this day it remains the most influential Protestant teaching

---

24. North, *No Other Standard*, xii, xiii.

25. As will be shown later, however, R. J. Rushdoony, the founder of the Reconstructionist school of thought, correctly recognized that the Reconstructionist perspective on civil ethics differed significantly from both Calvin and the Westminster Divines.

26. The views of Calvin, the Westminster Divines, and other Reformed writers are only summarized in this section. Chapter 5, "Reformed History and Theonomy," presents their views in detail and critiques the attempt of some Theonomists to establish a different understanding of their intent.

on the relation of Mosaic civil law to New Covenant-era states.[27] But Calvin was not writing in a theological vacuum: he contrasted his understanding of the New Testament relevance of the Mosaic civil laws in reaction to statements that his contemporaries had put forward—statements that, in at least one case, remarkably anticipated Bahnsen's position. Responding to the claims of some early Reformers who argued that no state could be "rightly framed which neglects the law of Moses, and is ruled by the common law of nations"[28] (a thesis almost identical to Bahnsen's Theonomic critique of the Calvin-Westminster position), Calvin introduced his reply with the following comment: "How perilous and seditious these views are, let others see: for me it is enough to demonstrate that they are stupid and false."[29]

Calvin's starting point was his belief that the Ten Commandments had been written on the hearts of every human being before they were promulgated at Mt. Sinai.[30] As such, they were God's requirements of humanity before Sinai, and they remain God's requirements through the New Testament age as both the pattern for individual sanctification and the basis by which to judge public laws. It is to the Decalogue alone that Calvin applied the term *moral law*.[31] But while Calvin believed that

---

27. For a fine survey of the viewpoints of Calvin, his contemporaries, and those who followed after, see Avis, "Moses and the Magistrate." Many of Avis' conclusions were echoed by James Jordan, then writing from within the Reconstructionist school, in "Calvinism and 'The Judicial Law of Moses.'"

28. Calvin, *Institutes*, book 4, chapter 20, paragraph 14.

29. Ibid.

30. For the scriptural evidence for this premise, see Ross, *Finger of God*, 61–79.

31. Calvin, *Institutes*, book 4, chapter 20, paragraph 16 reads, "the law of God which we call moral is nothing is nothing else than the testimony of natural law, and of that conscience which God has engraven on the minds of men, the whole of this equity of which we now speak is prescribed in it." Calvin derived this statement from Rom 1:32. That slander, insolence, boastfulness and deceit are deemed "worthy of death" by Paul shows that he is not here referring to the Mosaic civil code since that code did not assign the death penalty for all of these sins. Instead, Paul—and Calvin, following him—are referring to the moral law that God placed in human hearts centuries before he promulgated the commandments aloud on Sinai. Both Jews and Gentiles were already obligated to obey the moral law well before the Israelites left Egypt. When Jesus fulfilled the Sinai Covenant and inaugurated the New, the Sinai Covenant became obsolete and would soon disappear (Heb 8:13). The writing of the moral law on human hearts, however, has neither been changed nor abolished by the New Covenant, for nine of the Ten Commandments are clearly affirmed as continuing in the New Testament, and exactly how the Sabbath continues remains the subject of lasting debate. Gentry's argument (Gentry, "Civil Sanctions in the New Testament," 156, 157), that Paul is here not really

the civil laws of the Old Covenant *illustrated* the moral law, he did not believe that the civil laws were *included* within it. Rather, Calvin believed that the civil laws of the Sinai Covenant were intended specifically for Old Testament Israel and were framed to take account of Israel's particular national characteristics and special status as a people in a unique covenant with God. Since other nations, as political entities, are not participants in that covenant and their peoples have different national characteristics, the Mosaic civil laws may not always be the appropriate legislation to be applied to them.

Calvin states this plainly when he discusses the question of appropriate punishments. In contrast to those who, like Bahnsen, uphold the contemporary validity and immutability of all divinely unamended Mosaic punishments, Calvin allows that different nations may properly have different punishments for the same crimes, or even different punishments for the same crime at different times in their histories, in order to establish the same divine goal of social equity, even though the Bible nowhere authorizes such changes.[32]

Calvin's views on how to best apply Mosaic civil laws to Christian states were later codified in the Westminster Confession. As the Confession's framers sought to find the correct place for the Mosaic civil laws in the New Covenant era they were confronted by three problems. First, the scepter had departed from Judah with the coming of the one to whom it belonged (Gen 49:10): with the demise of Judea, the Mosaic civil laws were no longer the law code of an extant state. Second, since Peter had told New Testament Christians that they must obey the laws of their own states (1 Pet 2:13), the Divines knew that the Mosaic civil stipulations were not the civil laws that the believers were specifically commanded to follow.[33] Yet despite these observations, they also saw

---

assigning the death penalty to these offenses in themselves but rather as the distributive consequence of the fundamental sin of idolatry, cannot be sustained. For Paul not only concludes his remark with a plural statement "those who practice such things are worthy of death," his statement echoes the blanket statement of Ez 18:20 which also assigns death as the ultimate punishment for sins that are not capital offenses under Sinai.

32. Author's summary of *Institutes*, book 4, chapter 20, paragraphs 14–16.

33. These are the two Scriptures the Westminster Divines supplied as proof texts for their assertion in chapter 19:4 of the Confession that the judicial laws have expired. Since the scepter has departed from Judah with the coming of the Messiah, and since believers are commanded to follow the civil laws of their own states and not the Mosaic law, the good and necessary consequence that follows is that obedience to the Mosaic civil laws, as such, is no longer required of believers wherever those laws are not the

that the Mosaic civil laws were God's own commentary on how the Ten Commandments should be applied to one particular civil order. As such, the civil laws were "holy and righteous and good" (Rom 7:12)[34] and "profitable ... for training in righteousness" (2 Tim 3:16). Consequently, these laws could form a basis from which Christians could judge the laws of their own states. But how were Christians to recognize the eternal moral foundations of God's Old Covenant civil laws and gain the benefits of applying them within their states without making all of the Mosaic law valid in the New Covenant era, and perhaps thereby landing the church in the heresy of Galatianism? English covenant theologian John Ball demonstrated contemporary awareness of this problem when he argued that the Mosaic stipulations must not have continuing validity as an ongoing covenant. For "if [the law] did continue as a covenant, there could be no place for repentance, nor for the promise of forgiveness, or mercy reaching to the pardon of sin or the quickening of them that be dead in trespasses.[35]

Ball's comment brings us to a critical point; to avoid landing the church in Galatianism, the Westminster Divines could not ground whatever validity the civil laws retained in New Covenant–era states on their status as covenant stipulations of the Mosaic covenant, but on whether or not they would remain just if instituted in contemporary states.

The final problem the Divines faced was that they differed among themselves as to how many of the Mosaic civil laws and punishments still applied in the New Covenant era.

Despite these difficulties, they were determined to produce a statement that set fort critical doctrines "clearly, yet not so narrowly as to exclude brethren among themselves, who were likewise committed to generic Calvinism."[36]

---

law code of the state in which the believer lives. If the Mosaic civil laws had remained the single divinely commanded legal system in the church age, Peter's commanding his Jewish readers scattered throughout the Roman Empire (Gal 2:9, 1 Pet 1:1) to submit to Roman law and its significant differences from Mosaic law would be a command to submit to a sinful legal system rather than the righteous and still-applicable Mosaic law.

34. Scriptural citations are from the NASB unless otherwise noted.

35. Ball, *Treatise of the Covenant of Grace*, 15. Ball's work was published the year before WCF 19 was passed (Sept. 26, 1646), and two of the five Westminster Divines who jointly wrote the preface to Ball's work are critical witnesses for understanding how the Divines intended WCF 19:4 to be understood.

36. Ferguson, "Assembly," 345.

The Confession's framers addressed these problems by employing an old distinction in Christian theology: they distinguished between three different subcategories of the Mosaic law.[37] In chapter 19, sections 1–3 identify and define the term *Moral Law*, while section 4 refers to "sundry judicial laws." According to the Confession, the Moral Law was given initially to Adam in the garden, was subsequently written on the heart of every man and woman, and was later explicitly declared to Israel as the Ten Commandments. According to section 5, it is only the Moral Law that remains binding on all men and women today and until the end of the world. But in section 4, the Confession distinguishes between this eternally applicable Moral Law and the "sundry judicial laws" given to ancient Israel "as a body politic" that have "expired with the state of that people, not obliging any other [state] now."[38] The judicial laws, therefore, were specifically intended for ancient Israel, a national community in covenant with God as his chosen people, and were not directly intended as a civil code for states outside that covenant. Consequently, when Judea was conquered by Titus, the civil laws, as Judea's civil law code, expired with the Jewish state.[39]

But even though the Confession holds that the civil laws, as a class, expired with the destruction of Jerusalem in AD 70, the Divines also believed that some individual laws may continue to be valid despite the

---

37. There is no evidence that this distinction was known at the time of Christ. Despite some speculation that the advent of Messiah might change some stipulations, the Jews living under Sinai did not subdivide the Mosaic covenant, but experienced it as a unified whole.

38. All quotations in this paragraph are drawn from WCF 19:4.

39. In "Are the Mosaic Laws for Today?" 39–40, F. Nigel Lee argues that the meaning of "sundry" the Divines intended was that of "sundered or some . . . it would then follow that the 'sundry judicial laws' which 'expired' in A.D. 70 . . . were only some of the judicial laws (but by no means all of them). And this would then mean that apart from the 'sundry judicial laws' which expired, the rest of the judicial laws did not expire but are even today still to continue in the World" (40). Theonomists and critics who have assumed that Lee's argument is friendly to Theonomy have misread him, for Lee specifically notes that "the *non*-sundry judicial laws" that continue today are not Mosaic judicial laws but, instead, "are *Pre*-Mosaic" (39). While at least two important Westminster divines are on record as holding that pre-Mosaic judicial laws remains valid today, the text of the Confession does not explicitly allude to Lee's distinction. Nor does the Divines' use of pre-Mosaic stipulations or Mosaic civil law texts in the proof texts of the Confession and Catechism prove anything more than the Divines saw that these laws continued to be valid since their inherent equity rendered them as applicable in the New Covenant as they were in the Old.

change in covenants. So they continued their sentence on the civil laws by recognizing that the Mosaic judicial laws still "oblige . . . now [only as far as] the general equity thereof may require" (WCF 19:4). So the key question becomes, what exactly does the "general equity thereof" require today?

As Bahnsen recognized, at the time that the WCF was written, the term *general equity* was used in English law to mean an eternal ethical principle underlying and justifying particular laws. "When the particular political body for which the judicial laws were worded passed away, the literal wording or specific form of the laws was put out of gear. Only the underlying principle ("equity") of those historical illustrations continues to be obligatory."[40]

But Calvin and the Westminster Divines went further. They claimed that the foundational principles of equity underlying the case laws were the Ten Commandments, to which the Divines assigned the term "moral law" in WCF 19:1–3. And it would be the Decalogue that would determine whether or not a given Mosaic stipulation would remain valid in the New Covenant era.

Some Theonomists assert that WCF 19:4 was intended by the Divines to recognize that all Mosaic civil laws not amended by the Lawgiver remain valid in the New Covenant era. But this view accuses the Divines of self-contradiction, since in the previous clause the Divines had held that the judicial laws had expired.[41] In addition, the Divines' use of the word *may* in "may require" is an additional argument against this Theonomic premise. For if the Divines believed that all unamended Mosaic laws were necessarily required in the New Covenant era, they would have used a word such as *doth*, which avoids the implication of potential contrast inherent in *may*, which leaves open the possibility that general equity may not require the contemporary institution of some of these laws.

Bahnsen vigorously argued that WCF 19:4 was not intended to abolish either the Mosaic case laws or their penal sanctions and those who use it to do so are accusing "the Westminster Divines of blatant self

---

40. Bahnsen, "The Westminster Assembly and the Equity of the Judicial Law," under "Reading the Confession in Context."

41. Although it is not impossible that the Divines unwittingly contradicted themselves here, that possibility is highly unlikely, for, as Bahnsen correctly observed, the WCF is "the most cautiously worked out and carefully worded creed of the Evangelical Church" (Bahnsen, *Theonomy*, 517).

contradiction." Instead, he argued that "the Westminster view of civil authority requires all magistrates to observe and carry out the whole law of God as the standard of social justice and public righteousness."[42]

This is the crucial difference. For the Westminster view has nowhere claimed that every Mosaic judicial should be enforced today. Rather, it asserts that it is only those Mosaic judicials where the underlying "general equity [does] require" today that must be instituted.

James Jordan, writing from within the Theonomic camp, recognized that the Divines did not make all Mosaic stipulations automatically valid in the New Testament era. "What the [Westminster] Standards do not do is spell out to what extent and how these laws are binding and to what extent and how they have been loosed. This is doubtless because this was an open question, much debated at the time. Some [Divines] held, as we have seen, that whatever could be applied from these laws had to be applied, without any alteration. Others held more lax views regarding their binding nature. The Standards do not settle this issue in full."[43]

Instead, with WCF 19:4, the Divines provided a means of testing which laws expire and which laws remain valid. As the Calvin-Westminster view sees the matter, the Divines limited Christian obligation to the Mosaic civil laws to that of supporting laws and punishments of equivalent equity in the New Covenant era, as measured by the moral law, and working to change any laws which, measured by that standard, are unjust.

A major advantage of the Calvin-Westminster approach is that when anyone advocates instituting a Mosaic stipulation or punishment on this basis, the proposal can be presented on the basis of superior correspondence with the fundamental principles of equity enumerated in the Decalogue. When pressed to think matters through, unbelievers will recognize the justice of the measure—due to the Decalogue's being written on their hearts—and the proposals in question tend to become law. Calvin remade Geneva by applying more equitable biblical laws on a case by case basis; Wilberforce and the "Clapham sect" did likewise in their fight to outlaw the British slave trade. And since stating the rationale for the desired law in terms of its equity, rather than in terms of specific Christian premises, cuts the ground from under the feet of those who

---

42. Bahnsen, *Theonomy*, 516.
43. Jordan, "Calvinism and 'The Judicial Law of Moses.'"

object to laws based on Christian principles in a post-Christian context, Christian political activists might do well to use this approach.

The disagreement between the Calvin-Westminster view and Theonomy is not about whether one side uses general equity and the other side does not. Both sides utilize the concept, but each does so to a different extent. While both sides are happy to use general equity to apply the foundations of the moral law to situations that were unknown in ancient Israel yet present today,[44] Theonomists vigorously dissent when followers of Calvin and the Westminster Divines argue that scripturally unamended Mosaic stipulations need not necessarily be applied to contemporary recurrences of situations for which they were initially provided because the general equity of those laws is not the same when applied in the post-Sinai context.[45] We shall now examine the major reason why Theonomists have taken this view.

THE THEONOMIC PRINCIPLE

The reason that Theonomists do not accept the extent of general equity allowed by others is that they follow a different line of reasoning when defining the concept. Bahnsen's *Theonomy* offers the fullest explanation of their reasoning now available.

Unlike the Westminster Divines who advocated the continuing validity of the *ethical principles* underlying the Old Testament judicial laws, Bahnsen went further and asserted that the Bible mandated the continuing validity of all *divinely unamended OT judicial laws*, asserting that the "the whole law of God is to be enforced by the civil magistrate where and how the stipulations of God so designate."[46]

---

44. For example, Bahnsen famously observed that the same general equity behind the Mosaic stipulation requiring a parapet around a roof used as living space now requires a fence around swimming pools (Bahnsen, *By This Standard*, 138).

45. Calvin allowed the state to amend Mosaic punishments without Divine authorization (*Institutes* 4:20:16), and Westminster Divine George Gillespie allowed for the forbearing of a biblical punishment without biblical authorization for the change in "Wholesome Severity Reconciled with Christian Liberty." Gillespie's fellow Scottish Commissioner and friend, Samuel Rutherford, specifically denies Bahnsen's premise that the judicial laws are immutable unless Divinely amended when he wrote "a judicial, not a ceremonial law; that this should be perpetual because Christ in particular hath not abolished it, to me seems most unjust." Rutherford, *Divine Right*, 493–94.

46. Bahnsen, *Theonomy*, 36.

The Theonomy Debate and Why It Matters 15

Bahnsen begins his attempt to provide a scriptural foundation for his thesis by examining Christ's words in Matt 5:17–18. He believes that Christ was here "confirming" that the ethical stipulations of the law, down to the least detail, remain valid for the church age, except where the Lawgiver explicitly or implicitly amends them.[47] If that was Christ's intent, a number of consequences follow—consequences Bahnsen later attempted to summarize in the form of ten theses.[48] Four of these theses—numbers 4, 6, 9, and 10—are the heart of the Theonomy debate. Bahnsen believes that the

> . . . civil precepts of the Old Testament (standing "judicial" laws) are a model of perfect social justice for all cultures, even in the punishment of criminals.[49] We should presume that Old Testament standing laws [a term he defines in a footnote as "*policy* directives applicable over time to classes of individuals"][50] continue to be morally binding[51] in the New Testament, unless they are rescinded or modified by further revelation, [since the] standing laws are a reflection of [God's] immutable moral character and, as such, are absolute in the sense of being non-arbitrary, objective, universal, and established in advance of particular circumstances (thus applicable to particular types of moral situations).[52] [As such, the] general continuity which we presume with respect to the moral standards of the Old Testament applies

---

47. Bahnsen's controversial exegesis of this passage will be reviewed in chapters 3, 4, and 5.

48. The controversy resulting from the publication of *Theonomy* soon gave rise to a need for a second edition. Bahnsen's *Preface to the Second Edition (Theonomy, xxi–xxxvii)* was written to correct misunderstandings of his position. Included in the *Preface* were ten theses which form Bahnsen's invaluable attempt to "[draw] together, [clarify], and [state] in distilled form the vital teachings elaborated in the full text of Theonomy in Christian Ethics" (*Theonomy*, xxv, xxvi).

49. Ibid., xxvii, thesis 10.

50. Most of those writing on either side of the debate will agree that there is much work to be done analyzing many case laws to determine the subgroup—civil or ceremonial—to which they belong. For the purposes of this book, however, the terms "civil laws," "Mosaic civil stipulations," and "sundry judicial laws" are arbitrarily limited to those laws of the Sinai Covenant that clearly fall within Bahnsen's category of "standing laws" and, in addition, have divinely assigned punishments conjoined with them since these laws are clearly "judicial laws."

51. Whatever may be true of other Christian Reconstructionists, Bahnsen, with the words "morally binding," agrees with the entire Reformed tradition that the Mosaic judicials are no longer *covenantally* binding and thereby avoids the heresy of Galatianism.

52. Bahnsen, *Theonomy*, xxvi, theses 4 and 6.

just as legitimately to matters of socio-political ethics as it does to personal, family or ecclesiastical ethics[53] [for the] (standing "judicial" laws) are a model of perfect social justice for all cultures, even in the punishment of criminals.[54] Consequently the law for society today is the same as that in the Older Testament, and the officials of the state are responsible today . . . to enforce God's law.[55]

From these premises Bahnsen concludes that "the civil magistrate is obliged to follow the penal sanctions of God's law, for those sanctions are neither arbitrary nor temporary."[56]

Theonomists may offer four objections to critiques of Theonomy that are based on the aforementioned summary. First, they may adduce Bahnsen's statement "Calvin may not always have been consistent with these teachings [i.e., that the penal sanctions of the law are still valid and to be enforced in the present era] just as I am not thoroughly consistent with them either"[57] to invalidate such attempts. This attempt founders in two places. First, Bahnsen has misunderstood Calvin. The Reformer was not merely inconsistent with the premise that all judicials unamended by the Lawgiver remained valid in the present age, but denied that view altogether. Second, aside from presuming that Bahnsen was an incompetent summarizer of his own position, it is certain that the last clause of his remark cannot be pressed as far as these defenders wish. For Bahnsen's sole known disagreement with Mosaic penology[58] was his belief that "someone might convincingly argue that the method of execution (for example, stoning) is a variable cultural detail."[59] But since a belief that the method of execution may be variable does not change the degree and the equity or "justness" of the punishment that the criminal

---

53. Ibid., xxvii, thesis 9.

54. Ibid., xxvii, thesis 10.

55. Ibid., 453.

56. Ibid., 454. Although his theses do not mention Matt 5:17–18, Bahnsen's understanding of these verses is the essential foundation on which they rest.

57. Bahnsen, "God's Law and Gospel Prosperity."

58. As far as I have been able to determine, Bahnsen never advocated decriminalizing any Mosaic civil crimes, nor did he argue for any adjustments in the equity of Mosaic punishments.

59. Bahnsen, *By This Standard*, 278. These statements do, however, create an apparent contradiction with Bahnsen's understanding of Matt 5:17–20. We shall later discover whether or not the contradiction is real.

will receive, Bahnsen's difference from Mosaic penology on this point nullifies neither the accuracy of his summary nor the propriety of using it to construct critiques of Theonomy.

A second reason why Theonomists may object is that they believe Bahnsen had already replied to such critiques when he noted that, "a combination of . . . factors has misled some to maintain that *Theonomy*, because it often speaks of our obligation to the exhaustive details of God's law . . . cannot allow any change or advance over the Old Testament at any point, even by God Himself, and must follow without exception every single Old Testament precept, strictly, literally (even the cultural trappings necessitate verbatim application), and without qualification or modification."[60]

Bahnsen countered this misrepresentation by noting that *Theonomy* contains "no fewer than seventy pages that refer to the progress of revelation and redemptive history, God's right to change the law; exceptions to general continuity, laws which are laid aside, or advances over the Old Covenant. I mentioned 'radical discontinuities,' 'legitimate and noteworthy discontinuities' and 'laws which have become obsolete.'"[61]

Although Bahnsen's statement correctly rebukes critics who erroneously believe that he held *all* Mosaic laws to be immutable in the New Testament, Theonomists cannot use it to defend Bahnsen's view of the immutability of Mosaic civil stipulations from criticism, for in none of the seventy pages Bahnsen cites in *Theonomy* does he discuss any changes to these laws. Moreover, in a later book, after reiterating his point that some changes to the Mosaic law do occur, Bahnsen made it crystal clear that he saw no widespread or systematic changes to the civil laws. Instead, he believed that

> the New Testament does not teach any radical change in God's law regarding the standards of *socio-political morality*. God's law as it touches upon the duty of civil magistrates has not been altered in any systematic or fundamental way in the New Testament.
>
> Consequently, instead of taking a basically antagonistic view of the Old Testament commandments for society and the state, and instead of taking a smorgasbord approach of picking and choosing among those laws on the basis of personal taste and convenience, we must recognize the continuing obligation

---

60. Bahnsen, *Theonomy*, xxiii.

61. Ibid., xxiv. Page xxiv n. 9 lists pages 92, 211, 304, 306, 356, and 417 as the passages in question.

of civil magistrates to obey and enforce the relevant laws of the Old Testament, including the penal sanctions specified by the just Judge of all the earth. As with the rest of God's law, we must presume continuity of binding authority regarding the sociopolitical commandments revealed as standing law in the Old Testament.[62]

Since Bahnsen recognized no systemic changes to the Mosaic judicial laws, Theonomists may not object to criticism of Theonomy based on the above summary of Bahnsen's position.

The third objection Theonomists might raise is that Bahnsen's summary does not clarify an essential point. Does Bahnsen require explicit statements by the Lawgiver specifically changing a particular law before he will accept that that law has been amended? An oversight in *Theonomy* misled some to believe that he did require explicit statements authorizing such changes, for Bahnsen stated that it was the Christian's obligation to "keep the whole law of God as a pattern of sanctification"[63] without qualifying his statement by adding the words *unless amended by the Lawgiver in Scripture*.[64] Bahnsen seems to have assumed[65] that his readers would understand that his Theonomic principle was governed by the WCF's famous statement that "the whole counsel of God, concerning all things necessary for his own glory, man's salvation, faith, and life, is either expressly set down in scripture, or by good and necessary consequence may be deduced from scripture."[66]

Later, however, Bahnsen explicitly qualified the point: "Theonomic ethics does not maintain that Old Testament law stands 'until explicitly abrogated.' Many of the things which theonomists believe have been laid aside on the authority of the New Testament (e. g., breakdown of

---

62. Bahnsen, *By This Standard*, 3–4.

63. Bahnsen, *Theonomy*, 36.

64. Bahnsen wrote what became *Theonomy in Christian Ethics* as a Westminster Seminary thesis for his ThM degree under the title "The Theonomic Responsibility of the Civil Magistrate." Writing for that seminary, whose doctrinal standard was the WCF, he would not need to mention that his statements must be viewed within the bounds of the WCF as such a limitation would be taken for granted. But when Bahnsen's work was set before a wider readership than his Reformed seminary examiners, omitting to clarify that his apparently absolute principle was in fact so qualified left the door open for his position to be misunderstood.

65. Bahnsen, *Theonomy*, 35.

66. WCF 1:6.

Levitical orders and duties, prohibition of mixed-fiber clothing, the levirate institution) are not 'explicitly' abrogated in the New Testament, but rather discontinued on the basis of what is inferred by other statements."[67]

Clearly, Bahnsen intended to put forth two hermeneutical principles, not just one. While he urged the law's continuity in exhaustive detail unless amended, he also recognized that amendments need not be explicitly stated to be valid, but they may be valid because they are good and necessary consequences of other biblical statements. Yet granting the possibility of implicit amendments to the law on the basis of deductions from other biblical statements, however, does not blunt criticism of Bahnsen's thesis. Instead, it presents his thesis with three significant problems that he did not address.

The first problem Bahnsen faces becomes evident as he rightly recognizes that certain statutes are necessarily invalidated by the change in covenants from the Old to the New: the Levitical orders and duties expire (in an era in which Christ holds a better and permanent priesthood), the prohibition of mixed-fiber clothing (no longer necessary to identify God's people to the Gentiles), and the institution of levirate marriage (which runs afoul of Christ's restoration of the Edenic rule of marriage as for one man and one woman).[68] In effect, Bahnsen might argue that the justification for all of these changes lies in the change from the Mosaic covenant to the New Covenant, a claim with which no Christian will disagree. But in accepting such changes, Bahnsen thereby qualifies his understanding of Christ's words in Matt 5:17–18. If such covenantally wrought changes are legitimate, Christ, in these verses, cannot be prohibiting any changes to the law whatsoever, but is stating matters in such a way that will allow the Lawgiver to institute those changes to the law—the abrogation of the ceremonial laws and Israelite identity markers—that are inherent in the shift from the Old Covenant to the New, which is itself a change that the Lawgiver had previously announced would occur. But when Bahnsen explicitly considers whether or not the change in covenants creates an era in which, as a consequence of that same covenantal shift, the civil laws no longer govern God's people, he takes a different tack. Instead of arguing that such laws were not affected

---

67. Bahnsen and Gentry, *House Divided*, 75–76.
68. Ibid., 35, 75–76.

by the change in covenants, Bahnsen suggests that any view that the "*era governed by the law*"[69] ceased with Christ's advent suffers

> from the defect of imposing theological prejudice upon πληρωσαι [fulfill] and infusing it with content it cannot sustain, . . . [in addition] this view simply fails to take cognizance of verse 18 following where Jesus clearly states that the law he is discussing remains valid "until heaven and earth pass away." Furthermore, one must take account of the strong adversative ἀλλα [but] standing between καταλωσαι [destroy] and πληρωσαι [fulfill, complete] as well as Jesus' double assertion that he came not to abrogate the law—both appearing in the very verse under discussion.[70]

But Bahnsen did not realize that this argument does more than he wants it to do. If his objections are sustained, Christ is here prohibiting any change to any Mosaic stipulation until the end of the church age, a prohibition that necessarily renders the entire change in covenants illegitimate. To his credit, Bahnsen avoids such an unbiblical conclusion, but the only possible way he can do so is by positing that Christ intended his hearers to understand the words "the Law or the Prophets" as referring to "the *ethical stipulations* contained in the canon of the entire Older Testament."[71] But if Christ intended his words to refer either to the Old Testament Scriptures as a whole or to the covenant relationship between God and Israel that Moses instituted,[72] then the way that Bahnsen rejects the possibility that the civil laws have changed with the covenantal shift will necessarily lead to the conclusion that every detail of the Old Covenant stipulations must remain operative to this day.

The second problem Bahnsen faces arises when one attempts to determine the validity of conclusions inferred from various New Testament statements that would seem to amend particular civil laws. Although the New Testament does contain several statements from which readers may infer that a given civil law may have been amended, there is no case in which it is possible to demonstrate that the amendments supposedly entailed by such statements are true deductions following by necessary

---

69. Bahnsen, *Theonomy*, 58.

70. Ibid. In chapters 3 and 4 we shall discover that correct exegesis of Matt 5:17, 18 does not lead to Bahnsen's conclusions.

71. Ibid., 53.

72. As will be shown later, given the surrounding context of these words, Christ is almost certainly using "the Law or the Prophets" as a reference to the Sinai Covenant.

consequence from the statements made. Given that it is ultimately such "necessary consequence" that will determine whether any civil laws have been abolished, a Theonomist, when asked to say which Old Testament civil laws are abolished by necessary consequence of other scriptural statements, must answer the question by saying, "None."[73] Given that reality, Bahnsen's hermeneutic will, in practice, inevitably reduce to the premise that all Mosaic civil laws or punishments remain required today.[74]

The third problem Bahnsen encounters when he allows for the possibility that the law may be amended, is that it appears to run counter to "the absolutistic character of Christ's words in Matthew 5:17–19."[75] To this, Bahnsen's followers may reply that Christ was "using a common teaching device of laying down the general principle, but allowing for qualifications and refinements to be brought in later,"[76] something Christ clearly did in other incidents. "Does not Mark 10:11 appear to forbid *any* and *all* divorce, whereas Matthew 19:9 clearly allows divorce on certain grounds?"[77]

This Theonomic defense, however, fails to realize that the two situations are not identical. In Mark 10:11, Christ is providing his disciples with a fuller explanation of the answer he had previously given to the Pharisees, and his answer presumes their knowledge of his previous words. In that earlier discussion, he was answering a Pharisaic query about the lawfulness of initiating divorce for any non-adulterous but offensive reason; nowhere in that earlier discussion does he address the lawfulness of divorcing a wife when she commits adultery against her husband. Furthermore, in this discussion, unlike in Matt 5:17–20,

---

73. That the Sabbath laws were amended in the New Testament does not help Theonomists. For, in addition to being a creation ordinance, the Sabbath was a covenant sign between God and his people. See Rushdoony, *Law and Society*, 683.

74. Theonomists will often claim that their critics are erring when they claim that the Theonomic operating principle will, in practice, reduce to something similar to "All Mosaic judicial laws remain valid today." Yet those who have objected to this observation have never, to the present writer's knowledge, provided critics with counter examples of any Mosaic judicial laws that they believe do *not* apply in the present age. Until and unless examples of no-longer-applicable Mosaic laws are brought into the discussion by Theonomists, non-theonomists may logically infer that Theonomy's inevitable consequence is the re-institution of *all* the Mosaic judicial laws.

75. Bahnsen, *No Other Standard*, 274 n. 1.

76. Ibid.

77. Gentry, *Covenantal Theonomy*, 53.

Christ lays down no prohibition against qualifying his words by his statements elsewhere. Where Christ does not forbid qualification of his statements, we may use legitimate considerations of context and exegesis to harmonize discrepancies in his words without leaving a problem remaining at the end of our attempt. But in Matt 5: 17–18, Christ, in context, is addressing the charge that he has come to "destroy the law." By using the strongest possible form of Greek negation to announce that not a single change to any of the least details of the law would occur while it is in force, Christ creates a situation in which any subsequent changes to the law (while the rest of it remains in force) results in a full and formal contradiction that cannot be harmonized with his words in Matt 5:18. In addition, any such subsequent change would also prove him "guilty" of the Pharisees' charge that he was "destroying the Law."[78] Thus, this Theonomic attempt to deny the propriety of a critique based on Bahnsen's summary also fails.

The final objection that Theonomists may present to critiques based on the previously mentioned summary of Bahnsen's ten theses turns on their belief that Bahnsen's book was intended to be nothing more than a modern restatement of the Westminster view that it is only the principles underneath the Mosaic case laws that remain obligatory. To support this thesis, they point to passages such as the following: "God requires obedience to the underlying principles illustrated by Scripture's cultural expressions. *Theonomy* plainly observed: "the case law illustrates the application or qualification of the principle laid down in the general commandment," and it is "the underlying principle (of which the case law was a particular illustration)" which "has abiding ethical validity."[79]

Had Bahnsen limited himself to statements like the above, his work would not have been controversial. But when he attempted to show from his reading of Matt 5:17, 18 that Christ had confirmed the applicability of all divinely unamended Mosaic laws and punishments throughout the church age, he did not initially realize that by so doing, he had changed the subject of discussion from the continuity of Mosaic Covenant's ethical principles to the inescapable continuity of all divinely unamended judicial laws.

Followers of Bahnsen frequently don't see the problem this move creates until they are challenged on whether they hold to the abiding

---

78. This point is developed in detail in the review of Bahnsen's exegesis of Matt 5:18.

79. Bahnsen, *Theonomy*, xxiv, citing ibid., 306–8, 516–17.

validity of Mosaic judicial *laws* or to the abiding validity of Mosaic judicial *principles*. When Theonomists first assert "the abiding validity of [all Mosaic laws] . . . then [retreat] under scrutiny to a position which asserts [only] the abiding validity of 'principle,'"[80] the result is

> continual confusion when discussing the subject of theonomy. [The abiding validity of the judicial law is the] basic thesis which must be abandoned if the discussion is going to proceed to another level.[81]

Unfortunately Bahnsen must be held responsible for some of this confusion, for even after his critics pointed out that he had effectively moved to justifying the contemporary validity of Mosaic laws rather than justifying the contemporary validity of Mosaic principles, his subsequent books continued to make the point that the civil laws remained immutable unless changed by God himself.[82] His reductions of the Theonomic hermeneutic to axioms (e.g., as in his 10 theses), also continued focus on the immutability of all the "standing laws" rather than advocating for the continuity of the Mosaic principles. Ultimately, he reduced his Theonomic hermeneutic to this summary: "In all of its minute detail (every jot and tittle) the law of God, down to its least significant provision should be reckoned to have an abiding validity—until and unless the Lawgiver reveals otherwise."[83] This principle clearly differs from Calvin and the Westminster Divines, who reckoned the law to be abolished as a system, leaving only laws that are just by reason of general equity applicable today.

---

80. Winzer, "Objections," post 84.

81. Winzer, "Objections," post 97.

82. See Bahnsen, *By This Standard*, 3–4, Bahnsen, *No Other Standard*, 99, 121, 165, and 221 for representative statements in which Bahnsen continued to advocate the immutability of the OT *laws* rather than OT *principles*.

83. Bahnsen, "The Theonomic Position," 40–41. Bahnsen elsewhere noted that the Mosaic Law sometimes provides for flexibility in penalties. In addition, the lack of any police force in the Sinai system provided ample opportunities for apprehended criminals to negotiate with their victims before trial, which, as some Theonomists have correctly inferred, allowed victims of crimes the discretion to waive many punishments. But this is not the same thing as allowing states in the New Covenant era the freedom to recognize that individual Mosaic civil laws not amended by the Lawgiver are no longer necessarily valid or that the state has the right to amend punishments for those that remain—which is the Calvin Westminster view.

Having reviewed the views of both sides, we can now identify the key issue at the heart of the debate. Both sides utilize the same concept of general equity when considering situations analogous but not identical to situations addressed by the Mosaic law. But the two camps differ when considering situations specifically addressed by the Mosaic stipulations. Calvin and the Westminster Divines recognized that the destruction of the Jewish state caused the civil laws to expire with "the state of that people." Although they freely consulted the civil laws when seeking wisdom for Christian states, they dared not presume that all Mosaic civil laws remained God's righteous requirements for nations not in covenant with him in the New Covenant era. They therefore limited our obligation to instituting only those Mosaic civil stipulations whose equity is such that those stipulations will remain just despite the change in covenantal circumstances. In contrast, Theonomists believe that since Christ taught that all divinely unamended Mosaic laws continue to be valid to the end of the church age, the legitimately biblical meaning of general equity must require all Mosaic civil laws and punishments to be instituted in the church age unless such laws have been amended by the Lawgiver. Instead of the Westminster insistence on providing positive proof of a civil law's continuity, Bahnsen insists on the negative proof of discontinuity, thus reversing the Calvin-Westminster hermeneutic.

THE CONSEQUENCES OF THE DIFFERENCES

Although the hermeneutical differences between the two groups seem irrelevant when both advocate the adoption of given Mosaic civil laws or punishments, problems arise when the groups disagree on particular issues—disagreements that have serious effects on Christian political activity and evangelism. Many of the differences between the results of the two hermeneutics arise with respect to offenses against the "first table" of the commandments—those sins that involve sinning against God directly rather than sinning against a fellow human. These situations raise a profound question: Are the Old Covenant criminality of such actions and their Mosaic punishments applicable only within the covenant relationship in which the Israelites stood to God, or are they universally applicable? While the question is usually posed by members of the Calvin-Westminster school, it was Christian Reconstruction's seminal figure, Rousas Rushdoony, who put the problem in a particularly clear way. He first observes that the "concept of sacrilege rests on

God's sovereignty and the fact that He has an absolute ownership over all things: men and the universe are God's property. The covenant people are *doubly* God's property: *first* by virtue of His creation; and *second*, by virtue of His redemption. For this reason, sin is more personal and more than man-centered. It is a theological offense."[84]

Rushdoony then wonders whether the nature of some offenses changes depending on the type of relationship with God that underlies the situation. He writes: "the Sabbath is a sign, a covenant sign, between God and His people."[85] After citing Jaffa's observation that, in Israel, Sabbath breach was "an act of sedition,"[86] Rushdoony posed the following question: "Does this mean that in the modern world, Sabbath-breaking is punishable by death or should be? The answer is, very clearly and emphatically *no*. The modern state is not in covenant with God but is an enemy of God. Sabbath-breaking has no specific penalty of death just as there is no death penalty for adultery (Hos 4:14), because the nations are not in covenant with God . . . Because of this general and central indictment, the lesser offenses have no place. Covenant offences are one thing, enemy offenses another."[87]

Whatever one may think of his attempt to justify abolition of the Sabbath death penalty by citing Hos 4:14 in the face of the Mosaic death penalty for adultery,[88] Rushdoony is right to raise the possibility that some Mosaic judicial laws were covenant specific. Romans 14:5 implies that the Sabbath laws were specific to the Mosaic covenant and Christ certainly abrogated the Mosaic law concerning divorce in favor of the standard first set in Eden.[89] Moreover, the Mosaic law itself makes it plain that someone's status within or without that covenantal relationship may affect whether Mosaic civil laws apply to actions relating to such persons. Deuteronomy 23:20 prohibited Israelites from lending money at interest to fellow Israelites. But the same verse allowed Israelites to lend money to Gentiles.[90] Since it is certain that some Mosaic civil laws vary

---

84. Rushdoony, *Law and Society,* 28.

85. Ibid., 683.

86. Jaffa, "On Mano's 'Jews for Jesus,'" 1433.

87. Rushdoony, *Law and Society,* 685.

88. Deut 22:22. In addition, the Hosea text is specifically addressed to covenant breaking Israel, not to a state outside the Sinai covenant.

89. Matt 19:1–6.

90. That God permitted interest when lending to Gentiles proves that charging

with covenant status, Christians must employ a hermeneutic that recognizes differences in applicable covenant status. If Rushdoony is correct that a modern nation's non-covenant status entails non-applicability of the Mosaic crimes and penalties for Sabbath breaking, the necessary consequence (by parity of reasoning) is that all Mosaic stipulations for first table offenses are not automatically applicable outside the Sinai covenant.[91] Bahnsen implicitly repudiates this view when he claims that the "New Testament does not teach any radical change in God's law regarding the standards of *socio-political morality*. God's law as it touches upon the duty of civil magistrates has not been altered in any systematic or fundamental way in the New Testament."[92]

---

interest does not violate the moral law. Forbidding Israel to lend at interest among Israelites demonstrates that the Decalogue (moral law) and the Mosaic civil laws are not identical.

91. There is a key difference in sins against the first table of the Sinai covenant and sins against the second. Under Sinai, first table offenses were a sin directly against God in his capacity of Covenant Sovereign and, as such, they required him to exercise the retributive judgments against Israel which he had previously obliged himself to do as a condition of the covenant. Worshiping another "god" under Sinai was thus not only idolatry: it was treason against the Sovereign and the nation. Similar offenses occurring outside the Sinai covenant, although sins, are not rebellion against a covenantal suzerain; and while God may judge sinful nations in any way at any time and would be just in doing so, such sins do not (unlike Sinai) *covenantally oblige* God to impose the judgment of destroying the state in which these sins were committed. While first-table offenses remain sins in the New Covenant, the change in covenant relationships—between God and Israel then, and God and nation states today—raises a key question. Must Christians conclude that the Mosaic punishments for such sins remain required despite the change in political relationships brought about by the New Covenant? Or, to put the question another way, were Israelite idolaters under the Sinai covenant executed for treason or idolatry? If the former, such punishments may not be just today. (And even if contemporary Christians were to convince their fellow voters that tolerating sins against any point of the first table may render their nation more subject to God's judgment and thereby successfully achieve legislation against such sins that required Mosaic penalties, those Christian advocates would not be Theonomists, for they would not have followed Bahnsen's hermeneutic to justify their position.)

In second table offenses, on the other hand, while God, as Lawgiver, is indirectly sinned against, the one sinned against directly is another human. The relationship between a man and his neighbor is essentially unchanged despite the change in covenant situations. Christians may therefore justify the criminalization of Mosaic crimes and the application of Mosaic punishments to second table offenses on the grounds that such actions remain an equal violation of general equity today and deserve a punishment of equal equity to the same offenses committed under Sinai.

92. Bahnsen, *By This Standard*, 3, 4.

While many holding to the Calvin-Westminster school challenge the claim that God requires the institution of Mosaic first table crimes and punishments in Christian states today, those who follow Bahnsen's hermeneutic cannot do so. Until this difference between Calvin-Westminster advocates and Bahnsen's followers is resolved, many Reformed or evangelical Christians and Theonomists will be contradicting each other—the former attempting to persuade the electorate to take biblical positions only on second table commands while the latter proclaim the necessity of instituting Mosaic penalties for first table crimes as well.

The theological consequences of choosing the wrong hermeneutic are far more serious. If applying all unamended Mosaic judicials remains a Christian duty, eternal consequences follow. For if Theonomy is scriptural, non-Theonomic Christians hinder their sanctification and add to humanity's rebellion against God by not following, teaching, and promoting the civil laws. On the last day, they will be found among the least in the kingdom of heaven[93]—a judgment well worth avoiding, whatever the specific result of it may be. Yet, if Theonomy is unbiblical, Theonomists, by adding an unbiblical doctrine to their teaching, are hindering Christians from growing in grace, misrepresenting God's New Covenant requirements to unbelievers,[94] maintaining an unnecessary debate between Christians, and creating much unnecessary opposition to Christian evangelism. Finally, if Theonomy is unscriptural, its advocates are "generating God's displeasure [by] taking an erroneous teaching position with respect to the details of the law" and risk God's rebuke for adding to his word the thesis that obeying and promoting all unamended Old Testament civil laws is part of the Christian's New Covenant duty when God has not so demanded it.[95] All Christians, therefore, must give Bahnsen's work the most careful and thorough examination, one that must begin with a thorough test of the scriptural support for the Theonomic hermeneutic.

---

93. Matt 5:19.
94. On this see Olson, "Invitation to a Stoning."
95. Prov 30:6.

2

The Scriptural Foundation for the Theonomic Hermeneutic

MOST THEONOMISTS LIMIT THEIR application of general equity because Jesus says, "Do not think that I came to abolish the Law or the Prophets; I did not come to abolish but to fulfill. For truly I say to you, until heaven and earth pass away, not the smallest letter or stroke shall pass away from the Law until all is accomplished."[1]

Theonomists believe that Christ here teaches "the abiding validity of the law in exhaustive detail"[2] until the end of the church age (except for those points he would later amend).[3] Bahnsen saw this text as "the *locus classicus* pertaining to Jesus and the law"[4] and "one of the main supporting texts for the theonomic view,"[5] and implied it is the "fundamental scriptural support for the [Theonomic] thesis."[6] Yet he also denied that it is "the only text which could be used to substantiate the Theonomic

---

1. Matt 5:17–20.

2. The phrase is Bahnsen's title for the chapter in which he exegetes Matt 5:17–20 (*Theonomy*, 41–87). It is not a fully accurate summary of his position since it lacks the qualification "except where amended by the Lawgiver." But if Bahnsen's exegesis of Matt 5:17–18 is correct, "the abiding validity of the law in exhaustive detail" until the end of the church age is exactly what Christ taught.

3. If this was, in fact what Christ intended to teach, then general equity cannot be a ground for determining that a Mosaic stipulation no longer applies to the same situation it originally addressed when given; it may only be used to apply Mosaic stipulations to situations that the Mosaic law did not directly address.

4. Bahnsen, *Theonomy*, 41.

5. Bahnsen, *No Other Standard*, 163. Bahnsen also says the other main supporting text is Rom 13:1–7.

6. Bahnsen, *Theonomy*, 38.

operating premise."[7] Consequently, he believed that critics[8] who claimed that Theonomy could be proven unscriptural by demonstrating errors in his exegesis[9] of this passage were putting forth a straw-man argument, since, according to Bahnsen, the "fundamental operating premises of theonomic ethics could be—indeed, in my books, are—readily proven from any number of New Testament passages, only one of which is Matthew 5:17–19. Because it is such an explicit and important text and has often been made the center of discussion, [*Theonomy in Christian Ethics*] gives it detailed discussion. But the theonomic thesis could be demonstrated without any reference to this text at all."[10]

In support of this claim, Bahnsen and others have cited a number of Scriptures that, they say, establish the continuing validity of the Mosaic judicial laws in the New Testament age.[11] Yet unlike Matt 5:17–18, in which Christ identifies how much of the Mosaic law will continue until a certain point, and also identifies that point, none of the other texts mentioned by Theonomists establishes either of these supremely important details. Since texts such as Gen 49:10, 1 Pet 2:13, 14, and Heb 7:12 and 8:13 show that at least some of the Mosaic laws do not continue in the New Covenant, Theonomists must find at least one Scripture that tells us to what extent the Mosaic laws continue to be valid today. Upon examination, however, each of the additional texts that Theonomists have put

---

7. Bahnsen, "God's Law and Gospel Prosperity"; Bahnsen, *No Other Standard*, 273.

8. See, for example, Fowler, *God's Law Free from Legalism*, and House and Ice, *Dominion Theology*.

9. Exegesis is the art of discovering what an author or speaker meant by his words and the putting forth of reasons why particular understandings of such meanings are either correct or incorrect.

10. Bahnsen, "Response to Wayne G. Strickland," 297–98.

11. Bahnsen gives a number of these texts in *Theonomy*, 250–62, and Strevel cites many of them when attempting to disprove the Calvin-Westminster claim that the dispute concerns the difference in hermeneutics between the two camps. Strevel's other objection is that Theonomy's critics "are operating on the straw-man assumption that theonomic ethics does not allow for significant changes between the old and new economy. On the contrary, theonomy maintains that there are significant differences in the manner of observation of the Mosaic law" (Strevel, "Theonomic Precedent," 323). What nullifies Strevel's argument is that Bahnsen's version of Theonomy allows no changes whatsoever to Mosaic civil laws or punishments except where the Lawgiver amends them. Unfortunately, such amendments cannot be found in the New Testament and, if Bahnsen's exegesis of Matt 5:18 is correct, the necessary consequence (which Bahnsen rejects on exegetically insufficient grounds) is that the Lawgiver has specifically ruled out making any changes to the Law whatsoever until the end of the church age.

forward to justify their view fails to establish the point. Matthew 4:4, although laying down the general principle that we live by the Scriptures, does not tell us to what extent the New Covenant affects the contemporary applicability of Old Covenant Scriptures. This same omission also nullifies Theonomic appeals to 2 Tim 3:16. For while all the Old Testament remains profitable for rebuke, correction, and training in righteousness for believers, that Scripture does not tell us the extent to which scripturally unamended Old Testament judicial laws must be applied to civil governments not in covenant with God.

Although Christ cites the law as authoritative in numerous texts,[12] in each case he speaks directly to Jews living under the then-operative Old Covenant, a consideration that also invalidates any appeals to passages where those living under that covenant are commended.[13] Since the law would stand until at least Christ's crucifixion, and his citing of the law in these verses addresses situations occurring under the then-valid Old Covenant, rather than explicitly pointing to the forthcoming New Covenant context, we cannot presume that Christ meant us to understand him in these texts as teaching the exhaustive validity of the Mosaic law for Christians in the church age. The same consideration invalidates Theonomic appeals to any Old Testament passage referring to individual obedience, as well as to texts such as Matt 12:5, Mark 2:25–28, and John 7:23, in which Jesus vindicates his own behavior as a Jew living under the Old Covenant.

New Testament texts like 1 Cor 7:19 or 9:20 also prove insufficient to make the Theonomic point. Paul may have there intended "the commandments of God" and "Christ's law" to refer to the Decalogue. In the same way, texts outlining individual sanctification[14] simply do not address whether all unamended civil laws are meant to be applied in Gentile nations in the New Covenant era. In addition, although Christians are required to reprove the works of evil (Eph 5:11); understand the Lord's will and be wise (Eph 5:17); follow after righteousness (1 Tim 6:11); depart from iniquity (2 Tim 2:19, 1 John 3:4); and pursue righteousness and godliness (1 Tim 6:14), these truths say nothing about

---

12. Matt 12:3, 15:3–9, 19:17, 21:16, 42, 22:31; Mark 1:44, 2:25, 7:1–13, 10:3, 17, 11:17, 12:14ff., 28ff.; and John 7:19, 23; 8:17; 10:34.

13. Luke 1:6; 2:21–24, 27, 39; and 23:56.

14. Rom 6:12–19, 12:1, 2, 9–21; 2 Cor 7:21 and Gal 5:13–18, 2 Pet 2:21, and Rev 12:17; 14:12.

the extent to which the judicial laws continue—they are simply not mentioned.[15] The same objection also prevents Theonomists from anchoring Theonomy in Jas 3:18; 1 John 2:17, 3:3–5, 5:2f.; 2 John 6; and 1 Pet 4:17. James 4:11 does not establish a Mosaic judicial; its reiteration of the ninth commandment is merely a warning against breaking the moral law. Although Heb 10:26–29 teaches that the equity of the punishment for rejecting God is the same in both covenant eras, it does not follow from that Scripture that the standard by which obedience will be judged includes all dominically unamended Mosaic judicial laws.

When Paul (in 1 Cor 14:34) or James (in Jas 2:8–10) cites deductions from the law as valid in the New Testament, such use in itself does not settle the question about which hermeneutic they used to make that decision, and the texts say nothing about whether all divinely unamended civil laws should now be applied in states not in covenant with God. In some places (e.g., 1 Pet 2:17), although an Old Testament allusion may underline a New Testament command, the allusion is unclear and the command stands on its own without Old Testament support from specific civil laws.

Christ's teaching his disciples to pray "thy will be done on earth as it is in heaven" (Matt 6:44) does not settle the question of what is God's will for contemporary civil laws, nor can we find all unamended civil laws validated for the New Covenant in Matt 7:23 and 13:41, Mark 3:35, or Matt 28:19.

The several occasions where apostles apply an Old Testament stipulation in the New Testament, such as in 1 Cor 9:9–11 (in which the Old Testament principle of right treatment of one's animal is applied outside its original context in the covenant state to resolve a different situation within the covenant church), do not endorse Bahnsen's hermeneutic. Such applications to situations similar but not identical to the situation legislated in the Old Testament law (e.g., 1 Cor 9:7–10, 2 Cor 6:4) are not what the Theonomy debate is about: they are merely examples of that use of general equity upon which both sides agree. Paul's application of Deut 19:15 to protect elders from unsupported charges in 1 Tim 5:19 does not decide the matter, as his application of the Old Testament civil law is in the realm of the church, not the state. Nor do Scriptures like Matt

---

15. That the Decalogue or moral law remains valid in the New Testament and throughout the church age is taken for granted by almost all involved on either side of the Theonomy debate.

7:12 or Mark 12:31 shed light on the matter; since the individuals there described walk in the ways of God's moral law, they will never commit a Mosaic crime and will never encounter the civil law as a defendant.

Since the Mosaic law had been the operative covenant until a few weeks or months prior to Stephen's trial, his charge (Acts 7:53) that the Jewish leaders had broken the law is insufficient to establish the Theonomic case. For the most recent sin he charged them with was their role in Christ's death, a violation of the then-operative Old Covenant. Nor can Paul's defense before Festus settle the question; on trial in a Roman court before a Roman judge under Roman law, his unqualified comment in Acts 23:1–5 that "if I . . . have committed anything worthy of death I do not refuse to die" must be read as referring to offenses he may or may not have committed under Roman law, and thus cannot be held to be a reference to the continuity of all unamended Mosaic judicial laws in states other than Judea.

That everything is now under Christ's feet (Heb 1:8, 9) and that Christ inherited David's throne (Luke 1:32) are statements that also do not tell us which civil stipulations of the law remain valid in today's different covenantal context. And although Ps 2:10–12 exhorts pagan kings to "show discernment," to "take warning," to "worship the Lord with reverence," and to "do homage to the Son," it does not specify whether these rulers were to institute all Mosaic civil stipulations or whether they were to apply God's natural revelation of righteousness, written first on the heart of Adam in the garden and in the hearts of all who followed after him, to their non-covenanted contexts.[16] Romans 13:1–7 does not command Christian obedience to the Mosaic law; it commands Christian obedience to the civil laws of the states in which they now live. And for the initial recipients of Paul's letter, this meant Roman law, a system that differed from the Mosaic law at many significant points.

In recent years some Theonomists have attempted to justify their hermeneutic from 1 Tim 1:9–11.[17] Since Paul is clearly saying that the

---

16. None of the Old Testament (Bahnsen, *Theonomy*, 331–54) or New Testament (*Theonomy*, 55–388) texts Bahnsen discusses in his examination of the civil magistrate outside Israel address this issue. That Old Testament kings and states were judged for their violations of God's law does not answer this question since they were judged for their violations of God's moral law or for laws that they should have known were valid on the basis of general equity. Scripture never mentions a case of a nation judged solely because its civil law differed from Mosaic law.

17. Notable Theonomists holding this view include Bahnsen's former publisher, Gary North, and Gary DeMar.

law remains good if one uses it "lawfully," and he defines one lawful use as being "for those who are lawless and rebellious, the ungodly and sinners . . . and whatever else is contrary to sound teaching according to the glorious gospel of our Lord Jesus Christ," they argue that we may deduce the Theonomic hermeneutic from Paul's remark.

But when we look at these verses in context, we have to think again. In the first place, Paul's primary focus is not on the civil laws themselves; instead, Paul is using them, as a contrasting illustration, to emphasize a point he wants to make about another subject entirely. He is drawing a contrast between the right use of the law and the "strange doctrines" taught by "certain men" whom he tells Timothy to rebuke in verse 2. These strange doctrines focused on "myths and endless genealogies" of the law rather than how to achieve the goals of "love from a pure heart and a sincere faith." It is against this background of an unlawful use of the law that Paul contrasts the lawful use of the law: to restrain the evil behavior of unregenerate men. But the word Paul uses for "lawfully" is not the adjective *nomimos*, "conformable to law, lawful."[18] Instead, he chooses a different word, *nomimoos*, which means "*according to the rules or laws* of athletics."[19] Paul metaphorically pictures the law as having its own rules of usage to make the point that the Mosaic law must be used in "*its* intended way or purpose."[20] The false teachers, by focusing on what was unimportant, were breaking the rules of using the law in the same way that someone who uses a pool cue to make a golf putt violates the rules of golf. Paul is not requiring Christians to live by the Mosaic judicial laws; instead, he is rebuking the false teachers' foolish misuse of the law by contrasting it with the way God intended the law to be used. That intended use was then valid in Judea and within the social reach of the Jewish Diaspora, and it would remain so until the destruction of Jerusalem.

But if restraining the evil actions of unrighteous men is in accord with the rules governing the law's use, then Theonomists may ask: Doesn't that prove that the Mosaic judicial laws are the standard that must be used today? The answer is no. All that Paul is implying is that

---

18. Bauer, W., W. F Arndt, and F. W. Gingrich, *A Greek-English Lexicon of the New Testament and Other Early Christian Literature*, 2nd ed., 541. (Bahnsen used this edition.)

19. BAGD, 541; cf. 2 Tim 2:5.

20. Bahnsen, *Theonomy*, 196.

if someone made use of the law for such a purpose, that use of the law would be legitimate. And while such use of the law was indeed legitimate in Judea before AD 70, when the Mosaic judicial laws were the civil law code of the Jewish state, Paul here says nothing about whether the Mosaic stipulations remain the only legitimate means for civil governments not in covenant with God to use to achieve these ends. Since Paul neither commands the use of the judicial laws in the church age nor says that the judicial laws are the only lawful way of restraining unrighteousness, these verses also fail to establish the Theonomic hermeneutic.

THE HEART OF THE THEONOMY DEBATE: MATTHEW 5:17–20

Since none of the additional texts to which Bahnsen and other Theonomists have referred shows how many of the Mosaic civil laws are meant to continue throughout the church age, Bahnsen's exegesis of Matt 5:17–18 remains essential for establishing the Theonomic thesis. As T. David Gordon remarked,

> if Bahnsen cannot make his case from this test, his case is not made.
>
> We might go further and suggest that Bahnsen not only found in this passage a convenient defense of his hermeneutic, but that he could have found such a defense only here. The rest of the NT is so entirely silent on the issue, that it was necessary to Theonomy's case to establish itself on the basis of this text. Other NT passages provide counter evidence. The sweeping statement (covenantally conditioned) in Heb. 7:12 that where the priesthood changes, necessarily the law must change; Paul's general statement that believers are not "under the law" (Rom. 6:14), Paul's discussing the matter of civil obedience without any reference to the Sinai legislation (Rom. 13); and the evident suspending of the ceremonial legislation by the Jerusalem Council, Paul, and the author of Hebrews are matters which point compellingly away from Bahnsen's suggestion that the Sinai legislation is abidingly valid in exhaustive detail.[21]

---

21. Gordon, "Critique of Theonomy," 28. Gordon's list is not exhaustive. Christ's dealing with the woman taken in adultery (John 8:1–11); the fact that all of Paul's extended discussions of how believers are sanctified lack explicit reference to the law as a means of sanctification (and in the two critical discussions, Rom 6:1—7:6 and Gal 5:13–26, we find Paul explicitly stating that in sanctification the Christian is either "dead to" [Rom 7:6] or "not under" [Gal 5:18] the law). Paul's instructions to the Corinthian church (1 Cor 5:1–12) about how they were to deal with their incestuous member, also point away from Bahnsen's view.

The second reason that Theonomy's critics are correct to focus on Matt 5:17–20 becomes evident when one considers Bahnsen's attempt to provide an additional foundation for his thesis by presenting a series of deductions from other biblically sound theological premises, which, he claimed, supported his thesis. However, these attempts to prove his fundamental Theonomic premise either presume his exegesis of one of the above-mentioned Scriptures or his exegesis of Matt 5:17–18, or rely upon unsound reasoning. If his exegesis or his reasoning collapses, these theological justifications of his Theonomy fall with them. For example, the principal exegetical argument underlying the chapter in *Theonomy* titled "Covenantal Unity" stands only so long as his assertion: "Christ said in Matthew 5:17f. the epochal advent of the awaited Messiah did not have the effect of abrogating the law, rather the Mediator of the better covenant *confirmed* the Older Testamental *law*"[22] can withstand criticism. If that assertion fails, the fact that elements from Sinai continue in the New Covenant is no longer sufficient in itself to establish the Theonomic operating premise, since what remains unproven is whether the civil laws are included within the covenantal continuities rather than the discontinuities Bahnsen also mentions. In this connection, it is noteworthy that John Ball, the most significant English Covenantal theologian of the Westminster era, specifically denied that the Mosaic judicial laws remained valid because of covenantal continuity.[23]

Second, the argument that we can "anticipate that the law of the Mosaic covenant would have permanent validity from the fact (1) that *other* New Testament covenants have continuing significance in the New Covenant (e.g. Adamic covenant—Rom. 16:20, Noahic covenant—2 Peter 3:5–9, Abrahamic covenant—Rom. 4:16f, and Davidic covenant—Rom. 15:12),"[24] does not take into account the fact that none of these covenants is described in the New Testament as being the operative judicial laws which New Covenant era believers now live.

Consequently, until and unless Theonomists can provide an additional explicit scriptural foundation text for the Theonomic thesis that all unamended Mosaic civil laws remain valid in the New Covenant, thereby making good this deficiency, the sole scriptural support for

---

22. Bahnsen, *Theonomy*, 183.
23. Ball, *A Treatise of the Covenant of Grace*, 15.
24. Bahnsen, *Theonomy*, 184.

the Theonomic hermeneutic remains Bahnsen's understanding of Matt 5:17–18.

To those lacking firsthand knowledge of Greek or access to the basic tools of exegesis, Bahnsen's analysis appears to be intimidatingly thorough and unanswerable. Consequently, some Christians have too quickly believed that his understanding of Theonomy rests upon accurate scriptural exposition. Given that Bahnsen's understanding of these verses is crucial for the Theonomic hermeneutic, the lack of a full critique of his exegesis written from the historic Reformed perspective is a serious problem.

Our next step, therefore, is to examine the analysis of Matt 5:17–20 that Bahnsen put forward to justify his Theonomic hermeneutic. We shall consider both the initial statement of his thesis in *Theonomy* as well as some of his responses to critics with a view to answering this question: on how firm a scriptural foundation does his thesis rest? As we pursue our investigation, we shall find that Bahnsen makes numerous errors in exegetical procedure; he employs a number of doubtful or even impossible translations or implications for key words; and he fails to refute or discuss highly plausible alternative understandings of these words, even though all of them are found in the standard reference works of which he was known to be aware. In addition, he misrepresents several commentators, both directly and by implication, to make them appear to support his thesis at points where, in fact, they contradict him; and he gives superficial responses to some critical objections.[25] Finally, in a number of places, Bahnsen refutes his own arguments—without, apparently, realizing that he has done so. These procedural errors nullify the evidence for all of his major conclusions and fatally undermine his thesis.

THE SITUATIONAL SETTING OF MATTHEW 5:17–20

It is best to begin reviewing Bahnsen's work by considering certain aspects of the setting of the Sermon on the Mount. Then we will examine

---

25. This is not to suggest that Bahnsen attempted to mislead his readers. The present writer believes that Bahnsen's errors were largely due to overwork: when Bahnsen wrote his thesis (which is three times the customary length), he was recently married, had a newborn child, was simultaneously completing MDiv and ThM degrees in the time in which one degree is normally taken, and was working as youth director for a local church. See Bahnsen, David, "The Life of Greg L. Bahnsen," 12–13.

Matt 5:17–20 in detail, and show how Christ's teachings here relate to verses 21–48. As we work through this process, we will both critique Bahnsen's interpretation and advance another, which better fits the data. Throughout, we shall consider how critics have challenged Bahnsen's arguments, and we shall examine his attempted rebuttals.

Together with Bahnsen and many other Reformed and Evangelical scholars, the present writer considers the Sermon on the Mount to be a unified sermon.[26] But if we regard these chapters as a single sermon, we must keep in mind the characteristics and the limitations of the sermon format. One characteristic is the preacher's need to address different concerns in different members of the audience, often at the same time. This is a relevant consideration when analyzing this sermon since not only were Christ's disciples present, but in addition, "the multitudes were amazed at His teaching" (Matt 7:28). And since, in John 8, Jesus refers to "Jews who had believed Him" (v. 31) as "children of your father the devil" (v. 44), we cannot assume that all in the crowds following Jesus in those early days were indeed true disciples.

Three subgroups may be discerned within the crowd. The first group is Jesus' true disciples. The second consists of folks who are interested in Jesus but who have not yet fully understood the costs of being a disciple. Later, as his teachings began to include more challenging statements, many of these people would withdraw and "not [walk] with him anymore."[27] The last subgroup of the crowd is the scribes, the Pharisees, and their followers. While the Bible is silent on whether or not they were explicitly spying on Christ at this relatively early point in his ministry, Matthew does record that although Jesus was based in Galilee before the sermon was preached, he was being followed by large crowds of people from as far afield as Jerusalem.[28] This was a development that the Pharisees, who investigated John the Baptist early in his ministry (Matt 3:7), were unlikely to have ignored. Christ's first cleansing of the temple (John 2:13–25), his eating with tax collectors and sinners (Luke 5:27–32), his letting his disciples pick grain on the Sabbath (Luke 6:1–5), and his healing of the man with the withered hand (Luke 6:5–11) could

---

26. Compare Bahnsen, *Theonomy*, 46, n. 18; Carson, *Matthew Chapters 1 through 12*, 123–28.
27. John 6:66.
28. Matt 4:23, 25.

well have occurred before the sermon was preached.[29] Any one of these actions, which contradicted the Pharisaic understanding of the law, would have been enough for the Pharisees to believe that Christ was out to destroy the law—the latter miracle so enraged them that they plotted (on the Sabbath!) to kill him. So we cannot reject the possibility that some of the Pharisees or their surrogates or spies may have been in the crowd that day. Even if the Pharisees or their spies were not physically in the crowd when this sermon was preached, Jesus would have known that his teaching, laying out as it does the relationship between himself and the Mosaic law in explicit contrast to Pharisaical teachings, would be speedily brought to his enemies' attention. So for all practical purposes, Jesus knew that he was speaking directly to them.

That his enemies were present in some way in Jesus' audience reminds us of another point. Jesus does not speak all the truth all the time to all of his hearers. Explaining to his disciples why he teaches in parables, Jesus says:

> To you it has been granted to know the mysteries of the kingdom of heaven but to them it has not been granted . . . Therefore I speak to them in parables; because while seeing they do not see, and while hearing they do not hear nor do they understand. And in their case the prophecy of Isaiah is being fulfilled, which says:
> You will keep on hearing, but will not understand
> And you will keep on seeing, but will not perceive;
> For the heart of this people has become dull,
> And with their ears they scarcely hear,
> And they have closed their eyes,
> Lest they should see with their eyes,
> And hear with their ears,
> And understand with their heart and return,
> And I should heal them. (Isa 6:9, 10)[30]

If Jesus is prepared to speak obscurely to the crowds in general, who have not been given to know the mysteries, he must have seen himself as equally free to do so when speaking to the Pharisees, whom he called "blind guides of the blind."[31] So we cannot forget that Jesus, when

---

29. Luke, who may have recorded events in chronological order (Luke 1:3), recounts these incidents before the sermon takes place. Matthew's account of the latter miracle gives the detail that the Pharisees plotted to kill Jesus (Matt 12:14).

30. Matt 13:14, 15.

31. Matt 15:14.

addressing an audience that includes Pharisees, may intend to deliberately obscure his message.

The presence of these three subgroups raises some additional considerations to keep in mind as we proceed. First, we must consider whether or not Jesus is addressing any single subgroup or any combination of the three subgroups at any time. Second, we will have to examine whether or not he is crafting particular sayings to mean different things to different subgroups at the same time.

An additional temporal element also needs consideration. If Jesus had planned to fulfill the law in any sense, at any point sooner than the end of the church age, we must keep in mind that that point would have been either some months or some years after Jesus gave the sermon. Hence we must not forget that Jesus may well be addressing the relation of his teaching to both the Mosaic law and Pharisaic misinterpretations thereof, with respect to two periods of time: the period leading up to the fulfillment of the law, and the period after its fulfillment.

While Bahnsen correctly recognizes that Jesus contrasts his teaching with that of the Pharisees, he does not discuss the possibility that Christ may have regarded himself as free to employ a measure of obscurity in this sermon. Nor does he consider how the progression of Christ's thoughts may have been affected by a possible need to address his teaching to differing subgroups, or a possible need to address two temporal situations.

Finally, we must consider the immediate context. Up until verse 16 of the sermon, Christ has been speaking of his disciples. Now, he begins verse 17 by issuing a warning that his hearers should not think or even begin to think that his purpose was to destroy or abolish the law. Why does he change his subject? And why is this warning necessary?

Bahnsen believes that Christ knew "the danger that His hearers or scribal opponents might misunderstand or willfully distort His doctrine of the law, so He commands them not even to start thinking that the Messiah abrogates the law."[32]

But this answer does not explain why Christ would expect his hearers or his opponents to misunderstand or distort his doctrine of the law, something which, to this point in the sermon, he has not explicitly mentioned.

---

32. Bahnsen, *Theonomy*, 49.

The answer is found in verses 14–16. Even if the Pharisees had had no previous concerns about his view of the law,[33] Christ's statement that his disciples were "the light of the world" is, in itself, a statement that would have prompted his enemies to surmise that Christ would destroy the law, even if they had not come to that conclusion already.[34] For by calling his disciples "the light of the world," Christ applied to them a metaphor that the Old Testament famously attributes to God's words (implicitly the Mosaic law)[35] and that the Apocrypha attributes to Elijah (a prototypical scribe in post-Captivity Jewish thought).[36] By transferring the metaphor of light from the law to his disciples, Christ raises the following questions: Why now are the disciples the light of the world instead of the law, and why would their good works, rather than those of the followers of the law, glorify God?

By calling the disciples the light of the world, Christ has made an implicit claim that the law or its adherents were no longer the light of the world. The claim that his disciples were now that light would instantly raise the question of whether or not the teacher making such a claim was out "destroy the law or the prophets" by seducing Israel away from its covenantally required obedience to the Mosaic stipulations. Such a change would have the most serious consequences for the Jewish nation. For the covenant between God and Israel stated that if anyone ever seduced Israel away from its obedience to the Mosaic stipulations, God was covenantally obliged to destroy the nation. The Jewish people had once before suffered the destruction of their nation in the Babylonian Captivity, and only the Maccabean revolt had narrowly averted a second destruction.

The charge that Christ both posits and answers here, that he would abolish or destroy the Mosaic law, is itself a direct allusion to an account of the latter incident. In 167 BC, the Syrian monarch Antiochus abolished the Mosaic laws in Judea, and thereby precipitated the Maccabean revolt. The apocryphal book 2 Maccabees sums up the revolt thus: "The

---

33. If, as some commentators think, Luke's Gospel was written in chronological order, the Pharisees were already opposing Jesus by the time this sermon was preached (Luke 5:20–24, 29–32, 6:1–11).

34. In John 8:13, the Pharisees are very quick to challenge Christ's explicit claim to be "the light of the world."

35. Ps 119:105, 130; Isa 51:4–8.

36. Sir 48:1.

story of Judas Maccabeus and his brothers, . . . so that though few in number they seized the whole land and pursued the barbarian hordes, and recovered the temple famous throughout the world and freed the city and restored the laws that were about to be abolished (*kataluo*).[37]

It is unfortunate that Bahnsen did not discuss how Christ's words in verses 14–16 lead into, and set the stage for, verse 17. For Christ may well have intended his hearers to hear "Do not begin to think that I am come to destroy the law or the prophets" as his reply to an implied Pharisaic charge that he was a second Antiochus, out to seduce Israel to abandon its covenantally required obedience to the Mosaic law.

---

37. 2 Macc 2:19–22 The Apocrypha, Revised Standard Version. Since Antiochus had already formally abolished the Mosaic laws before the revolt began, translating *kataluo* by "destroyed" rather than by "abolished" is indicated, as the latter translation creates a contradiction with the actual events.

3

Is Christ "Confirming" or "Completing" the Law?
Matthew 5:17

IN THE FINAL ANALYSIS, Bahnsen's claim that Jesus taught the Theonomic thesis in these verses will stand or fall on whether he is correct in his understanding of verse 17. He believes that when Christ said, "Do not think that I came to destroy the Law or the Prophets; I did not come to destroy but to fulfill,"[1] he intended his hearers to understand him as teaching "Do not think that I came to annul the ethical stipulations of the Law or the Prophets; I did not come to abolish them but to confirm them." Bahnsen's argument for this understanding depends on five premises, of which the first three are:

1. By "the law or the prophets," Christ meant us to understand him as primarily referring to "the ethical stipulations of the law."

2. That the Greek verb *kataluo* here means "abolish" or "annul" and not "destroy" (another known meaning of the verb).

3. That the Greek word *alla* (but) always forces a contrast of exact opposites between the words it separates, in this case "annul/destroy" and "fulfill."

In order to sustain his view, Bahnsen must establish that all three of these premises are correct. For if Christ did not intend us to understand him as referring to the ethical stipulations of the law but to something else, Christ is not teaching what Bahnsen thinks he is in Matthew 5:17–20. Similarly, if Christ intended *katalusai* to mean something other than "annul" when used here of the Mosaic law, then the antonym "confirm" is not the only possible translation for *pleroosai*; its more common

---

1. Author's translation.

meanings of "fulfill" or "complete" may still apply. In addition, if *alla* does not always force a contrast of exact opposites, then even if Christ intended *katalusai* in the sense of "annul," we are not locked into translating *pleroosai* as "confirm" over and against its other known meanings.

In addition, Bahnsen requires at least one of two additional premises to hold in order to complete his argument. These premises are:

4. That *pleroo*, normally translated "fulfill," can be legitimately translated as "confirm" in the sense of "establishing the continuing validity of," *or*,

5. Even if *pleroo* cannot be legitimately translated as "confirm" in the sense of "establishing the continuing validity of the ethical stipulations of the law," "confirming" the law in the sense of "establishing the continuing validity of" its ethical stipulations is a legitimate implication of the more usual translation "fulfill," and thus a legitimate connotation of the word.

It is essential to Bahnsen's argument that at least one of these two latter premises be able to withstand criticism. For if *pleroo* is never used in the sense of "confirming" or "establishing the continuing validity of" something before the close of the New Testament era, then we lack the needed evidence to conclude that Christ was explicitly teaching the Theonomic thesis in these verses. And even though "confirmation" in the sense of confirming a prophecy's divine origin and the original prophet's inspiration is a legitimate implication of translating *pleroo* as "fulfill," that fact is not sufficient to validate translating pleroo by "confirm," For the Theonomic view requires a quite different sense of "confirm:" that of "establishing the ongoing validity of" the law's ethical stipulations. Theonomists must show that this latter sense of pleroo is an inherently necessary and legitimate implication of the known meaning "fulfill" before we can conclude that Christ was "implying" the Theonomic thesis here. If we cannot find this latter meaning documented in the literature before the close of the New Testament, or as a necessary logical consequence of the known translation "fulfill," then the fifth premise, which has become essential, also collapses.

At each of these five steps in his argument, Bahnsen must show that his chosen alternative is either the only possible meaning of the word in question or that it is superior to all other possibilities. Such an exercise is the art and science of biblical exegesis. Good exegesis will examine all relevant possibilities in each case and will demonstrate why a particular alternative is regarded as superior as well as providing valid reasons for rejecting others. In the rest of this chapter, we shall examine Bahnsen's exegesis and see how it measures up to this standard.

THE LAW OR THE PROPHETS

Since the theme of these verses is the nature of Christ's relationship to "the Law or the Prophets," understanding what Jesus means by this phrase is crucial. If we misunderstand him here, we will inevitably misunderstand his intent throughout the passage. At this point, Bahnsen makes two serious errors; he mistranslates one word in the phrase itself and he misunderstands what Christ intended by the phrase as a whole.

Nobody will challenge Bahnsen's claim that *ton nomos* ("the Law") usually refers to "more than simply those aspects of the Mosaic legislation (i.e., 'the Law') which have permanent moral application and sanction; the class of commandments traditionally termed 'ceremonial' or 'ritual' is also within the scope of the term . . . Hence τον νομοσ includes all of God's stipulations as revealed in 'the Law' of the Older Testament."[2] Similarly, nobody will take issue with him over his translation of *tous profetas* as "the Prophets," a phrase normally understood as a reference to the Old Testament's prophetic books.

The entire phrase "the law or the prophets" has been usually understood, like the companion phrases "the law and the prophets,"[3] "Moses and the prophets,"[4] and "the law of Moses, and the prophets and the psalms,"[5] to be "simply a Jewish designation for the whole OT."[6] Bahnsen initially appears to agree with this when he comments that "Jesus phrases His teaching in such a way as to embrace the entire canon of the Older Testament."[7] But when Bahnsen suggested that the phrase "the law or the prophets is best taken as focusing on the *ethical stipulations* contained in the canon of the entire Older Testament,"[8] he suggested a considerably narrower and more controversial meaning to the phrase.

---

2. Bahnsen, *Theonomy*, 51.
3. Matt 7:12, 11:13, 22:40; Luke 16:16; Acts 13:15, 24:14; Rom 3:21.
4. Luke 16:29, 31; 24:27.
5. Luke 24:44.
6. Hodge, "Exegetical Response," 7.
7. Bahnsen, *Theonomy*, 52.
8. Ibid., 53.

Bahnsen believes that there are six reasons supporting this understanding of Christ's intent. First, "the context [of Matthew 5:17] clearly demonstrates that both 'the law' and 'the prophets' refer to divine demand and not prophecy or promise."[9] Second, he noted that as "nobody would have expected the self-proclaimed Messiah to turn back the prophecies referring to Himself, it would hardly call for a specific and emphatic pronouncement to correct an unheld opinion."[10] Third, the preceding verse (v. 16) "deals with good works."[11] Fourth, verses "21–48 correct misinterpretation of the Divine demands."[12] Fifth, "Matt 7:12 (cf. Matt 22:40) uses 'the law and prophets' exclusively for moral demands." Finally, and "most telling . . . verses 18 and 19 following, which explain and apply verse 17 . . . mention only the law."[13] Each of these reasons needs to be considered.

The idea that the context of verse 17 rules out prophecy or promise is untenable; the point of verse 18 ("until heaven and earth pass away, not the smallest letter or stroke shall pass away from the law") is not merely a reference to God's ethical demands; it also hints at why God could not achieve reconciliation with man by relaxing the demands of the law. After having proclaimed a law of statutes of such righteousness "by which a man may live if he does them,"[14] altering them unjustly would besmirch God's own holiness. Since he could not justly justify, love, and bring into his family by means of altering his law those who had heretofore been rebels against him—and who, because of their sins, fully deserve an eternal hell at his hand—the only possible way for God to achieve his goal was the death of Christ for sinners. If reconciliation by the means of any other changes to the situation had been possible, Christ's death would not have been necessary.[15] Once we remember that the immutability of the law Christ here mentions is in itself a fundamental reason why Christ's atonement was necessary, planned, prophesied,

---

9. Ibid.
10. Ibid., 52.
11. Ibid., 53.
12. Ibid.
13. Ibid.
14. Lev 18:5.
15. Gal 2:21.

and achieved, we can no longer rule out the possibility that Jesus meant to refer to prophetic fulfillment in verse 17.[16]

Bahnsen supports the idea that Jesus meant the ethical teaching of the prophets while ruling out a reference to their prophecies by supplying a quotation from Meyer. "We are not to think of their predictions as such . . . as nobody could imagine that their abrogation was to be expected from the Messiah."[17] But Meyer is not entirely correct. While none of his opponents would have thought to charge Christ with intending to abrogate the Messianic prophecies at this relatively early point in his ministry—when he was still the darling of the crowds who had not yet realized that his agenda did not match their messianic expectations—his words (particularly if he meant *me nomisete* to be understood in the sense of "do not begin to think") do warn against an opinion that would arise later. For as Christ continued in his mission, two things would become increasingly evident. While the works he was doing testified his being the Messiah,[18] he would make no attempt to throw out the Romans and restore Israel to its former glory, something his contemporaries, misreading the messianic prophecies, expected the Messiah to do. So the following objection would arise: "This man cannot be the Messiah for he is not fulfilling the messianic prophecies." To such an objection, Christ's reply—"Do not think that I came to abolish the . . . prophets. I did not come to abolish but to fulfill"—makes perfect sense. For in effect, Christ is saying, "Do not judge by appearances. Trust me, I am the Messiah and I will fulfill all the messianic prophecies in the way they were meant to be fulfilled—which, however, is not how you expect that they are to come to pass."

But Meyer's statement does help us determine the nature of the hypothetical or actual charge that Christ was addressing. For Meyer correctly asserted that none of Christ's opponents could have plausibly charged him with intent to abrogate the messianic prophecies at this early point in his ministry. If, therefore, the charge to which Christ was

---

16. Gentry objects that whatever Christ means here, he "*cannot* mean that in the final analysis he actually *will* abolish the 'law or prophets'" (*Covenantal Theonomy*, 76). But Gentry's argument hangs on an erroneous assumption: that verse 18 teaches that the law expires at the end of the church age, an assumption that will be shown to be untenable in the next chapter.

17. Meyer, *Critical and Exegetical Hand-book,* 167, quoted in Bahnsen, *Theonomy,* 53.

18. Matt 11:4; cf. Isa 35:5ff.

addressing his reply had, in fact, been made, it is clear that it would have been limited to a charge that Christ was threatening "the law or the prophets" in some other sense of those words, and not an attack on the messianic prophecies. But if his enemies' charge would have been so limited, we encounter a crucial question. Since the prophets, whose role was not to promulgate the law but to enforce it, add no new ethical stipulations to the law, why did Christ add the words *or the prophets* to his denial of the charge if he wanted to focus on the law's ethical stipulations? In the same way, the good works mentioned in verse 16 were works enjoined by the law before they were enforced by the prophets as the law's requirements; the divine demands that the Pharisees had misapplied and Jesus here correctly applies were only enforced by the prophets because they were first proclaimed in the law. So if Jesus was "focusing on" the ethical stipulations of the Mosaic covenant, he had no need to mention "the prophets" here. But Christ not only mentions "the prophets" (when, if the Theonomic hypothesis is correct, he had no need to) but he also uses the disjunctive conjunction *or* to emphasize them.

Bahnsen's third argument for believing that "the law or the prophets" refers to the ethical stipulations of the law is that the context of the preceding verse deals with good works, but this reason is insufficient to make his point. For, while good works are mentioned in the previous verse, they are not its subject. The subject of the verse, as it has been from the beginning of the sermon, is Christ's disciples.[19] Christ teaches first what their character must be,[20] and then he turns to their relationship to the world around them.[21] After Christ called his disciples "the light of the world," in verse 14, he drew the corollary that it was because they were "the light of the world" that the good works they were to be seen doing would result in glory being given to God.[22] As we have seen, by using the metaphor of light to refer to the disciples, Christ would have caused his opponents to wonder whether he was a second Antiochus Epiphanes setting out to destroy the Mosaic law.

---

19. That Christ here is referring to his disciples, in particular, rather than the crowd at large is shown by his claim that his hearers are blessed when people insult, persecute, and slander them because of Christ (v. 11).

20. Matt 5:3–12.

21. Matt 5:13–16.

22. The correlative "thus" or "hence" that makes this point is overlooked by the NASB but is translated by the NIV as "in the same way."

Theonomists might argue that by calling his disciples the light of the world, Christ is confirming that the entire Mosaic law will continue in his new covenant. On this hypothesis, Christ is saying that even though the disciples are now the light of the world instead of the law, it is incorrect to infer from his statement that Christ would change the law. Rather, it was the disciples, and not the Pharisees, who would carry out the full demands of the law that Christ would elucidate in the following verses, and thus the disciples and not the Pharisees were the light of the world. Yet, this is not the only possible way to understand Christ's teaching, and it suffers from a major weakness. It does not explain why Christ, instead of contrasting the disciples with the Pharisees who were sinfully perverting the law, uses a metaphor that contrasts his disciples with the law itself.

On the other hand, if Christ was teaching that he was bringing the Old Covenant to its foretold completion and fulfillment in the institution of the prophesied New Covenant,[23] then, once the shift in covenants had been announced, the Mosaic law would no longer be the light of the world it had been under the Old Covenant, as it would be a way of life no longer fully following God's will. Given this change, Christ's disciples could well have been called the light of the world since they would now be the ones seeking the kingdom of God and proclaiming the covenantal shift as well as living by the true understanding of God's will—in contrast to the Pharisees and their followers, who were living by erroneous interpretations of it. Consequently, the disciples' good deeds would glorify God, whereas those of the Pharisees and their followers would not. Since this interpretation follows naturally from the preceding verses, Bahnsen's argument that the context in the previous verses is that of good works proves insufficient to limit our understanding of "the law or the prophets" as referring to the law's ethical stipulations.

We must therefore return to Matthew 5:17 to examine the disjunctive conjunction "η." All major Bible translations, and almost all commentators, translate this word as "or" in Matthew 5:17 so that the phrase reads "the law or the prophets." Bahnsen, in contrast, stands almost alone in that he believes that the phrase "functions just as" 'law **and** prophets' elsewhere in Scripture."[24] He offers four reasons for this

---

23. Jer 31:31–34.

24. Bahnsen, *Theonomy*, 53. Italics in all quotations are those of the original authors. Boldface in quotations is added by the present writer.

divergence. First, he argues that "Matthew is merely putting variety into his expression (not indicating distinctive emphasis),"[25] at which point he inserts the following footnote: "As suggested by some commentators, e.g., Meyer, *loc. cit.*"[26] But when we turn up the referenced passage in Meyer's commentary, we find Meyer writing "η never stands for *kai* [i.e., "and"] . . . but is always *distinctive*. Here (i.e., Matt 5:17), to abrogate one **or** the other."[27] By either incorrectly attributing his reference or misrepresenting his source, Bahnsen has enlisted Meyer in support of a view that the commentator had explicitly rejected with regard to the very verse under discussion!

We do not know whether or not Bahnsen ever realized that he had misrepresented Meyer. But he did attempt to refute the objection that "or" is normally used distinctively when he pointed out that "when [Matthew] intends the distinctive sense of 'either . . . or . . .' he always uses η ('or') twice in the phrase (Matt 6:24 and 12:33)."[28] But this statement is insufficient to prove the point. For Matthew limits his "double use of η . . . [to] positive statements"[29] such as those in 6:24 and 12:33, and he never employs the double use of "or" in statements that begin with a negative such as "do not think" (5:17). In such cases, the double use of η was unnecessary since, as grammarians Blass, Debrunner, and Funk have pointed out, a "disjunctive expression following a negative can be equivalent to *ou . . . oude,* or 'neither . . . nor' [the negative version of 'either . . . or'])."[30] and they cite Matt 5:17 as an example of this meaning.

Although we may not assume that the standard reference works are inerrant, careful scholars will make sure that they know what those works have to say on any grammatical point that their own work touches upon. If a standard reference disagrees with a writer's argument, good scholarly practice mandates that the writer note the objection to his argument and then go on to give reasons attempting to demonstrate the error

25. Ibid., 52.
26. Ibid., footnote 37.
27. Meyer, *Mathew*, 167. While *Theonomy* lacks a bibliography, and this quotation is there attributed to "Meyer, *loc. cit*," this is the only work by Meyer referenced in *Theonomy*'s footnotes, and the reference is confirmed in *Theonomic Responsibility* and properly credited in its footnotes and bibliography. Bolding is by the present author.
28. Bahnsen, *Theonomy*, 52.
29. Hodge, "Exegetical Response," 8.
30. Blass, Debrunner, and Funk, *A Greek Grammar of the New Testament and Other Early Christian Literature*, 231. This work is hereafter cited as BDF.

of the authority.[31] Bahnsen, by neglecting to provide any reason for disagreeing with Blass, Debrunner, and Funk, fails this test. His ignorance of their refutation of his position suggests that he neglected to perform the routine scholarly check of reviewing his proposed counterargument against the standard grammars and lexicons. More importantly, it also leaves their refutation of his view to stand by default.

Bahnsen's next argument for translating η by "and" instead of "or" is that the word "can be used where one related or similar term can take the place of or support the other. Matthew uses it in this way in Matthew 10:11, 14, 37; 17:25."[32] Although the standard lexicon of New Testament Greek, that of Bauer, Arndt, and Gingrich,[33] agrees with this meaning of the word, the lexicon does not support Bahnsen's conclusion that when used in this sense, η inevitably loses its disjunctive quality. Instead, the lexicon supplies other examples where η is used to relate terms or to have one term support the other where the concept of a disjunction was clearly meant (e.g., John 2:6). Thus, this argument also fails to prove that η must not be translated as "or."

Bahnsen's fourth argument for not taking η disjunctively is Alford's observation that ("'not . . . law or prophets' better expresses the negative correlative than 'not . . . law and prophets'").[34] But "or" is not always the expected conjunction to use when applying verbs to more than one noun in negative constructions. There are at least two forms of negative statement common to Greek and English. First, one may make a negative statement (e.g., "I am not come to destroy the law or the prophets"). In such cases, "or" may be the expected disjunctive conjunction. But when one refutes an otherwise positive statement (such as "The Nazarene is come to destroy the law and the prophets"), and negates it by preceding it with "do not think" or a similar beginning, then the disjunctive conjunction is not necessary to "apply the [verb] to each [of the following terms] severally"[35] since the original positive statement being quoted within the negation did not need the disjunction to do so. If a speaker is forbidding someone else to think a thought that uses the copulative "and" to link its direct objects, then "and" is the link one would expect between the

---

31. On this see Fee, *New Testament Exegesis*, 32, section 13.1.
32. Bahnsen, *Theonomy*, 52.
33. BAGD, 342.
34. Bahnsen, *Theonomy*, 52, citing Alford, *Greek Testament*, 42.
35. Alford, *Greek Testament*, 42.

Is Christ "Confirming" or "Completing" the Law? Matthew 5:17

The third essential reason for Jesus to add "or the Prophets" is that he himself, in his life and his teaching, was the necessary summing up, fulfilling, and transcending of the entire Mosaic covenant. And here we must return to Bahnsen's belief that since "Matt 7:12 (cf. Matt 22:40) uses 'the law and prophets' exclusively for moral demands,"[45] moral demands are therefore what Christ meant in Matt 5:17. Unfortunately for this argument, in Matt 7:12 and 22:40,

> where the expression [the Law and the Prophets] appears to focus on the ethical requirements of [the Old Testament] it is both the law and the prophetic administration of that law which are referred to.
>
> The significance of this observation is profound in its consequences for exegesis. Biblically "law and prophets" are conjoined. They are together in their function, and the prophets are in fact executors of the Sinai covenant. Their anticipation of Messiah's arrival is part of their declaration of judgment on Israel for her unfaithfulness to the covenant, because only the Messiah will be able to deliver from the curses of the Sinai administration."[46]

Once we realize that the prophets were the "executors of the Sinai covenant," it becomes clear that the phrase "the law or the prophets" was not only used to refer to the Scriptures but also to the Mosaic covenant itself. Certainly, this is what Jesus meant when he twice taught that "the Law and the Prophets" were temporary: lasting only "until John."[47] In these two incidents, Jesus could not have intended the phrase to confer scriptural status on these writings since "the Law and the Prophets" did not cease to be Scripture because John had come. Only if Jesus meant the phrase to refer to the Old Covenant itself could he truly say the Law and

---

45. Bahnsen, *Theonomy*, 53.

46. Gordon, "Theonomy," 29. When Gentry wonders whether this understanding "was what *Christ* was teaching in the Sermon" (Gentry, *Covenantal Theonomy*, 63), he is confusing what Christ was teaching with what his hearers already knew. While Christ was not specifically reminding his hearers of these facts in Matt 5:17, it is certain that his hearers already knew from the Old Testament that the prophets had prophesied Messiah's coming as God's response to Israel's unfaithfulness (e.g., Ezek 36:22–27), and they would have also recognized that if the Sinai covenant had not been superseded by the New Covenant announced by Jeremiah then Messiah had not yet come. More importantly they would also have known that if a deceiver were to seduce them into abandoning their covenanted obedience to God, God would reply by deploying the covenantally required judgments.

47. Matt 11:13; Luke 16:16.

the Prophets were "until John," for "in John, the Old Testament dispensation [covenant administration] began to die."[48]

This observation raises the following question: Could Christ have intended "the Law or the Prophets" to refer to the Sinai covenant as a whole? To answer that question, we must consider why Christ's enemies either had charged him with destroying the law or were on the verge of doing so. What exactly did this charge mean?

The Jews of Jesus' day stood in a corporate relationship to God as well as an individual one. Before the New Covenant was inaugurated, they were the one nation on earth that was in a covenant relationship with Almighty God. Ever since the events of the Exodus and the meeting with God at Mount Sinai, where God through Moses had initiated what we call the Mosaic or Sinaitic covenant, he had been their God and they had been his people. If they kept his covenant law, he would bless them as he had promised. But if someone were to deceive them into abandoning God for another god or gods, thus breaking the covenant, then God was covenantally committed to remove them from the Promised Land, and to enforce an additional barrage of covenant curses: something he had done once before in the Babylonian Captivity. Since Christ's calling the disciples "the light of the world" would have provoked the Pharisaic charge that he, like Antiochus, was out to abolish all the Mosaic laws and not just the ethical stipulations thereof, it becomes less likely that we can restrict the meaning of "the Law or the Prophets" to "the ethical stipulations of the Law." Rather, the charge that Christ would destroy "the Law or the Prophets" amounted to a claim that Jesus was a deceiver aiming to destroy the covenant relationship between Israel and God, together with the corollary that, if the people were to follow him, catastrophic judgments from God would ensue.[49]

Theonomists might argue that the disjunctive "or" separating "the law" and "the prophets" invalidates this covenantal understanding of

---

48. Henry, *Commentary on the Whole Bible*, 1259. For older Calvinistic commentators such as Henry, the word *dispensation* is often used to refer to a covenant era.

49. Gentry objects that if Christ was here referring to a change in covenants is correct, then "any Pharisaic complaint about his coming in order to effect a change in the Mosaic system would be legitimate and would not be denied by Christ" (*Covenantal Theonomy*, 63, 64). This objection fails to recognize that Christ was addressing the specific charge that he was a destroying the Law or the Prophets, not a charge that he was instituting a change in covenants. While Christ would have affirmed the latter charge had it been made, he rightly denies the former.

the charge to which Christ was responding, but this is not correct. A disjunctive such as "or" is not always enough to separate two elements of an (implied) single noun. When a waitress asks "Do you want ham or eggs?" no one thinks that the disjunctive in that sentence implies that only one of the two items, ham or eggs is included in the unmentioned underlying concept of breakfast. Her customer might well enjoy both. In the same way, Christ's Jewish contemporaries would have recognized that both law and prophets were included in the Mosaic covenant, the former as the source of its stipulations, the latter functioning as God's "covenant enforcement mediators,"[50] urging obedience to the covenant upon the people, announcing promises of blessings for obedience and curses for disobedience, and heralding the New Covenant yet to come. So, it is likely that Christ's hearers, steeped as they were in the history of the Sinai Covenant and the judgments God had carried out to enforce it, would have heard Christ's phrase as a reference to the Old Covenant itself. Nor could they have missed or misunderstood the serious covenantal implications inherent in the charge to which he was responding.

Theonomists may also object that this view makes Christ out to be dodging the hypothetical or actual charge that he was destroying the law by answering with the irrelevant statement that he has come to bring about the promised New Covenant. In fact, Christ's answer speaks directly to the charge he had placed before the crowd. Since the forthcoming change in covenants had been previously declared by God's prophets, then God cannot possibly be guilty of destroying the Law by implementing the change, nor can the One whom God has chosen to implement the change be guilty of that charge. That Christ will complete the time-limited Sinai covenant by inaugurating the New does not mean he is simply abolishing the Old Covenant. Rather, he is fulfilling it by bringing about the promised New Covenant to which the Old had pointed.[51]

---

50. This accurate description of the prophetic role is found in Fee and Stuart, *How to Read the Bible for All Its Worth*, 151.

51. Gentry believes that such a claim confuses categories. "Theonomists recognize that the Lord terminates 'the one covenant administration' in order to 'inaugurate a new one' . . . [but we may not equate] Mosaic *administration* with Mosaic *legislation*" (*Covenantal Theonomy*, 78). But Gentry errs; Gordon is not confusing categories, but is pointing out cause and effect. For when any covenant is legitimately terminated, its legislation is no longer in force unless it is reinstituted in a subsequent covenant. In the case under consideration, while the moral law and a few specific civil stipulations that

Realizing that mention of the "the law or the prophets" brings the Old Covenant into the picture helps us understand the biblical distinction between the sense in which "the law" vanishes in the New Covenant and the different sense in which it continues today. For "every time in the New Testament where it is said that the law has been 'done away' or rendered inoperative it always, in context, refers not to God's law as absolute, that is, contemplated as 'the law of commandments'... *it always refers to the Mosaic law as covenant law.*"[52]

So, if we take "'the law [or the] prophets' together as a reference to the Sinai covenant, or to the era in which God's people are governed thereby, then it makes sense to understand Jesus to be saying that he has not come (at least in his humiliated state) to abolish that covenantal administration, but to bring it to its conclusion."[53]

Bahnsen does not deny that the phrase "the law or the prophets" can refer to the Sinai covenant. He merely claims that it does not do so in Matthew 5:17. In his view, the possibility that

> Jesus came not to abrogate ... the law in the *past* period of redemptive history (for which it was intended) but now puts to an end the *era* governed by the law ... [suffers] ... from the defect of imposing theological prejudice upon πληροοσαι and infusing it with content that it cannot sustain, [also] this view simply fails to take cognizance of verse 18 following where Jesus clearly states that the law he is discussing remains valid "until heaven and earth have passed away." Furthermore one must take account of the strong adversative αλλα standing between καταλυσαι and πληροοσαι, as well as Jesus' double assertion that He came not to abrogate the law—appearing in the very verse under discussion.[54]

But as we move through these verses, we shall discover that each of these objections will fail. First, *pleroosai* has, among its known meanings, those of "bringing something to completion" or "complete, finish,

---

preceded the Sinai administration, were never terminated, and thus remain valid today, all Mosaic stipulations were terminated upon the demise of that covenant. Unless a Sinaitic stipulation is shown by general equity to be valid in New Covenant–era states, God does not require its application today.

52. Long, *Biblical Law and Ethics*, 19.

53. Gordon, "Theonomy," 30. Gentry's assertion that Gordon is confused between two meanings of Christ's phrase (Gentry, *Covenantal Theonomy*, 54) misses this point.

54. Bahnsen, *Theonomy*, 58.

Is Christ "Confirming" or "Completing" the Law? Matthew 5:17

bring to an end"[55] a time-limited condition; and since Christ finished the Sinai covenant by bringing it to its appointed completion and end, using *pleroo* in reference to completing it imposes no theologically prejudiced novelty of meaning or unsustainable content upon the word whatsoever. Second, Bahnsen begs the question of whether Christ intended *katalusai* to mean "destroy" rather than "annul." If he intended the former meaning, there is no problem with Jesus' assertion that, instead of destroying the law, his purpose was to bring it to its prophesied completion. Next, Bahnsen has overlooked the fact that *alla* does not always force an exact contrast of opposites between the words it separates, in this case *katalusai* and *pleroosai*. Thus, whatever Christ is doing with "the law or the prophets," it does not have to be a direct antonym of "destroy" or "annul." In addition, Bahnsen begs the question of the scheduled terminus of the law by assuming that "until heaven and earth disappear" refers to the same time as "until all things come to pass." As we shall later see, he rejects an alternative understanding of this phrase on insufficient grounds. Nor is this view refuted by Bahnsen's final argument that verses 18 and 19 mention only the law and therefore the "ethical stipulations of the law" is what Christ must have meant by "the law or the prophets."

For verse 18 is Christ's explanation of verse 17. The fact that the laws of the Old Covenant were immutable so long as it was in force is precisely why Christ announces in verse 17 that he has come to bring the covenant containing those laws to its promised completion. It is also why he instructs his disciples in verse 19 not to presume that any changes to the law would be made before the New Covenant was inaugurated—and why, in verse 20, he warns the Jewish religious leaders and those who would follow them in rejecting the New Covenant against placing their hopes in their attempt to live up to their amendments of the Old. For the righteousness thus obtained would prove insufficient to enter the kingdom of heaven.

At this point, Bahnsen's first premise must be rejected. Of the six reasons he gives for supporting his view that Christ was referring to the "ethical stipulations of the law," some are incorrect and none is compelling. In addition, Bahnsen fails to present a distinctive element of "the prophets" that Christ fulfills somewhat differently than the way he fulfills the law. By reducing his understanding of "the law or the prophets" from the Sinai covenant as a whole to the ethical stipulations of the law,

---

55. BAGD, s.v. "*pleroo*."

Bahnsen not only misunderstands Christ's words here, but he has also begun his journey into an exegetical blind alley, a mistake that will bedevil his understanding of the rest of the passage.

The words "the law" or the phrase "the law or the prophets" have been demonstrated to have been understood in the period as a reference to the Mosaic covenant, and it has also been shown that Bahnsen's objections are insufficient to reject this possible understanding of Christ's words. As we proceed, it will become clearer that the Mosaic covenant was exactly what Christ was talking about.

The failure of Bahnsen's essential first premise has consequences for the Theonomic thesis that go far beyond this point. If Christ was speaking of the Mosaic covenant in verse 17 rather than the ethical stipulations of the law, verse 18 will be his claim that not one stipulation of that covenant will be changed during the time that the Mosaic covenant is in force. Since Heb 7:12 tells us that changes to the law have already taken place, the expiration of the law indicated by the phrase "until all is accomplished" must have occurred before the Letter to the Hebrews was written. The conclusion is inescapable: the Mosaic covenant has expired, and its civil laws are no longer immutable even though divine authorizations for particular changes are lacking.

"TO DESTROY"

The basic meaning of *katalusai* is "*throw down, detach*, of a stone from a building [or] *destroy, demolish, dismantle*, of buildings. [It also has two figurative senses. The first meaning] "*tear down, demolish* [is what is meant in] Gal. 2:18 [and] of the body as an earthly tent . . . 2 Cor 5:1. [When used in a legal context it usually means] *do away with, abolish, annul, make invalid*."[56]

Bahnsen believes that "Jesus uses a vivid metaphor (drawn from the language sphere of physical objects) to teach that His relationship to the law is *not* one of invalidation or abrogation."[57]

Unfortunately for Bahnsen's argument, *katalusai* does not always carry the meaning of "annul" when it is used in legal contexts. In Galatians 2:18, for example, we find Paul writing specifically in reference to the Mosaic law that "if I rebuild what I have once destroyed [*kata-*

---

56. BAGD, 414.
57. Bahnsen, *Theonomy*, 50.

Is Christ "Confirming" or "Completing" the Law? Matthew 5:17

luoo], I prove myself to be a transgressor." Paul's antonymic use of the word *rebuild*, never used in Greek to mean "disannul,"[58] makes it utterly certain that he was intending *katalusai* to be understood in the sense of "destroying" something, rather than in the legal sense of "annulling" something. And whatever Paul is specifically referring to in this passage as first having been destroyed and later rebuilt somehow involves a breach of the Mosaic law;[59] for only if that law was breached could one be a "transgressor."[60] Since in Gal 2:18 *katalusai* clearly means "destroy" rather than "annul," Bahnsen needed to consider whether or not Christ might have been using *katalusai* to convey this more general metaphorical sense of "destroy" in Matt 5:17, as well, in order to make his case. This becomes especially necessary when we remember that the translators of the King James Version, men fully aware of the usual translation of "annul" for *katalusai* in legal contexts, chose to translate it by "destroy" in Matt 5:17. What reasoning prompted their choice?

The answer comes only a few words later when we find Christ using the word *pleroo* to describe his relationship to "the law or the prophets." This word has among its known meanings those of "complete, finish, and bring to an end,"[61] meanings that must be considered in the context of Matt 5:17 since there is a good deal of teaching in both the Old and New Testaments that the Old Covenant will come to an end. Since the winding up of the Old Covenant did involve annulling at least some of its stipulations,[62] if Christ here meant *kataluo* in the sense of "annul" rather than "destroy," he would have set up a situation in which he would have technically contradicted himself in the same breath. On the other hand, no contradiction results if Christ intended the verb in the sense of "destroy." Since even the poorest of preachers tries to avoid self-contradictions, Christ was not likely to have intended meanings that resulted in them, and therefore we, together with the translators of the King James Version, may well believe that Christ's intended meaning

---

58. See BAGD s.v. "*oikodomioo*."

59. See Bruce, *Epistle to the Galatians*, 142, and Longenecker, *Galatians*, 90–91, for lists of specific situations to which Paul could have been referring.

60. Wherever else in the New Testament this word appears, it is always in connection with "transgressing" the law. Cf. Rom 2:25, 27; Jas 2:11.

61. BAGD, 671.

62. Heb 7:12 uses the significant term "change of law" to describe the annulling of the Levitical priesthood.

for *katalusai* was more likely "destroy" rather than "annul." Instead of denying that he is annulling the law, Christ is denying that his intent was an unauthorized assault on the Old Covenant as a whole. Christ had no wish to be seen as setting himself "in opposition to the Mosaic Code, for his abrogation of the Law was to be by . . . fulfillment–not destruction."[63]

Since *katalusai* does not always mean "annul" when referring to the law, Bahnsen's later claim[64] that the meaning of *pleroosai* is established as "confirm" due to its antithesis with "annul" has suffered a severe blow. If Jesus meant us to understand *katalusai* not as "annul" but as "destroy," then "confirm" is no longer the only possible meaning for *pleroosai* open to us. By claiming that the only possible meaning for *katalusai* here is the technical usage of "abolish," and by overlooking the possibility of "destroy," Bahnsen is begging the entire question of Christ's meaning in this verse and setting up a situation in which Christ appears to contradict himself in the same breath. Bahnsen's second essential premise, therefore, is unproven and must be rejected.

"BUT"

What Jesus meant by this conjunction is important. For Bahnsen claims that "[perhaps] the best indicator of the meaning that should be extracted from *pleroo* ('fulfill') in Matt 5:17 is its antithesis to καταλυω."[65] This antithesis is created by *alla* (but) and, according to Bahnsen, the conjunction of *alla* and *katalusai* here forces the translation of *pleroo* as "confirm," the word whose meaning is *"directly contrary* to that of καταλυσαι."[66]

But the only support Bahnsen gives for *alla* being directly contrary is a quotation from Blass, Debrunner, and Funk and a parenthetical reference to Matt 10:34. But Bahnsen only quotes from Blass, Debrunner, and Funk's introductory statement concerning *alla* and ignores the wide variety of usages that *alla* has.[67]

This objection is critical. For when we examine the meaning of *alla* in the standard lexicons, we discover that it does not always create a

---

63. Hawkins, "Covenant Relations," 3.
64. Bahnsen, *Theonomy*, 64.
65. Ibid., 67.
66. Ibid., 68.
67. Hodge, "Exegetical Response," 28.

Is Christ "Confirming" or "Completing" the Law? Matthew 5:17

direct contradiction between the two words it separates. The word can be used when "introducing a contrast [or introducing] the main point after a question expressed or implied which has been answered in the negative."[68] Such contrasts are not always total contradictions—something evident even in Matt 10:34, Bahnsen's cited Scripture, which turns out not to support his point. In that verse, Jesus says: "Do not think that I came to bring peace on the earth; I did not come to bring peace but a sword." The suggestion that Jesus here intended *alla* in a totally adversative sense simply cannot stand.[69] For if that were so, Jesus would have meant his hearers to understand that he was to bring no peace on the earth at all—a view that, although it appears to be confirmed by the following verses, we must surely reject. For Jesus himself testifies to the contrary in John 14:27 and 16:33. As Bahnsen himself later remarked concerning Matt 10:34, this

> aphorism was not meant to be universally true for any and all senses of "peace," as commentators note. The Jews expected and supposed that the coming Messiah would suddenly in a single action (note the use of the aorist in Matthew 10:34) impose peace for them as the immediate and sole effect of His coming. Jesus utterly denied such an understanding. The sense in which He does bring peace must be supplied from somewhere else, not here. . . . Extracted from its context, of course, the denial of peace-giving in Matthew 10:34 would be an overstatement, to be tempered by revealed instruction elsewhere about the Prince of Peace.[70]

Unfortunately, Bahnsen failed to notice that he created a problem for himself when he conceded that the apparently absolute denial of peace-giving in Matt 10:34 "was not meant to be universally true for any and all senses of 'peace'" and must be qualified by Jesus' teaching elsewhere. By his concession, he effectively admitted that the presence of *alla* does not always force a meaning of total contradiction between the words it separates. Moreover, Bahnsen's comment is also an implicit recognition of a truth that any translator knows: as is the case with all words with more than one meaning, the precise sense of *alla* in Matthew 10:34 does not determine the meanings of the words it contrasts. Instead, its own meaning must be determined by the otherwise established mean-

---

68. BAGD, 38.
69. Contra Bahnsen, *Theonomy*, 68.
70. Bahnsen, "Exegesis of Matthew," 105.

ings of the words it separates. By conceding that the presence of *alla* does not force the total contradiction between "peace" and "sword" in Matt 10:34, Bahnsen has effectively refuted his own argument that *alla* necessarily forces a contrast of exactly opposite meanings between the words it separates in the grammatically identical Matt 5:17. Since one cannot maintain that Matthew 10:34 teaches "that there is no sense in which Jesus came to bring peace . . . [one cannot successfully argue that there] is *no* sense in which Jesus abolishes the law"[71] in Matt 5:17. Therefore one can no longer maintain that *alla* necessarily forces the translation of *pleroo* as "confirm" in this verse. Instead, the precise sense of *alla* that Christ intended in Matt 5:17 must be determined by his intended meanings for *katalusai* and *pleroosai*. We must therefore revisit the possibility that Jesus was setting up the "antithesis . . . not between 'annul' and 'confirm' but between 'destroy' and 'fulfill.'"[72] To sum up, we may well say that "even though *alla* indicates a strong contrast, it in no way *requires* a contrast of specific opposites . . . To override the normal meaning of *pleroo* and establish a meaning which has no or little lexical support, simply on the basis of *alla*, is a misplaced emphasis in exegesis.[73]

"FULFILL"

The last question that affects whether Matt 5:17 is to be understood in Bahnsen's sense is how *pleroosai* (fulfill) should be translated. If this word cannot be rightly translated as "confirm" in the sense of "establish the ongoing validity of," or if that meaning is not a necessary consequence of translating *pleroosai* as "fulfill," then it is certain that whatever Christ is teaching here, it is not the Theonomic thesis.

Bahnsen claims that the "sense of 'confirming, ratifying, validating and establishing' has been recognized as applying to 'fulfill' by past and present biblical scholars,"[74] including Calvin, Windisch, Campbell, Brown, Ridderbos, Spurgeon, and Murray.[75] But two considerations render these claims valueless for establishing the Theonomic thesis. Although the idea that Christ's intended meaning involved "confirm"

---

71. Carson, *Matthew*, 142.
72. Ibid., 143.
73. Hodge, "Exegetical Response" 29.
74. Bahnsen, *Theonomy*, 74.
75. Ibid., 73–74.

Is Christ "Confirming" or "Completing" the Law? Matthew 5:17

can be found as early as Calvin, that fact is insufficient to establish the contention that *pleroosai* meant "confirm" in Jesus day. For none of the men Bahnsen names as holding this view were lexicographers: all of them were preachers or commentators, and there is a significant difference between the disciplines. A preacher or commentator tries to decide what a word means on the basis of the immediate context in which it is found, whereas a lexicographer determines what meanings a word may have by a systematic study of every other use of the word in contemporary literature. Unless a commentator's suggested meaning can be supported by lexicographical evidence, it is nothing more than very late-dated speculation. And, as we shall shortly see, there is strong evidence that the Greek word Matthew used here had never taken the meaning "confirm" at the time that the New Testament was written.

The second reason that the belief held by some commentators that Christ intended "confirm" here does not help the Theonomic thesis is that Bahnsen does not mean the same thing by the words "confirm" or "law" as do the men he cites. For example, John Murray's view is summarized by Bahnsen thus: "Jesus refers to the function of *validating* and *confirming* the law and the prophets."[76] However, Murray actually wrote that "what Jesus means is that he came to realize the full measure of the intent and purpose of the law and the prophets. Jesus refers to the function of validating and confirming the law and the prophets and includes much more than the fulfillment of the predictions of the Old Testament regarding himself. He means that the whole process of revelation deposited in the Old Testament finds in him its completion, its fulfillment, its confirmation, its validation."[77]

This is something much more than merely "confirming . . . the ethical stipulations of the law." Murray specifically includes the fulfilling of the Old Testament prophecies as part of Christ's intended meaning, something Bahnsen specifically denies that Christ meant here.

Another point to consider is that while most of these men are assuming that the Mosaic laws that Christ is "confirming" are the Ten Commandments alone, Bahnsen expands his definition of that which Christ confirms to include the civil as well as the moral laws of the Old Testament. One may legitimately wonder whether the scholars he cites would agree with him when he redefines the term *law* to include the

---

76. Bahnsen, *Theonomy*, 74, summarizing Murray, *Principles of Conduct*, 150.
77. Murray, *Principles of Conduct*, 150.

civil laws, for many do not. This is brought out particularly clearly in the cases of Calvin—who in his commentary on Matt 5:19 makes it plain that he believes that Jesus has been referring to the moral law (i.e., the Decalogue) from v. 17 on[78]—and Murray, who disclaims Bahnsen's position that the regulatory penal provisions of the Mosaic economy must still continue when he writes, concerning the "eye for an eye" of Matt 5:38–42, that while "it would not be contrary to the analogy of our Lord's teaching elsewhere to regard Him as abolishing the regulatory penal provisions of the Mosaic economy (which could not be regulatory in the New Testament age) and in this respect doing what he had done to divorce in Matthew 5:31, 32."[79]

But even if the commentators do not exactly support Bahnsen's translation ("confirm"), Scripture may, and to Scripture we now turn. Sometimes, we do not need a great deal of evidence to determine whether or not a word in the Bible was intended to carry a meaning not previously known. If the matter is of little importance, one suggestive example is often enough to make the case for that meaning. But when the consequences made possible by the new meaning of a word include a complete revision of a major Christian doctrine that is certain to lead to a great deal of controversy within the church, and additional antagonism to the gospel by the unsaved, we need more than a single hypothetical possibility before we can regard the case as proven. Instead, we must be absolutely certain that the proposed new translation is correct. If Christians are to revise their understanding of the place of the Mosaic civil laws in the New Covenant based, in any measure, on Bahnsen's understanding of this passage, then we must be utterly certain that *pleroo* could have taken the sense of "confirm" in Jesus' day. Bahnsen believes that he has provided "sufficient and necessary grounds for the translation of *pleroosai* as 'confirm' over against the other alternatives."[80] We must now consider his evidence to see if he has achieved his aim.

The Structure of Bahnsen's Argument

When doing a word study in a foreign language, the first step is to examine the lexicons in order to determine the possible meanings of the

---

78. Calvin, *Harmony of the Gospels*, vol. 1. Online: http://www.ccel.org/c/calvin/comment2/hag1.htm.

79. Murray, *Principles of Conduct*, 174.

80. Bahnsen, *Theonomy*, 74.

Is Christ "Confirming" or "Completing" the Law? Matthew 5:17

word in question. When we look up *pleroo* in BAGD, we find that it had six basic meanings in prebiblical and biblical Greek. These are 1) *make full, fill*; 2) of time, *fill (up)*, complete a period of time, reach its end; 3) *bring something to completion*, finish something already begun; 4) *fulfill*. by deeds, to fulfill a prophecy; 5) *complete, finish, or bring to an end*; and 6) *complete* a number.[81] Bahnsen's "confirm" is not listed among these meanings, although BAGD does provide a gloss noting that some scholars have suggested (and other scholars have rejected) the possibility that "confirm" should be recognized as a possible meaning with reference to Matthew 5:17.

We can be certain that Jesus is not talking about filling up the Law or the Prophets in the sense of filling up water pots (sense 1) in these verses; however, Bahnsen does adduce the possibility that Christ may have intended the word metaphorically.[82] It is also clear that Christ never added to the laws (sense 6). So one might think that the debate would only be concerned with the remaining possibilities: the metaphorical use of BAGD's sense 1 and the literal meanings of senses 2, 3, 4, and 5.

But Bahnsen has a surprise for us. He does not derive his list of potential meanings from the lexicons. Instead, he quotes a number of English-language commentators who between them are cited as having adduced different interpretations of *pleroo*. These are: 1) "puts an end to" (perhaps an inexact and oversimplified understanding of BAGD sense 5); 2) "replaces" (another oversimplification of BAGD's sense 5); 3) "supplements" (BAGD sense 6); 4) "intends to actively obey" (possibly another inexact oversimplification, this time of BAGD sense 4); and 5) "enforce" (no exact BAGD equivalent).[83]

There are three major problems with Bahnsen's list of meanings found in the commentators. First, it is incomplete. He does not here include any commentators who support the meaning "fulfill" as in fulfill-

---

81. BAGD s.v. "*pleroo*."

82. Ridderbos believed that fulfill does not mean "completion of the law as the source of our knowledge of the divine will but the effectual assertion of the demands of the law. The word suggests a vessel that is being filled. The vessel of the law is being given its rightful measure." Ridderbos, *The Coming of the Kingdom*, 252, quoted in Bahnsen, *Theonomy*, 62. As the law had already been filled with its rightful demands when it was first given, a reminder of its demands would be properly called a refilling— a meaning that *pleroosai* had never before been given. If that was Christ's intended meaning, it would not have been so understood by his hearers.

83. Bahnsen, *Theonomy*, 55.

ing prophecy, even though there are many notable ones who do so.[84] We may reasonably assume Bahnsen's rejection of this possibility was due to his understanding that prophecy was not involved in the context,[85] and perhaps he believed that it would not make sense to speak of fulfilling the law but that it would make sense to speak of ratifying it.

Second, of the four remaining senses found in BAGD, Bahnsen has misleadingly simplified senses 2, 3, and 5, each time removing the important idea of "completion" from consideration. Bahnsen rejected this possibility that *pleroo* might mean "bring to completion, finish something already begun, [apparently on the sole ground that it] does not appear in the synoptic gospels at all (and its only use in John is with reference to the emotion of joy in an idiomatic sense—'my joy is fulfilled')."[86]

However, this is an extraordinarily weak argument. Throughout the New Testament we find words used only once or twice, and no competent scholar would claim, for example, that *mesituo* cannot mean "confirmed" in Heb 6:17 simply because it appears nowhere else in the New Testament, or that *allomai* cannot mean "leaping" in Acts 3:8 because it is used metaphorically of the water Jesus gives in John 4:14. If a meaning is known from elsewhere in the contemporary literature, New Testament lexicographers have no qualms in using it when it makes sense in the immediate context, especially if the source of that meaning can be shown to be widely known among those by whom the word was used. And there is no doubt that *pleroo* in the sense of a time-limited condition coming to its expected end was well known to Christ's contemporaries, for *pleroo* was the word the Septuagint translators used to refer to the end of a pregnancy in childbirth when they translated Gen 25:24 and 29:21 from Hebrew to Greek in about 160 BC. Given that this use of *pleroo* was documented in the BAGD article on *pleroo*, which Bahnsen is known to have consulted, we must regret that he failed to take it into consideration.[87]

In effect, Bahnsen has removed four of BAGD's listed meanings from serious consideration without informing his readers that he has done so. Ironically, he himself penned the only adequate refutation of

---

84. E.g., Henry, *Commentary*, 1222, and Lloyd-Jones, *Studies in the Sermon on the Mount*, vol. 1, 189–91.

85. See Bahnsen, *Theonomy*, 53.

86. Bahnsen, *Theonomy*, 62.

87. Bahnsen is not the only writer who has overlooked this possible meaning. Ross makes the same omission in *Finger of God*, 197–99.

Is Christ "Confirming" or "Completing" the Law? Matthew 5:17   67

this misguided procedure when he wrote that "the problem [of the correct meaning of *fulfill* in Matt 5:17] is only compounded, when in giving a multi-meaning interpretation of 'fulfill' . . . [four] proper [meanings are] left out of the list altogether."[88]

This is why Gordon is correct in saying that "Bahnsen's claim that πληρωσαι should mean 'ratify' rather than 'fulfill' [is the] . . . most daring dimension of [his] interpretation of Matt 5:17ff. [It] . . . reaches erroneous conclusions because some of the alternatives are not considered."[89] And another critic has drawn a disturbing possibility from this lapse: "It would appear that by dividing and simplifying alternative interpretations of *pleroo*, Dr. Bahnsen is creating straw men which are easy prey to a logician."[90]

Next, Bahnsen gives arguments supporting his rejection of the meanings that he does cite. These arguments will be discussed later when alternatives to Bahnsen's view are proposed. Finally, he adduces an argument to support the idea that if all his cited interpretations are insufficient, then any combination of them must also be wide of the mark since it "hardly needs mention that if the preceding series of suggestions as to the meaning of πληρωσαι in Matthew 5:17 cannot be accepted then any of these suggestions will be *a priori* unacceptable as well; a leaky bucket will not hold water any better if you simply contribute more faults or leaks to it."[91]

After removing all possible lexicographically accepted meanings of *pleroo* from consideration, Bahnsen goes on to propose another one. He argues that *pleroo* is meant to take the sense of "confirm" in Matt 5:17, and he demonstrates, by quoting a number of commentators, none of whom was a lexicographer, that the suggestion is not original. What differentiates Bahnsen from these commentators is his belief that he has

---

88. Bahnsen, *Theonomy*, 66 n. 74.

89. Gordon, "Critique of Theonomy," 29. Gentry (*Covenantal Theonomy*, 69) seems to have fallen into the error of selective quotation when he quotes the first clause of Gordon's remark without apparently noticing the significance of the sentence's conclusion. Although Gordon charitably claims that Bahnsen's argument "follows sound lexical considerations" it is hard to see how any lexical argument that fails to consider legitimate alternatives could be so described.

90. Fowler, "God's Law," 66.

91. Bahnsen, *Theonomy*, 66 n. 74. This argument, however, will hold only if all of BAGD's senses for *pleroo* must be rejected in favor of Bahnsen's possibility "confirm." As will be shown later, there are good reasons to reject that possibility.

provided reasons for thinking that Christ meant "confirm" "over against the other alternatives,"[92] something these commentators did not do.

Bahnsen next attempts to justify his translation. He starts with the incorrect premise that *alla* forces on *pleroosai* a meaning in absolute contrast to the legal meaning of *katalusai*, that is, "annul." Then, instead of consulting a Greek lexicon to determine which of *pleroo*'s known meanings is the most contradictory and the best fit in the context, Bahnsen turns to manuals of *English* usage to determine the antonym of *katalusai*, and he arrives at "confirm." However, as Fowler has observed, this is a

> *method* [that] *defies all the accepted rules for doing word studies in the Greek!* Neither etymology nor the use of *pleroo* in Matthew played a role in his search for its meaning. Moreover the meaning of *pleroosai* cannot be determined simply by contrast with *katalusai* for several reasons.
>
> One is that the meaning of *pleroosai* ("to fulfill") should first be determined by looking at the possible uses of *pleroosai* ("to fulfill"), not some contrasting word. It is a most inappropriate method to determine a word's meaning without first dealing with that word itself rather than a supposed antonym. . . . Dr. Bahnsen compounds this difficulty by reverting to *English* dictionaries of synonyms and antonyms to determine the precise meaning of *Greek* terms.[93]

Bahnsen replied to Fowler's charge by claiming that Fowler had misunderstood his argument. That Fowler had charge him with making "the confused schoolboy mistake of interpreting a Greek word by an English dictionary shows that [Fowler] has not grasped the technical linguistic argument at all. Given the syntactical setting of Matthew 5:17 (especially the operator *alla*), one needs to find a correct functional equivalence in the target language for *plarosai*; this is where the English language authorities necessarily come into the question."[94]

There are three errors in this attempt to refute Fowler's objections. First, it does not address all of Fowler's objections but only answers one of them, leaving unchallenged the objections that he has made no use of etymology and that he has ignored Matthew's normal usage of *pleroo*

---

92. Bahnsen, *Theonomy*, 74.
93. Fowler, "God's Law," 68.
94. Bahnsen, *No Other Standard*, 277–78.

Is Christ "Confirming" or "Completing" the Law? Matthew 5:17

in determining its meaning.[95] Second, it relies on the untenable view that *alla* forced on *pleroo* a meaning that is directly contradictory to *katalousai*—something that Bahnsen himself had earlier confessed was unfounded when applied to a grammatically identical passage.[96] Third, his refutation is inadequate. While he claims that Fowler does not understand the technical linguistic argument, it turns out that it is Bahnsen who does not understand Fowler's objection. Fowler's entire point is that Bahnsen has in effect skipped two necessary steps in the translation process, as we shall see as we examine the point in more detail.

Before translating any word, one must first adequately investigate the range of meanings of that word in its original language to determine which meaning best fits a given context. But Bahnsen did not take the usual first step in this process, that of consulting a Greek lexicon. While one can sometimes work around consulting lexicons by using English-language commentators, this method remains valid only so long as one includes all known meanings of the word in question in the list of possible meanings that they derive from the commentaries. Since Bahnsen's selected listing of meanings is incomplete, his use of commentaries is not an acceptable substitute for consulting the lexicons.

It is only when all the known meanings of the word in the original language are at hand that one may proceed to the next step of considering how that word is used in both in the immediate and the larger contexts of the writing in which it is found. At this second step, Bahnsen compounds his error by making another mistake. Consulting manuals of English usage to determine the English word whose meaning is an antonym to "annul," as Bahnsen does, is premature. While it is the appropriate step to take if one needs to find the Greek word to express a particular English meaning that one wishes to translate into Greek, it is the wrong step to take when, as here, one needs to determine which of the possible meanings a writer, writing in Greek, intended a given Greek word to convey to his Greek readers. Consequently, Bahnsen's attempt at this point to impose the meaning of the English antonym of an English translation of a Greek word upon another Greek word is simply wrongheaded.[97] Instead, Bahnsen needed to collect every known meaning of

---

95. While Bahnsen did address the issue of Matthew's normal use of *pleroo* in his response to Poythress, which forms an appendix to *No Other Standard* (291), it is unfortunate that he did so without documenting its relationship to Fowler's argument.

96. Bahnsen, "Exegesis of Matthew," 105.

97. Bahnsen's procedure here necessarily rests on the assumption that words in one

pleroo, and then determine which meaning best fit the context of Matt 5:17. Only after both of these steps are taken can the intended original meaning of the word in the passage in question be determined. And it is only after the intended meaning of the word in the original language is determined, that one can begin to look for words with correct "functional equivalence" in the target language. It is only at this last stage that "the English language authorities necessarily come into the question."[98]

By working from an incomplete listing of possible meanings for *pleroo*, and by turning too soon to the English-language authorities for antonyms of "annul," Bahnsen has begged the question of whether the word *pleroo* was ever used to mean "confirm" in Greek, thereby making the "confused schoolboy mistake" of which Fowler has accused him. Moreover, by omitting to quote enough of Fowler's objections for his readers to understand exactly what those objections were, Bahnsen, whether by accident or by design, has made it impossible for readers ignorant of Fowler's paper to discern whether or not Fowler's criticisms were correct.[99]

In the final analysis, however, it does not matter how brilliant Bahnsen's reasoning from English antonyms of *katalusai* to arrive at "confirm" might initially seem to be. Since Jesus does not define *pleroosai* in the context of Matt 5:17, he must have intended a meaning that he knew was known to his hearers. All Bahnsen's work will still come to naught if he cannot demonstrate that *pleroo* was known to have meant "confirm the ongoing validity of" in Jesus' day either directly or by im-

---

language will share every one of their meanings with a single word in another language. While this is sometimes correct—e.g., the Hebrew *mala* and the Greek *pleroo* have many meanings (especially the meaning "complete") in common—this happy state of affairs does not occur all the time: the resolution of the Arian controversy was delayed for several years, as the key words used to describe the nature of the Trinity did not mean all of the same things in the two languages involved. The Greek word *hypostasis* meant "person" with a secondary meaning of "substance," but the Latin word for person, *substantia*, did not carry the second meaning of "substance," but instead meant "actor or role," something that was not included in any of the meanings of *hypostasis*. See Brown, *Heresies*, 129.

98. Bahnsen, *No Other Standard*, 278.

99. Bahnsen's omissions were particularly unfortunate since Fowler's paper was privately published and distributed within a limited circle. It is hard to see how the readers of *No Other Standard*, otherwise ignorant of Fowler's paper, could have fairly considered Bahnsen's refutations of his arguments since those arguments were so poorly summarized by Bahnsen.

Is Christ "Confirming" or "Completing" the Law? Matthew 5:17

plication. Therefore, after having identified what he thinks Jesus meant by the word *pleroo* in 5:17, Bahnsen sets out to see if the meaning of "confirm" can be found in first-century Aramaic and Greek texts.

The Meaning of Pleroo in Aramaic and Classical Greek

Bahnsen begins by considering the question of an Aramaic original of Matthew's Gospel. He rightly concludes that there are weighty arguments against the idea that the Gospel was originally written in that language. But when he turns to other Aramaic texts, he asserts that "when one searches for the Aramaic background he comes, or can come, to the conclusion that Christ's original words meant 'confirm, validate.'"[100] It is unfortunate, however, that Bahnsen overlooked an article written by C. F. D. Moule that records Ljungman's challenge to "the view, which had become almost an axiom ever since the time of Dalman, that the Semitic equivalent of πληρωσαι in this saying would be a part of the verb קום ['confirm'] ... Ljungman's painstaking examination of the facts shows that we have no right to assume, merely on the basis of the Targumic usage [as Dalman seems to have done], that Matthew's πληρωσαι (supposing there were a Semitic original behind it) would represent קום [*qum*, 'confirm'] rather than מלא [*mala*, 'fill, be full']."[101]

The Targumim were Hebrew Scriptures translated into Aramaic for the purpose of being read in the synagogues—a necessity since Aramaic had become the everyday language of the Jews of Jesus' day. The essential problem with Dalman's argument is that while the Targumim began to be used long before Christ's birth, the Targumim in question were not written down until two hundred years after Christ. Consequently, late-dated Targumim, translating the Hebrew word for "complete" by an Aramaic form of "confirm," are not sufficient to establish that *pleroo* could have taken the meaning "confirm" in the minds of Jesus or his hearers two hundred years earlier.[102] Therefore, there is insufficient evidence to conclude that *pleroosai* may have meant "confirm, validate" in Matthew 5:17 from the Targumim alone.

When we turn to classical Greek of 300 BC and earlier, we find that the Liddell and Scott *Greek English Lexicon*, the standard classical

---

100. Bahnsen, *Theonomy*, 56 n. 52.
101. Moule, "Fulfillment Words in the New Testament," 313, 314, citing Ljungman, *Das Gesetz*.
102. Moule, "Fulfillment Words," 314. See also Carson, *Matthew*, 143.

Greek/English lexicon, lists eight meanings for the word.[103] Bahnsen's "confirm" is not included. Instead, we find *pleroo* used in classical Greek in a moral sense only when referring to the carrying out or fulfilling of promises, not of confirming the ongoing validity of a previously established agreement. There is therefore no evidence in either Aramaic or classical Greek that *pleroo* ever took the sense of "confirm" in Jesus' day.

The Septuagint

The next source we must consider is the Septuagint (LXX) translation of the Old Testament into Greek made sometime between 285 and 247 BC.[104] The LXX translators' normal practice was to translate words of the מלא ("fill up," "complete") family as *pleroo*, since "fill up" and "complete" were among the usual Greek meanings for that word.[105] Nowhere in the LXX do the translators use it to translate the Hebrew קום ("confirm"). House and Ice extend this observation further and claim that a review of "a concordance for the Septuagint reveals that none of the Hebrew terms for 'confirm' are translated by any of the Greek terms for 'fulfill' and none of the Hebrew terms for 'fulfill' are translated by the Greek terms for 'confirm.'"[106]

But Bahnsen supplies a number of Old Testament Scriptures in which, he believes, *pleroo* is required by the context to take the sense of "confirm."[107] How should we resolve this contradiction and determine who is right? Or, to put the question another way, how do lexicographers do their jobs?

When lexicographers receive a possible new definition for a word together with a list of Scriptures such as Bahnsen provides, they insert the suggested translation into the passages the suggesting scholar has provided, and then consider what the passage now says. The suggestion may turn out to be a worse fit than already recognized meanings. This will be shown when the new insertion creates new difficulties in the immediate verse or in the surrounding context. Such suggestions are almost always rejected at once since they leave our understanding of the

---

103. Liddell and Scott, *A Greek-English Lexicon*, 1227.

104. Douglas et al., eds., *New Bible Dictionary* s.v. "Texts and Versions" J. N. Birdsall.

105. BAGD, 671.

106. House and Ice, *Dominion Theology*, 108. See also C. F. D. Moule, "Fulfillment Words," 314.

107. Bahnsen, *Theonomy*, 70.

Is Christ "Confirming" or "Completing" the Law? Matthew 5:17

text worse off than it was before. The second possible result is that the suggestion seems to fit as well as the currently recognized meanings. We might think such an equal fit would be enough to establish the suggestion as a genuine meaning, but a little thought shows us that an equal fit is not enough. An equal fit only shows us that the word seems to fit well for us, but that is insufficient to establish the meaning. The question we need answered is whether the ancients really did use the word in the way that has been suggested. And the only way we can be certain that the ancients must have used a given word in a way not previously recognized is when there is at least one case in which the new suggestion demonstrates a clear superiority to all currently accepted meanings of the word, both in the phrase in which it is found as well as in the surrounding context of that phrase. Such a discovery is like finding a missing piece to a jigsaw puzzle: it not only makes sense in itself but it also makes better sense of the surrounding context.[108] Ultimately, whether a suggested meaning passes this latter test determines whether or not the suggested meaning is accepted as correct.

With these things in mind, we are ready to consider Bahnsen's examples. The first thing to notice is that Hebrew word for "confirm" is not found in any of the passages Bahnsen suggests. In all of Bahnsen's examples, we find the word for "fulfill" or "complete" used instead. With that in mind, we turn to the Scriptures in question. Bahnsen begins by examining 1 Kings 1:14. According to Bahnsen "the translation [of the LXX] is clearly: . . . 'Behold, while you are still talking there with the king, I also will come in after you and confirm ($\pi\lambda\eta\rho oo$) your words.'"[109]

Putting the verse in context, we find Nathan telling Bathsheba about an event, telling her also to report it to the king, and while she is still speaking he will come in and "complete" her account. When we first read the verse in isolation, the word *complete* appears to be a clearly inferior translation of Nathan's intent than "confirm" would be.

---

108. Such discoveries do not happen often nowadays, but they do sometimes occur. A friend of the present author was studying in Cambridge in the 1950's when her Hebrew professor divided an Isaiah passage so as to include a four-letter root rather than following the then-prevalent assumption that the passage was a succession of three-letter roots with an extra letter that had somehow been corrupted into a textual mess whose meaning translators could only guess at. The professor's reading made so much better sense than any previous reading that it has been accepted by all translations made since the 1960's and the previous "best guesses" are not even footnoted.

109. Bahnsen, *Theonomy*, 70.

So it is not a great surprise to discover that both the Brown, Driver, and Briggs Hebrew-English lexicon and the Koehler and Baumgartner lexicon assign the meaning "confirm" to *mala* in this passage,[110] as does the article on *pleroo* in the *New International Dictionary of New Testament Theology*.[111] When we find that this translation is supported by at least four major Bible translations, we might be excused for thinking that the matter is settled in Bahnsen's favor.[112] And if we looked no further into the rest of the incident we would never need to revisit our conclusion.

But when we do look at the rest of the story, we have to think again. When we compare what Bathsheba tells David in verses 17–21—information she has received from Nathan himself—with Nathan's own report to David in verses 24–27, we find that the two accounts differ. In his account to David, Nathan adds a couple of additional details that, apparently he did not tell Bathsheba, as they are not found in Bathsheba's account. When Nathan adds his own name, as well as the names of Beniah, Zadok, and Solomon to those not included in Adonijah's guest list (verse 26), he is going beyond merely supplying a general confirmation of Bathsheba's account to explicitly completing it. Since "complete" was a known meaning of *mala* at this date,[113] Nathan's inclusion of the additional names supports the possibility that Nathan had earlier told Bathsheba he would "complete" her account. Since "confirm" lacks the additional and necessary nuance of "adding additional details," something Nathan did with his report, "complete" is a better translation for *mala* in this verse than "confirm" would be.[114] The meaning "confirm," therefore, cannot be established as a possible meaning for *pleroo* over against "complete" from this passage alone. And since this is the only

---

110. Brown, Driver, and Briggs, eds., *A Hebrew and English Lexicon of the Old Testament*, s.v. מלא. See also Koehler and Baumgartner, *The Hebrew and Aramaic Lexicon of the Old Testament*, s.v. מלא.

111. Brown, ed., *New International Dictionary of New Testament Theology*, s.v. "Fullness" subsection "*pleroo* and *pimplemi*" R. Schippers.

112. The KJV, RSV, NASB, and NIV translate *mala* as confirm.

113. Gen 29:27, 28.

114. After the information in this paragraph was brought to the translators' attention, recent editions of the ESV and TNIV have noted the possibility that "complete" may have been Nathan's intended meaning by adding paraphrased statements implying the idea of completion; the ESV gives "expand on" as an alternative, and the TNIV translates the clause as "add my word to what you have said." Ross (From the Finger of God, 359) also noticed that Nathan could have had "complete" in mind.

Is Christ "Confirming" or "Completing" the Law? Matthew 5:17

example in which any translations use "confirm" to translate *mala*, there is serious reason to question whether the ancient Hebrews ever used the word to mean "confirm" before this date.[115]

Even if we assume that Nathan may have intended, and Bathsheba understood him as planning to "complete" her report, we also have to consider whether or not *mala* acquired the meaning "confirm" from its use in this passage—for Nathan's completion of Bathsheba's account of events did have the inherent result of confirming her news. To this question, the translators of the Septuagint, working around six hundred years later, provide an important witness. When they translated this passage into Greek, the Greek word they chose had the known meaning of "complete" and had never before carried the meaning of "confirm." The translators' choice of *pleroo* suggests that they thought that Nathan was proposing to complete rather than confirm Bathsheba's account, which, as we have seen, is exactly what he did. If the translators did understand Nathan to mean "confirm" in this verse, then we must ask why they rejected the available and well-known words *istemi* (confirm) or *bebiaoo* (establish), which the translators well knew were the appropriate Greek words to carry the meaning of "confirm."[116] Since the LXX translators knew and usually used the normal Greek words to render the Hebrew word for "confirm," why then did they reject these words in this one passage in favor of a word that had never previously carried that meaning if they thought that "confirm" was what Nathan had meant? Bahnsen neither poses nor answers this question. Since the LXX translation is known to contain some Hebraisms, this argument is not entirely conclusive, but the translation of *mala* by *pleroo* still points away from understanding "confirm" as the meaning of Nathan's intended thought.

When we see that "complete" was a known meaning of the word *pleroo*, that it is a better fit in the immediate context, that the LXX translators chose *pleroo* rather than the known Greek words for "confirm," and that "confirm" is not a meaning given to מלא in modern Hebrew dictionaries, even as a lapsed meaning, there remains no solid evidence supporting Bahnsen's claim that "confirm" was explicitly meant by

---

115. The more usual Hebrew word for "confirm" predates this incident being found in Num 30:14, Deut 27:26, and Ruth 4:7 and so was available for Nathan's use, had "confirm" been his intended meaning.

116. On this see Hatch and Redpath, eds., *A Concordance to the LXX and Other Greek Versions of the Old Testament*, s.v. ιατημι and βεβιαω.

Nathan, or was so understood by the LXX translators. Those who have supported the translation of מלא or *pleroo* here as "confirm" rather than "complete" have not realized the significance of the details that Bathsheba omitted in her account to David, and how, by providing them, Nathan completed her account.

Bahnsen, however, has provided other examples that we must also consider. "The translation of 1 Maccabees 2:55 (LXX) is 'Joshua while he confirmed the word, was made ruler in Israel'; here *pleroo* is used. Taken in historical perspective, this activity of Joshua's obviously refers to his taking a stand for God's ability to grant Israel their promised land. It is not that Joshua obeyed the word (for the word was one of promise, not a demand), but that he confirmed it by his testimony."[117]

It is not, however, as obvious as Bahnsen makes it out to be since "the promise to enter into the land still had to be obeyed for them actually to enter into it. 'Fulfilling the word' cannot mean 'be confirmed by his testimony' since the writer . . . says that of Caleb in the next verse using different words: 'Caleb for being a witness before the congregation received an inheritance in the land.' Joshua 'fulfilled the word' by bringing it into effect."[118]

Or, as Poythress remarks,

> Joshua's faithfulness to God's word, not the fact of confirmation, seems to be preeminent. Hence, this use of the word *pleroo* may well match one of the normal senses of the word, namely, "fulfill" an obligation (sense four in Bauer's lexicon). Moreover, in Numbers 14:6–9 . . . Joshua is recorded as saying, "Only do not rebel against the Lord." Thus Joshua construes his own response as a question of loyalty instead of rebellion. "Fulfilling the word" in 1 Maccabees 2:55 may mean, "fulfilling God's word calling for loyalty to himself"[119] [i.e., the first of the Ten Commandments].

Since both Joshua's obedience in leading the conquest of the land and his calling for loyalty to God rather than rebellion can be fittingly said to "fulfill the word," Bahnsen fails to make his case from this text as well.

---

117. Bahnsen, *Theonomy*, 70, 71. While 1 Maccabees may have been originally written in Hebrew the origingal Hebrew text was lost and the earliest surviving texts, including the Septuagint, are in Greek.

118. Hodge, "Exegetical Response," 19.

119. Poythress, *Shadow of Christ*, 371.

Is Christ "Confirming" or "Completing" the Law? Matthew 5:17

Bahnsen's third example is 4 Macc 12:14, in which "we read that in martyrdom men 'fulfill' righteousness before God; yet martyrs are not actively involved in performing a deed, accomplishing a task or doing the law; rather they have something *done to* them. The fact that these individuals are selected for execution, and the fact that they endure it without apostasy, *confirms* that they are righteous.[120]

Yet, "as the text says, they did choose to die bravely. They could have died cowardly, or renounced their religion and not have died at all. The term εὐσέβεια should not be translated as 'righteousness' as Bahnsen does. BAGD indicates that ευσεβεια means 'in the LXX only of the duty which man owes to God: piety, godliness, religion.'[BAGD, 326] 'These men completed their final duty to God, which was their martyrdom.'"[121]

Thus "the use of *pleroo* here matches sense five in Bauer's lexicon, 'complete, finish, bring to an end.'"[122] Here, too, since "completed" is an equally or more valid translation, Bahnsen fails to make his case.

When Bahnsen next claims that the LXX uses *pleroo* to mean, "establish, set" (e.g., in 1 Sam 20:3 and Song 5:14),[123] his argument is not successful. In 1 Sam 20:3, the reference is to the literal filling of space and time: David literally says, "It is filled up between me and death" to make the point that he is in great danger. And "filling" is a known Greek usage for *pleroo*. Only in Song 5:14, where the beloved's hands are as rings "filled with beryl," could we properly translate that into English as "set." However, "filled" is an equally possible translation. "Bahnsen simply overlooks this usage when he claims that Song of Solomon 5:14 contains the sense 'establish, set.'"[124]

Finally, Bahnsen argues that *pleroo* takes the sense of "ordain" "in Num 7:88; Judges 17:5, 12, 3 Kgs [1 Kgs] 13:33; 2 Chron 13:9; and Sirach 45:15."[125] However, "the references Bahnsen cites where the word takes the sense of ordain all use a particular Hebrew idiom which is translated

---

120. Bahnsen, *Theonomy*, 71.
121. Kittel and Friedrich, eds., *Theological Dictionary of the New Testament*, s.v. "*pleroo*," quoted in Hodge, "Exegetical Response," 20.
122. Poythress, *Shadow of Christ*, 372.
123. Bahnsen, *Theonomy*, 71.
124. Poythress, *Shadow of Christ*, 372.
125. Bahnsen, *Theonomy*, 71.

'the filling of his hands.' None of these verses even have a hint of the idea of 'establish, confirm.'"[126]

Once again "filling" is a recognized meaning for *pleroo*. One wonders why Bahnsen even bothered with this argument. For in all the verses Bahnsen cites, what was occurring was not "ordaining" a law but consecrating an individual. This is not the same thing as the confirming of a covenant previously made.

We have seen there is no certain evidence in favor of the view that the Septuagint translators ever used *pleroo* in the sense of "confirm" and a great deal of evidence against it. Nor is there any evidence that they used *pleroo* in the sense of "establishing the ongoing validity of" that Bahnsen requires in order for his fourth premise to stand. Therefore, Bahnsen's claim that since "the Septuagint was . . . well known to Palestinian Jews . . . the use of *pleroo* for 'confirm' . . . was available to Jesus and Matthew"[127] must be rejected as unfounded.

New Testament Usage

But the Septuagint is not the only witness we must consult. Bahnsen also claims that in a few New Testament passages in which *pleroo* is used, those verbs can take

> the sense of "confirm, establish." James 2:23 says, "The Scripture was fulfilled saying Abraham believed God and it was imputed to him for righteousness. The quotation . . . to which James alludes is Genesis 15:6 yet the activity which James has in mind is Abraham's willingness to offer up Isaac (James 2:21) and this does not occur in Genesis until chapter 22. Abraham's activity does not fulfill a prophecy, for . . . Genesis 15:6 is an assertion, not a prediction. What James tells us, therefore, is that Abraham confirmed his righteousness by obedience to God; this is the theme of James 2:14–26.[128]

But, as Hodge points out, this passage will fit

> easily into regular usages for pleroo . . . Abraham's good work does fulfill the statement of imputed righteousness in the sense that good works complete, not confirm salvation . . . This is not to say that works are necessary for salvation but that works are a

---

126. Hodge, "Exegetical Response," 20, and Poythress, *Shadow of Christ*, 373.
127. Bahnsen, *Theonomy*, 71.
128. Ibid., 71, 72.

necessary result of salvation. In the preceding verse [2:22] James says, "Do you see that faith was working with his works, and by works faith was made perfect?" . . . As faith is made perfect by works, so imputed righteousness is made complete by righteous works, just as a tree is perfected by its fruit.[129]

If the already well-established meaning "complete" will make good sense in this passage, one cannot choose the not-yet-established meaning of "confirm" over against it. Similarly, when in Rom 15:19b, Paul says that "from Jerusalem and round about as far as Illyricum I have fully preached the gospel of Christ," Bahnsen believes that this must mean that "Paul had *established* the message of Christ's gospel"[130] in the area. However, this use of *pleroo* "in a pioneering sense . . . is not evidence for Bahnsen's use of *pleroo* with Jesus and the law since [in Matt 5:17] the law was already in existence. In any case, *pleroo* here does not mean 'to establish' but 'to complete' in the same category as James 2:23; 2 Cor. 10:6; and Rev 3:2."[131]

While Paul had not preached the gospel in every place in those regions (Rom 15:23), he had completed the commission given to him, that of founding enough churches in the area in question that there was no more pioneering to be done. Since "completed" is again an equal or better fit with the text, this example, too, fails to prove Bahnsen's point. This is also the situation with regard to Col 1:25, in which Paul is called to "fully carry out the preaching of the word of God." "Paul's preaching is not primarily functioning merely to confirm the truth of the gospel but to fulfill God's plan that the gospel should be communicated and spread to the Gentiles (1:27)."[132]

Bahnsen's next candidate for *pleroo* in the sense of "confirm" is 2 Corinthians 10:6, which reads, "being ready to punish all disobedience when your obedience is complete." Yet, as Poythress notes: "Bauer's sense three is used here, 'bring something to *completion*.' Bahnsen virtually agrees with this interpretation in his comments. 'Punishment will be restrained until it is not needed . . . Obedience is not established as such until it is completed.'"[133]

---

129. Hodge, "Exegetical Response," 23, and Poythress, *Shadow of Christ*, 374.
130. Bahnsen, *Theonomy*, 72.
131. Hodge, "Exegetical Response," 25, and Poythress, *Shadow of Christ*, 375.
132. Poythress, *Shadow of Christ*, 376.
133. Poythress, *Shadow of Christ*, 374, quoting Bahnsen, *Theonomy*, 72.

In addition, Poythress makes another important point with reference to Bahnsen's conclusion to the above-quoted sentence, which reads "to fill up obedience is equivalent to confirming or establishing obedience."[134] Poythress observes that while

> completion of obedience may imply confirmation and establishing of obedience . . . the two, nevertheless are not semantically equivalent, as if confirm were an exact synonym for complete. Evidence for an implication must be distinguished from evidence for a new sense of the word.[135]

Since the more usual translation and recognized meaning of "complete" fits as well or better here than Bahnsen's "confirm," Bahnsen's claim fails due to lack of support.

The final passage to consider is Rev 3:2 ("I have not found your deeds completed in the sight of my God"). Bahnsen claims that "the Sardisians . . . efforts to date had not confirmed the status of obedient servants in God's sight and judgment."[136] But the "church of Sardis does not need to confirm-establish their works . . . for the text says that their works were already found not complete or lacking . . . Rather they needed to complete their work, to fill up something that was lacking."[137] In such a setting, "the word *confirm* does not work very well as a substitute, [it] makes much less sense than the alternative . . . complete."[138]

Summary of the Evidence against Bahnsen's Translation

Bahnsen has not only failed to establish either an Aramaic or Septuagintal usage of *pleroo* in the sense of "confirm, establish the ongoing validity of," but he has failed to do so from the New Testament as well. Poythress fittingly concludes: "In summary, none of the texts that Bahnsen puts forward offers substantial evidence in favor of a distinct new sense of 'confirm' for the Greek word *pleroo*. The texts can all be understood on the basis of already well-established senses of the word."[139]

---

134. Bahnsen, *Theonomy*, 72.
135. Poythress, *Shadow of Christ*, 375.
136. Bahnsen, *Theonomy*, 72.
137. Hodge, "Exegetical Response," 25.
138. Poythress, *Shadow of Christ*, 375.
139. Ibid., 376.

Bahnsen's response to this conclusion is one of his most striking lapses from good scholarly practice. Although he does not quote, outline, or refute Poythress' arguments, Bahnsen dismisses his concerns. "The reasons he offers against the (commonly accepted) translation of 'confirm' in 1 Kings 1:14 are really nothing more than quibbles."[140]

Unfortunately, there are two errors in this attempted rebuttal. While "confirm" may now be an "accepted" *English* translation of the Hebrew מלא in 1 Kings 1:14 (see KJV, NIV, ESV and NASB), if "confirm" was the meaning intended here it would have been understood in the sense of "establishing the truth of an account," a different sense than that of "establish the ongoing validity of," which Bahnsen requires to make his point in Matt 5:17. We have also seen that the difference between Bathsheba's and Nathan's accounts of Adonijah's actions are such that Nathan may well have meant that he intended to "complete" rather than "confirm" her account. Taken together, these reasons are far more than quibbles: rather they are very strong reasons to doubt that *pleroo* would have meant "confirm" to a first-century, Greek-reading Jew, who had never before seen the word used in that sense.

Bahnsen extends his argument to Poythress' critique of his other examples: "Indeed when we examine his responses to the examples I have provided where *pleroo* could be translated 'confirm' . . . we find basically the same thing. He does not demonstrate that this translation cannot be correct, but simply offers his own reasons for taking the word in a slightly different way. This is more autobiography than refutation."[141]

Here, too, Bahnsen misunderstands Poythress' point. In every other case Bahnsen had provided, Poythress had demonstrated that already established meanings of *pleroo* are a better or equal fit than "confirm," by the usual criteria of lexicographical practice, thereby proving that the translation "confirm" cannot be justified. Poythress' objections, therefore, are certainly "more than quibbles." Indeed, they are so telling that BAGD, the standard lexicon of New Testament Greek, deliberately refused to accept the suggestion that *pleroo* can take the sense of "confirm." Their action is highly significant, for, as Poythress correctly notes,

> the testimony of the standard lexicons must be allowed to carry great weight in cases like this one. A massive amount of literature exists in ancient Greek, and the lexicons have endeavored

140. Bahnsen, *No Other Standard*, 320 n. 32.
141. Ibid.

to summarize it ... Many known instances exist for the established senses of the word *pleroo*. We ought to have firm evidence for some hypothetical new sense, if we are to believe that such a sense is not merely a queer, unexplainable exception, but was firmly established in the minds of Greek speakers through repeated usage. Hence it is safe to say that *pleroo* does not have the sense of "confirm" in Greek.[142]

Bahnsen's reply does not fully come to grips with the force of this conclusion. Instead he objects that "the standard New Testament lexicon by Arndt and Gingrich [BAGD] glosses 'confirm' as one possible translation for *pleroo*—precisely at Matt 5:17! They may not favor that view, but they had no qualm with glossing it as a legitimate possibility."[143]

While BAGD does gloss "confirm" at Matt 5:17, Bahnsen's remark does not answer Poythress' point. Meanings that BAGD believes to be established appear either in numbered definitions or, in specific cases where the intent is unclear, BAGD lists a number of possible meanings for the specified word in the particular verse under discussion.[144] When we turn up *pleroo* in BAGD, we find that the possible meaning "confirm" appears neither in the numbered definitions, nor in the list of BAGD's possible meanings of *pleroo* for Matt 5:17. Instead we find that the possibility that *pleroo* means "confirm" is only mentioned in a gloss, which is where BAGD summarizes debates between scholars who have advanced or denied a possible meaning for a word that Bauer, Arndt, and Gingrich did not accept. And since "confirm" only appears as a gloss rather than being discussed as a numbered meaning, or as a named possibility, it is clear that the lexicon's editors do not accept the translation of "confirm" for *pleroo*. If BAGD had accepted "confirm" as a possible meaning for *pleroo*, "confirm" would have been mentioned in their discussions of established meanings for the word, and not glossed among proposed meanings that the authors of the lexicon did not accept.[145]

Poythress' point is not a denial that some scholars have suggested translating *pleroo* by "confirm," but a claim that Arndt and Gingrich do

---

142. Poythress, *Shadow of Christ*, 377.
143. Bahnsen, *No Other Standard*, 320.
144. BAGD, s.v. "*pleroo*."
145. The articles mentioned in BAGD's gloss include viewpoints of those who advocate the translation "confirm," such as Dalman, and those who reject it, such as Ljungman.

Is Christ "Confirming" or "Completing" the Law? Matthew 5:17 83

not favor the view that "confirm" is a valid translation themselves. And it is their lexical judgment, and that of their colleagues, who do not accept "confirm" as a possible translation, that "must be allowed to carry great weight"[146] here. Either Bahnsen did not understand BAGD's formatting, or he failed to realize that the substance of Poythress' objection was a reference to the lexical judgment of Bauer, Arndt, Gingrich, and Danker who, by glossing this possible meaning, regarded it as doubtful rather than accepting it as established. The latter explanation seems more likely, for Bahnsen did concede that BAGD "may not favor"[147] the possibility that *pleroo* meant "confirm" without, apparently, realizing that by writing those words, he has conceded Poythress' entire point!

Next, Bahnsen deploys an additional argument. He writes, "The distinction between common verbs for 'fulfill' and 'complete' . . . in Hebrew and Greek is utterly irrelevant, for this does nothing to preclude the use of one word as a precising definition of the other in suitable contexts."[148]

Unfortunately, this objection has a serious problem. Using one word as a "precising definition" of another will only work in one of two situations. Either the word used to specify a narrower meaning of the first word has a known meaning that serves as a precising definition of another and thus could be used without the speaker specifically defining the broader word by the narrower, or else the speaker must so define his chosen word. Neither of these conditions is present in Matt 5:17: the Hebrew and Greek words for "fulfill" seem never before to have been used to mean "confirm," thus Christ could not have used *pleroosai* here and expected his hearers to understand it to mean "confirm" unless he went on to so define it, something he did not do. Given that there is no evidence that "confirm" was a known meaning of *pleroosai*, and that Christ did not go on to so define the word, we must assume that he did not intend his audience to understand his word to be taken as "a precising definition" of "fulfill" but rather as "fulfill" itself.

At this point we must address another question. If Christ spoke in Aramaic, why did Matthew, who knew all of the local languages,[149] not

---

146. Poythress, *Shadow of Christ*, 377.
147. Bahnsen, *No Other Standard,* 320.
148. Ibid., 278.
149. Matthew was a capable writer in the three languages of Galilee: Hebrew, Aramaic, and Greek. Cf. Carson, *Matthew*, 18–19.

translate the Aramaic[150] word used by Jesus with *pleroosai* instead of *istemi* or *bebaioosai* to give the meaning "confirm" if he thought that Jesus meant "confirm" in 5:17? These were the words commonly used by the LXX to express that meaning, and thus were far more familiar to readers of the LXX. *Istemi*, for example, "occurs twenty times [in the New Testament] . . . and either means literally 'set, place, bring' or figuratively 'establish, confirm.'"[151] More importantly, *istemi* has a long history of being used "to establish" the Mosaic law. In Exod 6:4, God says, "I established my covenant with them [the patriarchs]"—a usage picked up by Paul who, in Rom 3:31, asks, "Do we then make void the law through faith? God forbid, yea we establish (*istemi*) the law." Here, *istemi* was used to communicate the idea of establishing, rather than destroying the law. If Christ was trying to convey Bahnsen's idea of "confirm or establish"[152] in Matt 5:17, then he could easily have used *istemi* to do it.[153] That Christ did not use this word, pregnant with the very connotations needed to establish the Theonomic thesis in Matt 5:17, is a very strong argument that he had in mind to teach that he had come to do something other than "confirm, establish" the law in these verses.

However, Bahnsen has observed that in view of

> the corruption that the ethical stipulations of the Older Testament had suffered at the hands of the scribes and the Pharisees . . . , it can be seen why the word πληροο was used instead of the simpler and less expressive (or pithy) word ιστημι . . . [Jesus] did not merely establish the law . . . but confirmed it and restored it to full measure. As Ridderbos has observed, "fulfill in Matthew 5:17 does not mean to abolish or replace the Mosaic law, but to make plain its full demand, true content and purpose in contrast to the [later] Jewish [mis]interpreters"[154] . . . πληρow has a wealth of connotations not associated with ιστημι which make it the most appropriate word for the context of Matthew 5.[155]

---

150. In the period before 70 AD, the distinctions between meanings of the "confirm" and "fulfill" word groups seem to have been common to the three languages involved. Cf. Koehler and Baumgartner, eds., *The Hebrew and Aramaic Lexicon of the Old Testament*, vol. 2, 584; vol. 3, 1086; and vol. 4, 1915, 1968.

151. BAGD, 138.

152. Bahnsen, *Theonomy*, 70.

153. Hodge, "Exegetical Response," 26.

154. Ridderbos, *When the Time Had Fully Come*, 37, quoted in Bahnsen, *Theonomy*, 74.

155. Bahnsen, *Theonomy*, 74.

Is Christ "Confirming" or "Completing" the Law? Matthew 5:17

Unfortunately for this argument, Bahnsen has forgotten that he has specifically rejected all but one of the known meanings of the word *pleroo*[156] in order to establish his proposed sense of "confirm/restore . . . the ethical stipulations of the law and the prophets" "over against" these additional meanings.[157] After specifically ruling these known meanings of *pleroosai* out of consideration, Bahnsen cannot now argue that Christ had need of the "wealth of connotations" associated with *pleroo* over against words with fewer connotations, especially when one of the words with fewer connotations is exactly what is needed to establish the Theonomic thesis. Since it "is illogical to reject the evidence for one point and then use it to prove another,"[158] Bahnsen may be rightly faulted for trying to have his cake and eat it too: something as impossible in exegesis as it is in dessert.

Since all of Bahnsen's lexical arguments have failed, we can only conclude that there is no lexical case for translating *pleroo* as "confirm" in the sense of "establishing the ongoing validity of" anywhere in the Bible. Of all of Bahnsen's examples, none is strong enough to show that *pleroo* would have been so understood by first-century hearers in the sense required by Bahnsen's fourth premise.

Given that all of the previous four premises have failed, if his thesis is to have any hope of standing, Bahnsen must now prove the last premise: that "confirming" the law is a legitimate implication of Christ's words. Picking up Poythress' remark that in "nearly all cases the theological idea of fulfillment implies confirmation,"[159] Bahnsen argues from it that since "confirmation is an *implication* of many of the legitimate translations of . . . *pleroo* . . . the significant thing about the theonomic . . . treatment of Matthew 5:17 is not some linguistic point about preferred translation, but rather a substantial theological conclusion about the relationship of Jesus to the Old Testament law. If . . . Jesus did not

---

156. Of the known meanings and connotations of *pleroosai*, the single connotation that Bahnsen did not specifically reject was Ridderbos' suggestion that *fulfill* was used metaphorically, i.e., to (re)fill the law with its original intent. But Ridderbos' suggestion is incorrect: the law already was filled with its original intent when it was originally given. Had it been Christ's intent to restate the law's original content metaphorically, he would have said he had come to "refill" it rather than "fill" it. One unrejected possibility, however, is not a "wealth of connotations."

157. Bahnsen, *Theonomy*, 74.

158. Hodge, "Exegetical Response," 27.

159. Poythress, *Shadow of Christ*, 364.

'say' that He confirms the Old Testament law but . . . 'implied' . . . that He came to confirm the Old Testament law . . . [the] crucial theological point has still been established."[160]

But Bahnsen has here fallen into an old error in logic: that of equivocation, changing the meaning of a syllogism's terms between its premises and its conclusion. He is premising that since the "fulfilling" of a prophecy "confirms" its divine origin and the prophet's truthfulness (which was Poythress' point),[161] that one may therefore conclude that fulfilling the law or the prophets in that sense necessarily implies "confirming" the law's commandments in a different meaning of "confirm," that of establishing the law's ongoing validity in the church age. But this is not so. Equivocation renders any arguments using it invalid,[162] and since a term in Bahnsen's argument changes meanings between the argument's premise and its conclusion, Bahnsen's argument fails by equivocation.

This fallacy in Bahnsen's argument can be also be demonstrated from the Scriptures. While all fulfilled prophecies are "confirmed" by their fulfillment in the sense of being divinely originated and spoken by a true prophet, not every prophecy is automatically "confirmed" in the different sense of being a continuing obligation either for the one who fulfills the prophecy or for the fulfiller's followers. Although the divine origin of Zechariah's prophecy and his status as a true prophet were both confirmed by Christ's fulfilling of his prophecy, Christians do not believe that Christ, after his resurrection, was (or the church after his ascension, is) guilty of neglecting an ongoing obligation to continue riding donkeys into Jerusalem in obedience to Zechariah 9:9. Even though the fulfillment of his prophecy confirms that Zechariah's statement was a genuine prophecy having its origin in the mind of God and spoken by a true prophet, Christians universally recognize that it is not thereby "confirmed" in the different sense of requiring messianic or Christian repetitions.

Bahnsen, therefore, cannot argue that a fulfilled prophecy or law "confirmed" in the sense of being a true word of God, is thereby automatically "confirmed" in the different sense of being a continuing requirement for God's people. The consequence for Bahnsen's thesis is clear. If Christ, in Matthew 5:17, meant to imply that he "fulfills" the Old

---

160. Bahnsen, *No Other Standard*, 321.
161. Poythress, *Shadow of Christ*, 364–65.
162. Luce, *Teach Yourself Logic*, 162.

Is Christ "Confirming" or "Completing" the Law? Matthew 5:17

Testament in himself, the only thing he is automatically "confirming" in so doing is that the laws and prophecies he is coming to "fulfill" were divinely originated laws and prophecies spoken by true prophets. He is not, however, thereby "confirming" the ongoing obligatory nature of some or all of these Scriptures for the church age, since, as we have seen, not all fulfilled prophecies were to be confirmed in the sense of continuing obligation. Since Bahnsen's argument has been shown false on both logical and scriptural grounds, his fifth premise also cannot stand. Therefore, the "crucial theological point" remains to be established.

At the beginning of this chapter we saw that Bahnsen's view of Matt 5:17 would depend on whether at least four of five key premises could be established. Having examined each of Bahnsen's attempts to show that his chosen alternatives are either the only possible meaning of the words in question or are superior to all other relevant options, we now can evaluate his argument as a whole.

Bahnsen's first premise, that Christ meant his hearers to understand "the law or the prophets" as referring to "the ethical stipulations of the law," has been shown to be flawed by a number of methodological errors, including insufficient supporting arguments and a notable misunderstanding of lexicographical procedure coupled with an apparent ignorance of what the standard reference tools say about key words. When we draw the logical conclusion and wonder why Christ bothered to add "or the prophets" at all, Bahnsen's explanations are unsatisfactory. And Bahnsen does all this, in spite of Christ's deliberate use of "or" (the meaning of which, Bahnsen, by misrepresenting a source, misrepresents), which makes his reduction of the meaning of "the law or the prophets," from the entire Mosaic covenant administration to its "ethical stipulations," less likely. In addition, Bahnsen's refutation of the more likely meaning of the phrase "the law or the prophets," that is, the Mosaic covenant, has been shown to be inadequate on two of his three grounds: shortly the third will be shown to be equally flawed. Thus Bahnsen's first premise, already highly suspect, presently hangs by a thread soon to be cut.

Bahnsen then failed to discuss why *kataluo*, which certainly took the meaning "destroy" rather than "annul" when used of the law in Gal 2:18, cannot mean the same thing in Matt 5:17—a particularly significant omission given that the KJV translators thought "destroy" was a better fit in the Matthean verse. By making these errors, Bahnsen leaves unproven his second essential premise, that *katalusai* must mean "annul."

Moreover, even if *katalusai* was intended to mean "annul" here, *alla*, as Bahnsen himself later recognized, does not always force a meaning of total contradiction on the words it separates. Thus Bahnsen's required third premise, that *katalusai* must force the translation of *pleroosai* as "confirm," collapses.

Bahnsen's next error is his rejection, without sufficient discussion, of four known and decidedly relevant meanings of "fulfill" for *pleroo* despite the substantial scriptural support that they enjoy, and the demonstrable relevance that each has in the context of Matt 5:17. Instead, he proposes the unlikely possibility of "confirm" in the sense of "establish the ongoing validity of," a possibility made considerably weaker by the lack of solid evidence that either the Hebrew *mala* or the Greek *pleroo* ever meant "confirm" in that sense in or before the New Testament era. This lack of evidence discredits any possibility that *plerousai* ever meant "confirm" in that sense, which is Bahnsen's fourth premise.

Finally, Bahnsen's last premise—that "confirm" in the sense of "establish the ongoing applicability of commands" is a logical and legitimate implication of translating *pleroo* by "fulfill"—has been demonstrated to be both illogical and false to the Scriptures. Of Bahnsen's five premises, his first now hangs by a thread, his failed second premise has been made irrelevant by the failure of his third, and both of his final two premises have been shown to be insupportable.

Finally, Bahnsen makes Christ out to have made a massive error in his choice of words by using the misleading *pleroosai* to mean "confirm," rather than the far more fitting *istemi* (confirm/establish), which was well known, available to him, and would have established the Theonomic thesis beyond any possibility of doubt. In short, by inserting the meaning "confirm" for *pleroo* with no real lexical grounds for doing so, it is Bahnsen, not Poythress, who is "overlook[ing] the obvious" and "importing preconceived ideas into the text (and context), rather than reading them out of the text"[163] and doing violence to the context.

Since Bahnsen has misunderstood the subject of Christ's thought, the relationship between the two verbs brought about by the conjunction, and the meanings of both of the key verbs in this verse, his exegetical case for the Theonomic thesis has not met the burden of proof.

---

163. Bahnsen, *No Other Standard*, 322.

Is Christ "Confirming" or "Completing" the Law? Matthew 5:17

Already it is clear that Bahnsen's Theonomy is one thesis that Christ is not teaching here. Instead, he is teaching something else in these verses, and to that teaching, we must now turn.

HOW JESUS FULFILLS "THE LAW OR THE PROPHETS"

After having determined that *pleroosai* never was used to mean "confirm" in the sense of "establish the continuing validity of" at any point before the close of the New Testament, the question we must consider is, what then does *pleroosai* mean in Matt 5:17? As a first step to answering this question, let us examine how BAGD defines *pleroosai* in this verse. In BAGD, this verse is discussed separately, for its editors believe that the word is to be taken "in the broadest sense and in contrast to καταλυειν . . . depending on how one prefers to interpret the context πληροο is understood here as *fulfill* = do, carry out, or as to *bring to full expression* = show it forth in its true mng., or as *fill up* = complete."[164] BAGD is not alone in proposing a broad understanding of *pleroo*'s meaning here. Hendriksen, writing before Bahnsen's thesis became public, also makes an extended and strong case against too narrowly defining the meaning Christ intended for this word:

> It was [Christ's] aim that *in the lives of his true followers* the spiritual requirement of the Old Testament would receive its due, that is, that in these lives the vessel of the law's . . . demand would become filled to the brim.
>
> However, it does not appear . . . that the explanation given so far *fully* satisfies the meaning of the passage. It is hard . . . to believe that in saying "I have not come to set aside but to fulfill" Jesus was thinking *only* of fulfillment in *his followers*. [In addition Jesus may have been thinking of fulfillment in his own experience as well. Such a possibility] brings the passage in harmony with such other sayings of Jesus in which he presents himself as the fulfillment of the Old Testament; not only with the words uttered at a much later time (Matt 26:56; Luke 18:31; 24:25–27, 44), but also and especially with those who probably belong to the very year when this sermon was delivered.
>
> It is hard to believe that he who had very recently revealed himself to the woman of Samaria as the realization of mankind's hope (John 4:25, 26, 42) and who very shortly would describe himself to John the Baptist and to the people of Nazareth as the

---

164. BAGD, 671.

fulfillment of prophecy (respectively Matt 11:1–16 and Luke 4:16–30), would in this sermon have been able, without thinking of any realization *in himself*, to speak about fulfilling the Old Testament.

Now if the fulfillment was to be in relation to himself also, then was it to be with respect to his teaching *only*, setting forth the true meaning of the law and revealing himself as the fulfillment of the Old Testament types and predictions, so that he would stand out as *the chief prophet* (Deut 18:15, 18)? Or with respect to his vicarious suffering and death *alone*, by which through his active and passive obedience he would satisfy the demands of the law as his people's *sympathetic high priest* (Ps. 40:6, 7; Jer. 23:6)? Or exclusively with respect to his royal rule, thereby delivering his people from the power of the enemy and holding sway over their lives as their *eternal king* (Gen. 49:10; II Sam. 7:12, 13; Ps. 72)? But why not all three? Does not the Old Testament itself lead the way to a fuller interpretation of the concept "Messianic Fulfillment" when in describing the coming Redeemer it does not always restrict itself to the manner in which he would function in one office? See Ps. 110:4; Isa. 53; Zech. 6:13. Conclusion: in *all* he was and was to do he had come not to set aside or annul the Old Testament but to fulfill it. The context does not require—perhaps it is not erroneous to say "does not even permit"—any restriction to be made as to the meaning of this majestic statement. Moreover the passage itself, by means of its disjunctive "or" ("the law or the prophets" instead of "the law and the prophets") emphasizes breadth of meaning, causing the mind to linger a little longer on the two distinct parts, and probably indicating that Jesus had not come either to lift the demand of the law, or to invalidate the words, including the predictions, of the prophets. He had come to fulfill both.[165]

If Hendriksen is correct, we must examine the possibility that Christ came to fulfill the law in more than one sense. Four distinct possibilities must be considered.

Fulfilling Prophecy

As we have already seen, Bahnsen believes "there is no reason to see any *distinctive* mention of the predictive prophecies of the Older Testament in Matt 5:17 or its context."[166] In addition, he offered a number of rea-

---

165. Hendriksen, *Exposition of the Gospel according to Matthew*, 289–90.
166. Bahnsen, *Theonomy*, 52.

sons for denying the view that "'fulfill' in Matt 5:17 should be assimilated to the other uses of 'fulfill' where it applies to prophecies of the Old Testament. . . . [First,] the specific context of the Sermon on the Mount simply does not deal with Old Testament prophecies."[167]

The word *pleroosai* is usually translated "fulfill" when connected with prophecy and is so translated by all major translations at 5:17. Combined with "or the prophets" it is enough to bring "distinctive mention of the *predictive* prophecies of the Older Testament [into] Matt 5:17" itself, let alone its context. Such a view is only confirmed by the assertion in verse 18 that "not one jot or one tittle shall disappear from the law until all is accomplished," which is, as we have earlier seen, a major reason why the fulfillment of the messianic prophecies was necessary. Bahnsen, therefore, begs the question when he did not provide a detailed examination of whether Jesus intended us to understand *pleroosai* in this commonly used sense of "fulfill." When we also consider that the idea of fulfilling prophecy is also the most common use of *pleroo* in the New Testament, in Matthew's Gospel, and on the lips of Jesus himself, we would be seriously remiss if we did not examine the possibility that Christ meant us to understand *pleroosai* in Matt 5:17 in the sense of "fulfilling" prophecies.

In the Septuagint, we find seven times where "*pleroo* is used of fulfilling divine prophecies or promises."[168] Turning to the New Testament, *pleroo* is used thirty-two times in the sense of "fulfilling" Old Testament prophecies against Bahnsen's suggested four possibilities for "confirm"—none of which, as we have seen, can withstand scrutiny. A number of these are in Matthew alone and they are highly significant.[169] As Guthrie has noted, "Matthew's major purpose in writing his gospel is to prove that the Messiah is in complete fulfillment of OT prophecy."[170] "Of the sixteen times πληροω occurs in Matthew, twelve times are clearly for prophetic fulfillment of Scripture. Every major event in the life of Jesus is characterized by fulfillment of Scripture: the infancy stories (1:22; 2:15, 17), His dwelling at Nazareth (1:23), the move to Capernaum (4:14),

---

167. Bahnsen, *No Other Standard*, 322.

168. 1 Kgs [English versions] 2:27; 4:15, 24; 2 Chr 6:14, 15; 36:21, 22. Hatch and Redpath, eds., *A Concordance to the LXX*, 1147–48.

169. Matt 1:22, 2:15, 17, 23, 4:14, 8:17, 12:17, 13:35, 21:4, 26:54, 27:9, 35.

170. Hodge, "Exegetical Response," 31, quoting Guthrie, *New Testament Introduction*, 25.

His healing work (8:17, 12:17), His explanation of parables (13:35), His triumphal entry (21:4), and His passion (26:54, 56; 27:9)."[171]

Since there can be no doubt that Christ's explanation of his relationship to the law is of equal importance to his explanation of the parables, Christ may be using the same formulaic explanations for his relation to the law as he did when explaining the parables. Thus it is far more likely that Jesus is announcing that his purpose is to "fulfill" the old covenant rather than announcing he has come to "confirm" the law or the prophets.

Bahnsen seemed to be attempting to minimize the problem Matthew's normal usage of *pleroo* created for the Theonomic thesis when he wrote that

> even when πληροω is used of the actualization [Bahnsen avoids the more usual translation "fulfillment" here] of a prophecy (as it often is) the word has the unmistakable connotation of "confirmation." A primary purpose of prophecy was the accreditation of a messenger from God or of his (His) message; prophecy was meant to inspire faith in those who witnessed its fulfillment. Jesus indicates this in John 14:29, "And now I have told you before it comes to pass, that when it comes to pass you may believe." This double sense for πληροω (i.e., actualization and confirmation) is witnessed in the LXX and extensively in the New Testament.[172]

There are two problems with this argument. First, neither "actualize" nor "fulfill" is truly synonymous with "confirm." Bahnsen cannot, therefore, automatically use the fact that "fulfill" sometimes connotes the meaning of "confirm" to justify the change in translation from the former word to the latter since that change causes the loss of key nuances. As Poythress rightly notes of "fulfill" (and his comments will be valid for "actualize," also):

> we might say that . . . *fulfill* implies or connotes "confirm." But the words *fulfill* and *confirm* are not absolutely identical in meaning. . . . If we simply replace *fulfill* by *confirm* we lose the distinct nuances of realization, completion and consummation
>
> *Confirm* suggests a static maintenance of an existing rule, whereas *fulfill* suggests an advance toward realization. Accordingly, English dictionaries do not say that "confirm" is

---

171. Hodge, "Exegetical Response," 31.
172. Bahnsen, *Theonomy*, 71.

Is Christ "Confirming" or "Completing" the Law? Matthew 5:17

one of the senses of *fulfill* or that the two words can replace one another without loss. The theological and logical fact that *fulfill* implies "confirm" must not be confused with the linguistic question about the distinct senses of the English word *fulfill*.[173]

But Bahnsen believes that Poythress has "unjustifiably narrowed what I say about the word [*pleroo*] in that passage reducing it merely to 'confirm' and then (on top of that) portraying confirmation in a linguistically shallow and connotatively sparse manner (e.g., 'purely static continuation' . . . and other phrases with purposely negative and unwarranted connotations). By setting up this straw man the critics can then berate theonomy for ignoring the richness of the word 'fulfill' in Matthew 5:17."[174]

To this "unsound" charge, Bahnsen protests that he had already claimed that "Jesus says . . . He came to confirm and restore the full measure, intent and purpose of the Older Testamental law . . . [and] sees the whole process of revelation deposited in the Older Testament as finding its validation in Him—its actual embodiment . . . *Pleroo* is subject both to the norm both of literal Older Testamental wording and the meaning of salvation manifested in Jesus Christ."[175]

Yet, once again, Bahnsen has forgotten that it was he himself who so limited the meaning of *pleroo* to "confirm" in Matthew 5:17 when he made such a point of arguing that it meant "confirm" in that verse, "over against" any other meaning usually suggested, by specifically rejecting every other known meaning of the word used in first-century Greek.[176] And Bahnsen only confirmed that limitation when he claimed that Christ meant us to take the phrase "the law or the prophets" "as focusing on the *ethical stipulations* contained in the canon of the entire Older Testament."[177] Such limitations would seem to rule out including "the meaning of salvation manifested in Jesus Christ," in any other sense. It is therefore no wonder that his critics have objected that he has narrowed the meaning of the word *pleroo*. He has not left any other possible option open that will let his readers come to a different conclusion so far as its meaning in Matt 5:17 is concerned. After limiting the meaning of

---

173. Poythress, *Shadow of Christ*, 365.
174. Bahnsen, *No Other Standard*, 318.
175. Bahnsen, *No Other Standard*, 318, quoting Bahnsen, *Theonomy*, 67.
176. Bahnsen, *Theonomy*, 74.
177. Ibid., 53.

the word, he cannot complain that his critics err in charging him with so doing.

But Bahnsen's objection fails for another reason as well. My dictionary defines "confirm" as follows: "to make stronger or more persistent . . . to corroborate . . . to ratify, endorse by writing; to make (something provisional) definite."[178] None of these definitions has the specific connotation of "advance toward realization" that is essential to the meaning of fulfill. Therefore, Bahnsen's belief that Poythress has defined "confirm" in a "linguistically shallow and connotatively sparse manner" over against "fulfill" does not hold up.

Bahnsen also argued that the "prophetic" interpretation of "fulfill" should be rejected since it took

> every connotation or association [that can be drawn] to the word "fulfill" in Matthew's gospel and . . . packed [them] into . . . [the] use of the term . . . at 5:17. This interpretive method is fallacious from the standpoint of both logic and literature (despite its popularity among some theologians.) Poythress wants to say that "fulfill" in 5:17 should be assimilated to the other uses of "fulfill" when it applies to prophecies of the Old Testament . . . We get into real trouble when we overlook the obvious. . . . Poythress (and others) who try to import prophetic . . . "nuances" into the word "fulfill" in Matthew 5:17 are doing just that—importing preconceived ideas into the text (and context), rather than reading them out of the text. . . . The violence done to the context of Matthew 5:17 by importing prophetic and topological objects of "fulfillment" is astounding, obvious to any simple reader.[179]

Unfortunately, this attempt at refutation contains two errors. First, the theological method here decried is simply that of comparing Scripture by Scripture. Should we never check the meaning of a word in one passage by its usage in another? Bahnsen, good Calvinist that he was, would be the first to say, "Of course not," because the direct consequence would be that "world" in John 3:16 would have to be taken to mean "all persons without exception." Such an answer, anathema to Calvinists, can only be refuted by demonstrating from elsewhere in the Bible that the word *world* can mean more than one thing.

---

178. *The New Lexicon Webster's Dictionary of the English Language*, 1989, s.v. "confirm."

179. Bahnsen, *No Other Standard*, 322, 3.

Is Christ "Confirming" or "Completing" the Law? Matthew 5:17

Second, the refutation misunderstands Poythress' point: he is not taking "every connotation or association [of] fulfill . . . and [packing them] into . . . [the] use of the term . . . at 5:17."[180] Rather, Poythress is only suggesting that we translate *pleroo* in 5:17 by one of its recognized meanings, that of "fulfill by deeds"—a meaning we have good lexical and contextual reason to prefer, being the meaning most often used to translate *pleroo* in Matthew and the meaning most often given to it when it is found in the same context as the word *prophets*. It is an especially appropriate meaning in this case when, in the same context, we find a major reason why a number of prophecies were not only later fulfilled, but made in the first place as well.

Next, Bahnsen wonders why Matthew would "commit the silly *faux pas* of using his 'code word' [*pleroo*] for fishing nets? [13:48] If this is really a code word for Matthew, why does he not use it more frequently in obvious places where it might be suspected?"[181]

But this question is easily answered; *pleroo* is not a code word, but one with a number of recognized meanings. As we have seen from our study of the lexicons, its basic meaning in classical Greek was that of "filling" something or someone, and that meaning remained valid in biblical Greek.[182] It was, therefore, the appropriate word for Matthew to use in the particular verse where the context was filling fishing nets. In fact, Bahnsen himself provided the decisive answer to his own objection on the same page on which he voiced it when he wrote, "The verb 'fulfill' will have slightly different linguistic senses depending upon the object which is said to be fulfilled—whether it is a prophecy . . . or a fishing net."[183] Second, Bahnsen seems to have forgotten for the moment that Matthew does use *pleroo* in the sense of "fulfill" in "the obvious places where it might be suspected," that is, almost every time Jesus fulfills Scripture.[184]

---

180. Readers unaware of Poythress' "multiperspective theology" will not realize that Bahnsen here deploys *ad hominem* arguments attacking that perspective in both this and the following argument. These attacks are especially ironic since Bahnsen apparently did not realize that Poythress' argument derives not from "multiperspective" premises but from classic word study technique.

181. Bahnsen, *No Other Standard*, 322 n. 34.

182. As seen in both the Septuagint (Eccl 9:3) and the New Testament (Luke 3:5).

183. Bahnsen, *No Other Standard*, 332.

184. One is forced to consider whether or not Bahnsen was being disingenuous here, since the only way he could have confirmed that the translation "confirm" for *pleroo* is

Bahnsen's next step is to quote from an article by David Wenham to support the view that the context in Matt 5:17 is not one of prophetic fulfillment but rather that of confirming or establishing the law.

> We may agree . . . that *pleroosai* is normally used in Matthew to mean fulfill (especially of the fulfillment of prophecy), **and that quite possibly that thought is present here in Matthew 5:17—not only the prophets but also the law are seen as pointing forward to Jesus and finding their fulfillment in him.** But whereas Banks believes that Matthew's thought is of "fulfilling and so transcending" the context suggests rather that the thought is that of "fulfilling and so establishing. The contrast in verse 17b "I came not to abolish but to" . . . favors this view: "abolish-fulfill/establish" are a more natural pair of opposites than "abolish-fulfill/transcend." And the subsequent context also favors this interpretation: the fact that Jesus is the fulfiller of the law leads on to the practical "therefore" of v. 19. Jesus' followers are to uphold and not abolish the law.[185]

While it is true that "abolish-establish" may be a more common pair of opposites than "abolish-transcend," "abolish-transcend" is not an impossible contrast. For we have already seen, in our examination of *alla*, that the contrast that it sets up need not be absolute. And Wenham's other point about the subsequent context will only hold true if the terminus of the law, "when heaven and earth pass away" is not a different point in time from when "all is fulfilled." If those two points are not identical, Wenham's second point fails. We shall come back to this when examining verse 18.

In an argument designed to refute the notion that prophetic fulfillment is involved in the meaning of *pleroo* in this verse, it is not entirely fair to Wenham to substitute an ellipsis, as Bahnsen does, while omitting the words given above in bold. These words make it clear that although Wenham believes that the thought here is primarily that of "confirming and establishing," he does not share Bahnsen's denial that the idea of prophetic fulfillment is present at all. Instead, the prophetic fulfillment

---

"not the statistically most common use" for the word (Bahnsen, *No Other Standard*, 320), is by examining a concordance and totaling up the different New Testament uses of the word. Had Bahnsen done that routine check, he could hardly have avoided realizing that the vast majority of New Testament examples of the use of *pleroo* are cases of Matthew recording Christ's fulfillment of yet another scriptural prophecy.

185. Bahnsen, *No Other Standard*, 319, quoting Wenham, "Jesus and the Law," 93. Bolding by present author.

Bahnsen denies is, for Wenham, a possible precondition for the establishing of the law. For Wenham, Jesus may well fulfill prophecies as well as the law.

Some other questions need to be considered. We must ask whether it is only a confusing circumstance that it was essential for Christ to "fulfill" both the law and the prophets in order to achieve our salvation while he meant to teach something else in Matt 5:17. Or was Christ indeed referring to this need when he announced that his purpose in coming was to fulfill the law and the prophets? And if Christ did mean to coin a new usage for *pleroo*, why did he not go on to qualify or redefine the term so his hearers could understand his intent? If Christ had no intention of referring to his upcoming fulfillment of the messianic prophecies in Matt 5:17, why did he, arguably the master teacher of the ages, use *pleroosai*, if speaking in Greek; or if speaking in Aramaic, use a word that Matthew believed was best translated by *pleroosai* there? His use of such a word, instead of those available to him that point directly to the Theonomic thesis, points away from the meaning that he, on Bahnsen's hypothesis, supposedly wanted to convey and directs us exactly to the meaning that he supposedly did not want us to understand. In addition, we must explain why he later increased the confusion when he used the word *pleroo* in Luke 24:44. In this verse he reminded his disciples of his pre-crucifixion teaching that he would fulfill the messianic prophecies—in a way that appears to be directly alluding to what he had said in Matt 5:17: "'These are my words which I spoke to you while I was still with you, that all things which are written about me in the Law of Moses, and the Prophets and the Psalms must be fulfilled' [*pleroothemai*]. Then He opened their minds to understand the Scriptures, and He said to them, 'Thus it is written, that Christ should suffer and rise again from the dead the third day.'"[186]

It appears that Christ is quoting an earlier teaching he gave on the subject of how he would "fulfill" the law and the prophets in which he used the word *pleroo*. While Christ often used that word when he spoke of fulfilling individual prophecies of Scripture, Matt 5:17 is the only place recorded in the gospels in which he used it when speaking of "fulfilling" the law or the prophets as a class. It is therefore the only recorded earlier teaching Jesus could have been referring to in Luke 24:44. Nowhere does Bahnsen reply to this argument.

186. Luke 24: 44–46.

Finally, there is also present an element of bringing the law and the prophets to their full expression by fulfilling prophecies that Bahnsen fails to take into account.[187]

> In the prophets Isaiah, Jeremiah, and Ezekiel, a . . . contrast emerges between the old covenant with its "Sinai Torah" and the new covenant with its "Zion Torah" . . . With these exilic prophets comes the promise expressed in Jer 31:31–34 as the "new covenant," the self revelation of God and the Law "written on the heart" and in Ezek. 36:25–27 expressed as the cleansing forgiveness, a "new heart" and "spirit" connoting a new relationship between God and his people and their obedience of his will. This motif of God's redemptive activity, often associated with Zion, runs through Isaiah (cf. 2:2–6, Mic. 4:1–5) and reaches its culmination with Isa. 56:1, "keep justice and do righteousness for my salvation comes and my righteousness . . . will be revealed."[188]

When the "Zion Torah" arrived, the ability to walk according to God's will would come as a gift, the product of the divine initiative in the end times. Consequently, the "'Zion Torah' . . . stood in contrast to the 'Sinai Torah' but did not annul it. The 'Zion Torah' superseded the 'Sinai Torah.'"[189]

So Jesus may have intended to "fulfill" the law and the prophets by filling them up and completing them, since by his coming he "fulfills" and "brings to completion" the "full realization of the personal relationship [between God and His people] involving an ethical and moral 'fulfillment of God's will.'"[190]

After examining his counterarguments, we conclude that Bahnsen has failed to make the case for rejecting the meaning of "fulfill" in the sense of fulfilling prophecies. Since Christ is clearly engaged in fulfilling the prophets in this sense, Bahnsen's view that "there is no reason to see any distinctive mention of the predictive prophecies of the Older

---

187. Bahnsen had encountered scholars who saw Christ teaching a "New Torah" replacing the old. But, according to Bahnsen, the New Torah ethic mentioned by Burrows is an attitude rather than a detailed code and must be rejected since it is an abolishing of the law prohibited by Jesus' words in Matt 5:17 (Bahnsen, *Theonomy*, 59). While he was correct to reject this view if a mere "replacement" before all the law and prophets were fulfilled was meant, Bahnsen's view will not necessarily stand if Christ meant that the change would occur when the Old Covenant was replaced by the New.

188. Guelich, *Sermon*, 140.

189. Ibid.

190. Guelich, *Sermon*, 140, quoting Moule, "Fulfillment Words," 317.

Is Christ "Confirming" or "Completing" the Law? Matthew 5:17

Testament in Matthew 5:17 or its context,"[191] must be rejected as "a good example of poor exegesis."[192] We must keep our minds open to the possibility that Christ meant "fulfill" to be understood in the sense of fulfilling prophecy in Matt 5:17.

Obeying the Law

The second way Christ will "fulfill" the law is by the active and passive obedience to it he performed throughout his life. For it is only as Christ perfectly fulfilled the demands of the law that he could achieve a righteousness under the Old Testament law that could be credited to sinners.[193] Therefore, Jesus' holiness and good works are crucially involved in Matt 5:17–18.

Bahnsen advances two reasons for rejecting this view. First, he argues that the existence of "three more commonly circulated words which more directly and explicitly expressed that thought [of obeying commandments] makes this interpretation unlikely."[194]

But an additional consideration nullifies this objection. If Christ is engaged in fulfilling the law or the prophets by his deeds, he will be both keeping commandments and fulfilling prophecies. Therefore, the word he needs to use must be equally suitable when used in reference to both commandments and prophecies. While *pleroo* is usually found used of fulfilling prophecy, it is also, as Bahnsen recognized, sometimes used to refer to "the keeping or doing of a commandment (e.g., 1 Macc. 2:55; Rom. 13:8, 8:4; Matt. 3:15)."[195] On the other hand, since the three words Bahnsen cites as better possibilities for "keeping" commandments had never before been used in the sense of fulfilling prophecies, *pleroo* was clearly a better choice for our Lord to employ, as it had already been used to refer to both keeping commandments and fulfilling prophecies.

---

191. Bahnsen, *Theonomy*, 53.

192. Hodge, "Exegetical Response," 32.

193. Matt 3:15; 2 Cor 5:21. "It is a question worth pursuing, whether the righteousness by which a believer is justified is in any way the righteousness of the Law. Within the right understanding of the terms employed there, there can be no hesitation in affirming that this is so. The doctrine of the imputation of Christ's active obedience to the believer is beyond all doubt an establishing of the Law in this manner." Kevan, *The Moral Law*, 82 n.

194. Bahnsen, *Theonomy*, 63.

195. Ibid.

Bahnsen also noted that "the idea of fulfillment by *doing* is usually expressed in the passive voice, whereas in Matt 5:17 πληροω appears in the active voice."[196] But "usually" is not the same as "always," and there are two New Testament passages in which *pleroo* is used in the active voice to express fulfillment by doing. First, in Matt 3:15, Jesus, referring to his proposed baptism, tells John the Baptist that "in this way it is fitting for us to fulfill [*pleroosai*] all righteousness." Similarly, in Romans 13:8, we find that "he who loves his neighbor has fulfilled [*peplerooken*] the law." These examples are enough to establish that it is entirely possible that Jesus may have intended to "fulfill the law or the prophets" by his deeds in keeping the law also.

Showing Forth the Law's True Meaning

While some commentators have argued that Jesus was here inaugurating new teaching that supplements or replaces the Old Testament because of its own insufficiencies in its ethical content, Bahnsen correctly reminds us that the Old Testament law was biblically recognized as being "perfect, complete (Ps. 19:7f, 119:28)" in its ethical content.[197] Nor did it "fall short of informing God's people of the need for inward heart righteousness in contrast to mere external legalism."[198] One need only look at Ps 51:6, 10, and 17 to be disabused of this error.

What Bahnsen overlooked, however, is that the Old Testament law, while perfect and complete as to the content of its legislation, did not spell out an explicit perspective that would resolve all questions of apparent conflict between its laws. If you foolishly vow your resources to God, does the law's requirement that vows be paid bar you from using those resources to help your parents as the law commands? Is it lawful to do good on a Sabbath day, or is that work, hence forbidden? The Pentateuch did not explicitly answer these questions, which is why they became the subjects of later Jewish debate. It is by providing answers to these questions involving apparent conflicts between various laws, that Jesus provides the necessary framework to complete the law and show it forth in its true meaning.

---

196. Ibid., 64.
197. Bahnsen, *Theonomy*, 60.
198. Ibid.

Christ, however, did not introduce a totally novel system of interpretation. It had already been hinted at in passages such as Hosea 6:6, but since the prophets were not explicitly promulgating additional stipulations to the covenant,[199] the debate raged on. Perspectives found in the prophets could settle such debates only after the lawgiver announced that the prophets were as authoritative as the covenantal law. By ascribing to the prophets an equally canonical status as the law, Jesus may have intended to "fulfill" the law and the prophets by showing them forth in their true meanings as well.

Completing the Old Covenant's Time in Force

According to Bahnsen, the idea that Jesus came to "put an end to" the law and the prophets fails since when *pleroo* "is used in the sense of 'finish or end,' it always appears in a context where the thought of advancement, or moving on, as well as a temporal element are explicit . . . [and] both these elements are absent in the present passage with reference to the fulfilling done by Jesus."[200]

This objection, however, fails to recognize that the thought of advancement and a temporal element are both present if Matt 5:17–18 is taken to refer to the transition from Old to New Covenant. For the New Covenant features two significant advances on the Old: in the New Covenant, the law will be written upon the heart of the believers, and the Gentiles will be brought into the covenant together with the Jews. Also, the temporal element is present: Christ twice makes temporal references in verse 18. Since both allegedly missing elements are present in the context, Bahnsen's objection does not hold good.

Bahnsen also claims that this view is an "attempt to force a distinction between the conceptions of 'dismantling' (καταλυω) and 'abrogat-

---

199. Paul points out in Gal 3:15 that once even a human covenant is made it cannot be changed by others, and the word *even* in that verse implies that the same holds true for a covenant made by God. The only way a change to the Mosaic covenant was possible was for God to exercise his sovereignty and make a new covenant, thereby superseding the old. Such a change is not ruled out by Paul in Gal 3:15, since all covenants between a sovereign and a subject could be superseded at the whim of the sovereign. Since no prophet between Moses and Christ made a covenant with God that altered the Mosaic covenantal conditions, the Mosaic covenant was not superseded, and therefore no prophet's ethical observations could be as authoritative for Israel as the ethical stipulations of the law until and unless the Lawgiver directly so pronounced them.

200. Bahnsen, *Theonomy*, 57.

ing' (πληροω) e.g., to abrogate the law while repudiating the spirit of a destroyer."[201]

This objection, however, fails to reckon with critical data: although *pleroo* has never taken the sense of "abrogate" in Greek, both the Hebrew *mala* and its Greek counterpart *pleroo* were used for the expected completion of a time-limited condition such as a pregnancy; for example, Genesis 25:24's "when her days to be delivered were fulfilled." If the Sinai Covenant had a divinely given limited period of applicability, Christ is not unlawfully abrogating it, but rightfully completing the time of its applicability. So, we need to ask two questions: did the Sinai Covenant have a rightful end, and when that end was achieved, could it be described as "fulfilled" in the sense of being completed? Indeed, it did have such an end, and it could be so described. Although Moses had announced that "the Lord your God will raise up for you a prophet like me,"[202] it was clear that this prophet was not one of Moses' immediate successors since none of them had initiated a new national covenant as Moses had done. And while Jeremiah 31:31 records God's announcement to Israel that he would make a New Covenant that would supersede the covenant he had made through Moses, Christ's contemporaries were still waiting for that Covenant to be made.[203]

Jesus, who announced the establishment of the New Covenant (Luke 22:20), also announced the forthcoming superseding of the Old with his statement that "the prophets and the Law prophesied until John" (Matt 11:13). Paul echoes the point with his remark that "the Law . . . was added . . . until the seed should come to whom the promise had been made," the seed being Christ.[204] The author of Hebrews confirmed that the early church as a whole understood that the New Covenant superseded the Old.[205] The institution of the New Covenant, superseding the Old, was not a destruction of the former covenant. Instead, it was the bringing of that covenant to its rightful completion.

---

201. Bahnsen, *Theonomy*, 57, referencing Bruce, *The Synoptic Gospels*, 104.

202. Deut 18:15.

203. That the promised prophet had not come by Christ's time is shown by the Jews asking John the Baptist if he was "the Prophet" in John 1:21. The early church saw that this prophet was Jesus (Acts 3:22, 23).

204. Gal 3:19. It is a major flaw in his argument that Bahnsen does not discuss this most significant verse in either *Theonomy* or *No Other Standard*.

205. Heb 7:18–19; 8:6–13.

By his metaphorical placing of his disciples in the place heretofore reserved for the law, Jesus has given an unmistakable hint that he was the one who would establish Jeremiah's New Covenant. In view of these facts, we must reject Gentry's claim that "nothing in Matthew 5 suggests Jesus is teaching his hearers about a change in covenantal administration."[206]

THE MEANING OF PLEROO IN VERSE 17

Having studied Bahnsen's work, we have seen that he failed to consider the possibility that Christ meant us to understand *pleroo* or its Aramaic original in the sense of "bringing a time-limited covenant to its prophesied completion." This omission is critical, for there is considerable evidence in the context and in the rest of the scriptures that this was the sense in which Jesus intended *pleroo* to be understood.

As we examined the evidence behind each of BAGD's suggested meanings for *pleroosai* in Matt 5:17, we have discovered that every one of them can muster far stronger scriptural support than Bahnsen's "confirm." The scriptural evidence supporting each possibility is so strong that none of them can be ruled out of court. We can therefore conclude that in Matt 5:17, Christ used *pleroosai* to convey that he would "fulfill" the law in every one of these meanings. For by bringing the Old Covenant to its prophesied completion in the New, Christ both fulfilled the law by his required obedience to it and fulfilled the messianic prophecies that foretold these changes and made them possible. Along the way, Christ showed forth the Old Covenant's true meaning, by providing the perspective from which to resolve conflicts between laws, and opened the way to the deeper encounter with God promised by Jeremiah. This view is in accordance with the known usage of comparative negation for *alla*, and is the only possibility that is "consistent with both 'law' and 'prophets' . . . does not require a *de facto* 'washing out' of one or the other, . . . is consistent with how the verb is regularly related to 'prophets'; . . . [is] consistent with Matt 11:13; and it is consistent with the portrait of Christ elsewhere in the NT as functioning within the Sinai covenant until he established the new by his death and resurrection, and therefore requiring his disciples to obey the Mosaic law until the New Covenant was inaugurated (Matt 23:2, 3)."[207]

---

206. Gentry, *Covenantal Theonomy*, 63.
207. Gordon, "Theonomy," 30.

In addition, since winding up the Sinai covenant required Christ to fulfill "the law" and "the prophets" in different ways (fulfilling the law by his obedience to it, and the prophets by accomplishing their prophecies), it is this understanding that both links and distinguishes the law from the prophets in Matt 5:17, and finally explains Christ's use of "or" rather than "and" in this verse. It also explains why the apostles could exempt the Gentiles from keeping whole divisions of the law.[208] Finally, this view employs only known meanings for *pleroosai* instead of introducing a hitherto unknown meaning for that word. And since this understanding "would be the natural and normal way to understand . . . the verse as a whole, the burden of proof remains on Bahnsen and those who would maintain otherwise to demonstrate differently."[209]

---

208. See Acts 15:28–29.
209. Hodge, "Exegetical Response," 32.

4

When Will the Law Disappear?
Matthew 5:18

"For truly I say to you, until heaven and earth disappear, not one smallest letter nor one least stroke of the pen shall by any means disappear from the Law, until all things come to pass."[1]

This verse is divided into two parts; the first clause and then the last three clauses taken together. Throughout, Christ takes great pains to emphasize the importance of what he is saying. In the first clause, he achieves this by using *amen* ("truly"), a word signaling "that the statement to follow is of the utmost importance."[2] In the second clause, the emphatic note is struck by the phrase "until heaven and earth pass away," which, in that "cultural-literary milieu [was] . . . a graphic and strong way of saying 'never.'"[3] In the third clause, we find Jesus employing the "double negative *ou mē* [i.e., "no wise" or "by any means"], the most definite form of negation regarding the future"[4] in Greek. His repetition of the word *one*, to emphasize that "not one smallest letter nor one least stroke of the pen shall by any means disappear from the Law,"[5] only adds to the impact. Whatever Jesus is teaching here, he is pressing it in the most serious and emphatic terms possible.

---

1. Author's translation.
2. Carson, *Matthew*, 145.
3. Bahnsen, *Theonomy*, 79 citing Broadus, *Matthew*, 100.
4. BDF, 184.
5. Matt 5:18.

THE FIRST CLAUSE: VERSE 18 EXPLAINS VERSE 17

With "for truly I say to you," Jesus links verse 18 to verse 17. Bahnsen has correctly observed that there is "complete harmony between Matthew 5:17 and 18. Verse 18 gives the reason for the teaching in verse 17; the two verses are connected with the conjunction γαρ [*gar* (for)]."[6]

Since the "for" in this clause is explanatory,[7] we know that the rest of verse 18 will give the reason behind the teaching of verse 17. In verse 17, Jesus has told us that he has come to fulfill the law or the prophets; the last three clauses of verse 18, therefore, must be Christ's explanation of why he has come to do so.

According to Bahnsen, Jesus here explains why he is confirming the Mosaic laws; the "reason why Jesus could not presume to invalidate the law is that the law remains binding to the end of the world."[8] But we have already seen that Christ, rather than setting forth the continuing validity of the Mosaic law in verse 17, was instead teaching that his purpose in coming was to wind up the Sinai Covenant. If this view is correct, with verse 18, Christ will explain why he has come to fulfill the law or the prophets and when that fulfillment will take place.

Bahnsen correctly recognizes that with "truly I say unto you," Jesus "is impressing the following assertions upon us with supreme authority."[9] Unfortunately, he also overlooks a significant pattern in Christ's use of the phrase. In almost every case where Jesus uses "Truly, I say unto you," he is about to say something he particularly wants to be understood as a statement that is not to be qualified by later exceptions. In Matt 5:25–29, for example, Christ teaches that we must agree with our adversary before we are thrown into prison, never to get out until we have repaid an impossible debt. From Christ's teaching elsewhere we know that it is God who is actually our Adversary—and we know that he is not teaching a general principle that admits of exceptions: for once in hell there is no escape. In the same way, when, in Matt 10:15, Christ says, "Truly I say to you it shall be more tolerable for the land of Sodom and Gomorrah in the day of judgment" than for a town that rejects the disciples, we do not

---

6. Bahnsen, *Theonomy*, 75.
7. Carson, *Matthew*, 145.
8. Bahnsen, *Theonomy*, 75.
9. Ibid.

read him as leaving open the option that perhaps Gomorrah might have a harder time on Judgment Day than a town that rejected the disciples.[10]

This observation has a significant consequence for the Theonomic thesis. Since Christ in no other text uses the phrase "truly I say unto you" to prefigure a truth to which he will subsequently admit exceptions, his statement "For truly I say to you, until heaven and earth disappear, not one smallest letter, nor one least stroke of the pen shall by any means disappear from the Law, until all things come to pass," should not be read as a categorical statement establishing in principle the general continuity of the Mosaic law in a way that can be elsewhere qualified. Instead, Christ is teaching that so long as the Mosaic law is in force, it is totally unchangeable.

The remaining three clauses of the verse answer two questions: How long shall the law's validity extend (the second and fourth clauses), and why must Jesus fulfill the law (the third clause)?

Bahnsen's understanding of these three clauses will stand or fall on the correctness of the following propositions:

1. The third clause "not one smallest letter nor one least stroke of the pen shall by any means disappear from the Law" although referring to all the law, is not as absolute as it appears to be.

2. The second clause "until heaven and earth disappear" refers to the end of the church age when Christ returns to bring all human history to a close.

3. The last clause "until all things come to pass" refers to the same point in time as the second clause.

These three premises must be established in order for Bahnsen to make his case.

It is essential for Bahnsen's argument that the third clause means something that is not as absolute as it appears to be. For if it means what it appears to say, then Christ is confirming all the law (verse 17) which

---

10. John 6:53, in which Christ speaks about eating his flesh and drinking his blood, is not an exception to Christ's normal practice, for Christians must eat Jesus' body and blood (in some sense) in order to have eternal life. When Christ later explains what he meant by his teaching (John 6:63; 14:21–24), he does not qualify his statement by exceptions; instead he explains the metaphor he used. This is in contrast to the situation in Matthew 5:17–18, in which Christ either institutes every single detail of the law until the end of the church age or He does not.

then remains valid until the end of the world (which is Bahnsen's understanding of the second and fourth clauses of verse 18), and absolutely no changes to it can be expected. This creates a real contradiction with the rest of the New Testament, which features the Apostles amending not only "one, but several of the Mosaic laws, and not merely the least, but several of 'major' laws, to wit, circumcision, the Jewish calendar, and the dietary laws."[11] In addition, if this clause cannot be shown to be less absolute than it appears, Bahnsen's attempt to limit Christians' divinely required "obedience to the underlying principles . . . laid down in the general commandment'" which have "abiding ethical validity"[12] cannot hold.

Similarly, if "until heaven and earth disappear" does not refer to the end of the church age but to something else, the law may not be meant to be in force in the church age. Even if this clause does refer to the end of the church age, it does not establish the inviolability of the law for the church. For it is the last clause that truly establishes the termination date of the law, and if "until all things come to pass" does not refer to the end of the church age but to something occurring earlier, then the law may not be immutable today. We shall now examine the evidence for each of these points.

THE THIRD CLAUSE: THE IMMUTABILITY OF "THE LAW"

The clause, "not one smallest letter nor one least stroke of the pen shall by any means disappear from the Law," explains why Christ must fulfill the law or the prophets.

The "smallest letter . . . least stroke"

Yod was the smallest letter in the Hebrew alphabet, "and the least stroke of the pen" may have been any one of a number of possibilities. These include the Hebrew letter *waw*, the projection that distinguishes certain Hebrew letters, an ornamental stroke, or "a hendiadys with 'jot' referring to the smallest part of the smallest letter."[13]

Bahnsen correctly notes that Christ's use of these words "emphasizes minute detail . . . [So long as the law remains valid, not] . . . even the

---

11. Gordon, "Theonomy," 30.
12. Bahnsen, *Theonomy*, xxiv.
13. Carson, *Matthew*, 145.

least extensive number of the very least significant aspect of the Older Testamental law will become invalid.[14]

"by any means"

These words translate the Greek words *on me*, which form the double negative "never, certainly not,"[15] "the most decisive way of negativing someth. in the future."[16] Taken together with Christ's negative repetition of the word *one* before both "smallest letter" and "least stroke," Bahnsen comments that it "is hard to imagine how Jesus could have more intensely affirmed that *every bit* of the law remains binding in the gospel age."[17] But while we can agree that every bit of the law would remain binding for at least some time after the Sermon on the Mount was preached, we must test Bahnsen's exegesis of the second and fourth clauses of Matt 5:18 to determine the period during which the law remains binding.

"disappear"

The word *parelthe* (disappear) has a number of meanings. Bahnsen, like many scholars, recognizes that it means "disappear" in the second clause. In the third clause, he believes that Christ meant us to understand the word in another sense, that of "lose force, become invalid."[18]

There are three reasons why his view is unlikely. First, the same words in adjacent clauses are usually held to have the same meaning unless the context gives strong indications to the contrary. For instance, Bahnsen does not assume that the meaning of the word *katalusai* changes meaning between the two clauses of Matt 5:17 in which it appears. Since there is no indication in the context that the meaning of *parelthe* has changed between clauses in verse 18, it remains the better part of wisdom to read the two words as meaning the same thing.

A Theonomist might counter that Bahnsen's comment on the parallel statement in Luke 16:17 [But it is easier for heaven and earth to pass away than for one stroke of a letter of the law to fail'] explains the change in meanings; "there the *keraia* is said not to '*fall*' (from πιπτω

---

14. Bahnsen, *Theonomy*, 75, 76.
15. BAGD, 517.
16. Ibid.
17. Bahnsen, *Theonomy*, 76.
18. Ibid., 80.

[*piptoo*] 'become invalid, come to an end')."[19] But *piptoo* can also mean "disappear," a meaning that Christ may have intended in the Luke verse also. "Pass away" in the sense of "disappear" makes just as much sense in the context of Luke 16:17 as it does in both clauses of Matthew 5:18.

One good reason to suspect that *parelthe* does not change meanings here is that if its meaning does change in this third clause, it destroys the pattern of parallelism between clauses that Christ established in verse 17 and reinforced in verse 19, as shown in the following lines:

v. 17: come to destroy . . . / . . . not come to destroy . . .

v. 18: heaven and earth disappear . . . / . . . not one jot and one tittle shall disappear

v. 19: whoever . . . shall break . . . and teach . . . shall be called least / whoever . . . shall do . . . and teach . . . shall be called great.[20]

These word repetitions were a common memory aid of the period and are most effective if the common words in different clauses have the same meanings.

Finally, had Christ intended to use *parelthe* in the sense of "lose force or become invalid," he would have most likely not added the phrase "from the law" after it. When something heretofore valid becomes invalid, it becomes invalid in its own right and not invalid "from" something else; but when something "disappears," it disappears from something or somewhere.

The Meaning of "the Law"

What did Jesus mean us to understand by "the law" in this clause? Bahnsen believes that Jesus' change of focus, from "the law or the prophets" in verse 17 to simply "the law" here, proves that he has been referring to the ethical stipulations of the law all along.[21] But it is equally possible that Christ merely intended "putting variety into his expression"[22] without moving the subject of his thought away from the Mosaic covenant, which, as we have seen, was the real subject of the charge to which Christ

---

19. Bahnsen, *Theonomy*, 80, quoting BAGD, 660.
20. The NIV is cited here, as it correctly brings out the parallelisms.
21. See Bahnsen, *Theonomy*, 53.
22. Ibid., 52.

was responding in verse 17. The case for this alternative becomes stronger when we remember that once God's demands in the Sinai covenant had formalized and institutionalized the relationship between God and Israel, God had sent prophets to foretell the means by which he would achieve the needed full reconciliation with Israel and with humanity as a whole. Once the messianic prophecies were made, however, it became essential that every "smallest letter [and] . . . least stroke of the pen" of the prophecies that announced the end of the Old Covenant and the inauguration of the New, not disappear from the Scriptures until they had been brought to pass. We cannot, therefore, restrict Christ's use of the term "the law" here to the ethical stipulations of the Pentateuch. Instead, we must consider the possibility that he is still referring to the least details of the Old Covenant, all of which were required to receive their fulfillment in the winding up of the Old Covenant and the inauguration of its replacement.

"from"

It is easy to overlook the word *apo* (from), yet its use by Christ has immense significance. By saying that "not one letter nor one least stroke of the pen shall by any means disappear from the law," Christ is not so much teaching that the entire Law will continue until the end of the age as he is teaching that not a single particular stipulation may be removed from the Law while the rest of it remains in force. The addition of the phrase "from the Law" to the phrase "not one jot or one tittle shall disappear" serves to identify the target group in the crowd to which this saying was primarily addressed. Christ's words spotlight an abuse of the Law by the Pharisees who had misinterpreted conflicts between the Law's ethical stipulations in such a way as to "invalidate the word of God for the sake of your tradition" (Matt 15:6).[23] Consequently, although theoretically they remained orthodox, in practice they were changing many of the law's provisions and effectively causing many provisions of the law to "disappear."[24] By teaching that while the Old Covenant remains in force, "every letter or . . . stroke of the pen" of it remains in force, Christ lays the

---

23. Christ would later "strongly [denounce the Pharisees] . . . publicly for their neglect of the law for tradition (Matt 15:1–10). No answer was possible against this charge; clearly the leaders of the people had set aside the law by means of their humanistic legal tradition" (Rushdoony, *Institutes*, 702).

24. See Matt 5:21–48.

groundwork for his countercharge in verse 20 that the Pharisees were outside the kingdom of heaven due to their not keeping the commandments of the law.[25]

One consequence of Christ's teaching is crystal clear: since "not one smallest letter nor one least stroke of the pen shall by any means disappear from the Law" during the time that the Law is in force, it would seem that any view that permits the slightest change in the Law while insisting that the Law as a whole continues to be in force would contradict his teaching here.

THE SECOND AND FOURTH CLAUSES: WHEN WILL THE LAW'S IMMUTABILITY END?

For Bahnsen, the two clauses "until heaven and earth disappear" and "until all come to pass" together tell us how long the law shall continue unchanged. Bahnsen believes that Jesus is teaching that the law will continue until at least the end of the church age. To support this view, Bahnsen begins by providing extensive documentation to show that this was the common Jewish view of the period:

> Wisdom 18:4 speaks of "the incorruptible light of the law" given to the world through Israel, and Tobit 1:6 talks of "fulfilling the law that binds all Israel perpetually." Of this incorruptible, perpetual law 2 Esdra 9:37 says, "The Law perisheth not, but remaineth in its honor." And Baruch 4:1 parallels this in declaring "This is the book of the commandments of God, the Law that stands forever." In the Mishnah Coholeth 71:4 we read "The law shall remain in perpetuity forever," and Josephus calls the Mosaic law "immortal" (*Against Apion* II. 277). Rabbi Shemoth got even more specific. "Not a letter shall be abolished from the law forever" (VI) and . . . the Exodus Midrash harmonized by maintaining that "The smallest tittle will not be erased from thee." These last statements sound much like what Christ Himself declared on the Mount. So also does the statement from Rabbi Bereshith in the Midrash for Genesis sound similar to Christ's teaching, especially in that there is a common standard of comparison: "To

---

25. The countercharge is implied in the syllogism derived from verses 18 and 19: Those who keep the law are great in the kingdom of heaven. Yet since a righteousness superior to that of the Pharisees is needed for entry (v. 20), the Pharisees must be outside the kingdom of heaven. Therefore, the Pharisees must be breaking the commandments so seriously as to be denied access to the kingdom—a charge Christ supports with the six antitheses of vv. 21–48.

everything is its own end, the heaven and the earth have their own end; only one thing is excepted which has no end, and that is the law." In the Biblical Antiquities of Philo it is said that "It is an everlasting Law by which God will judge the world. Men will not be able to say 'We have not heard!'"(XI: 2) and "It is an eternal commandment which shall not pass away" (XI:15). Christ also speaks of the commandments not "passing away." However, there is an even more impressive parallel between Matthew 5:18 and Philo's *On the Life of Moses*, there Philo says that the Mosaic laws are "firm, unshakable, immovable . . . remain secure from the day when they were first enacted to now, and we may hope that they will remain for all future ages as though immortal, so long as the sun and moon and the whole heaven and universe exist . . . not even the smallest parts of the ordinances has been disturbed" (II. 14–15).[26]

Since all of Bahnsen's sources are non-canonical, we may not assume that these writers' understanding of the duration of the law's validity is necessarily correct. Yet, even though quotations from rabbinic Judaism are not normally accepted as authoritative for Christian exegesis, Bahnsen provides a reason for taking them seriously here. Since Christ's words "so closely resemble what must have been the pervasive Jewish teaching on the length of the law's validity, and from the fact that He did not go on to qualify or redefine his terms (or explain that there was a broader model that his hearers had to keep in mind as modifying His apparent agreement with the common teaching) we can expect that the above quotations help us to understand (in the historical and literary pedagogical context of the saying) what Christ was actually telling his audience in Matthew 5:18."[27]

This, however, is not as strong an argument as it seems to be. Ever since the declaration recorded in Jer 31:31–32, the Jews had known that the Sinai covenant would be superseded by a "new covenant" that God would make with Israel. Christ's statement that he would fulfill "the law or the prophets" could easily have been heard as telling his hearers that he would bring about the fulfillment of Jeremiah's prophecy, as easily he might have been momentarily misunderstood as confirming the noncanonical writers' view of the eternity of the law.

---

26. Bahnsen, *Theonomy*, 77–78.
27. Ibid., 78.

The Second Clause

Commenting on the second clause, Bahnsen observes that

> Christ certainly taught that heaven and earth would pass away (Matt. 24:35) . . . Even when we do take into account the actual ending of heaven and earth we see that Scripture teaches it to be at the return of Christ: there will be a great conflagration and noise (2 Peter 3:10) and separation of mankind into those who no longer experience death and those who experience the second death eternally (Rev. 21:1–8; cf. Isa. 66:22–24) . . . Christ is stating . . . that the law will remain valid *at least* as long as the physical universe lasts, that is until the end of the age or world . . . At least until that point the details of the law will remain.[28]

There are two shortcomings in Bahnsen's argument. First, even if his understanding of "until heaven and earth disappear" is correct, Bahnsen here begs the question as to whether this clause of verse 18 refers to the same event as the last clause. Only if the two clauses refer to the same event will the law remain in force as long as the physical universe lasts. In addition, since Christ's hearers did not have Matthew 24, 2 Peter 3, or Revelation 21 resonating in the back of their minds when Christ preached the Sermon on the Mount, we cannot presume that they would have heard the two clauses as referring to the same event.

Instead, we must consider whether "until heaven and earth disappear" would have been understood as a reference to the awesome spectacle of the end of the church age or whether Christ knew that his hearers would have thought of something else when they heard his words. Against the view that Christ meant the words literally, there is an alternative that Bahnsen did not discuss, and it must be examined. We need to ask whether Christ meant this clause to be understood as a metaphor for "never." Bahnsen's failure to address this possibility is particularly surprising since he recognized that "the idiomatic use of the phrase for strong comparison should not be overlooked in understanding [Christ's] words,"[29] and he also believed that this clause in that "cultural-literary milieu . . . is quite likely a graphic and strong way of saying 'never.'"[30] Yet if Christ intended "until heaven and earth disappear" merely as a metaphor for "never," rather than as a factual statement

---

28. Ibid., 79.
29. Ibid.
30. Bahnsen, *Theonomy*, 79.

of when the law terminates, then both "until" clauses in verse 18 no longer necessarily refer to the end of the church age. Instead, the verse is only a statement that the law will not change "until all things come to pass," thus making the termination of the law dependent on the fourth clause alone.

There remains one last possibility to consider. For it is also possible that Christ intended his hearers to understand the words "until heaven and earth disappear" literally, as a reference to the end of the church age, and "until all things come to pass" as a reference to his completing the Sinai Covenant's time of applicability by instituting the New Covenant at the cross.

If this view is correct, Matt 5:18 recounts Christ's warning to those who would reject his messianic deliverance by denying his claim to bring to pass "all things," that they would thereby be obligated to keep every Mosaic stipulation, unamended, until the end of the world. A decisive point in favour of this possibility is that it leads naturally into verses 19 and 20 in which Christ outlines the consequences of attempting to revise the law.

Even if we agree that "until heaven and earth disappear" must be taken to refer to the end of the church age, we may not automatically conclude that Bahnsen's view that all Divinely unamemded Mosaic laws remain in force today is correct. For these laws will only remain in force to the end of the church age if the last clause of Matt 5:18 refers to the same event as the second clause.

Bahnsen, however believes that the second and fourth clause of v. 18 do refer to the same event. To support his view, he first claims that if the second clause "is taken to refer to an event in the present order, then the entire verse would be made self-contradictory; we know from the previous εος [eos, "until"] clause [i.e., the second clause] that the details of the law remain in force as long as the world lasts."[31]

To support this assertion, Bahnsen deploys an argument from grammatical structure, claiming that "'until all things have taken place (are past)' is functionally equivalent to 'until heaven and earth pass away.' These two εος clauses parallel (a common literary device) and explain each other . . . [thereby giving the verse] another note of emphasis."[32]

---

31. Bahnsen, *Theonomy*, 81.
32. Ibid., 83.

Although parallelism was a common Hebrew literary device, most notably found in the Psalms, the second and fourth clauses of Matt 5:18 are not a true example of Hebrew parallelism: parallel clauses in Hebrew thought follow one after the other; they are not separated by an intervening clause, as is the case here, a factor that nullifies the force of Bahnsen's argument.

While "until heaven and earth disappear" is more likely to be a reference to the end of the church age than to the other possibilities we have considered, the failure of the preceding argument means that we must now examine the possibility that Christ intended the two clauses to refer to different events: the first clause referring to the end of the church age in the Day of Judgment, and the fourth clause referring to something else.

The Fourth Clause

The fourth clause, *eus an panta genetai* (until all things come to pass), finally establishes the point at which the law is no longer unchangeable. As Bahnsen correctly notes, "Εως is used with the aorist subjective and αν to indicate that the commencement of an event is dependent upon certain circumstances[33] . . . In Matthew 5:18 the commencement of the law's passing away is made dependant upon παντα γενεται [*panta genetai* (until all things are accomplished)]."[34]

The key questions here are: What does "all things" mean? What does "all things are accomplished" mean? And what would happen to "the law or the prophets" when "all things are accomplished"? Once again, we shall examine Bahnsen's view of these questions and see how well his case stands up.

"all things"

Bahnsen believes that the usual translations of this clause "until all is fulfilled or accomplished" are "misleading."[35] He believes instead that the phrase should be translated by "all things have taken place (are past)"[36] in the sense of the passing away of heaven and earth. His first reason

---

33. See BAGD, 48.
34. Bahnsen, *Theonomy*, 82–83.
35. Ibid., 80.
36. Ibid., 83.

for believing that the usual translations of this clause are inaccurate is that the translation "until all is fulfilled or accomplished" . . . "makes it appear that 'all' [*panta* (all things)] refers to the commandments of the law: however, it cannot do so since *nomos* is masculine gender while *panta* is neuter gender."[37]

While Bahnsen is right to point out that *panta* does not have an antecedent, he has momentarily forgotten that Greek does not require explicit grammatical agreement with an antecedent to establish a referent—something he will later remember when, in analyzing verse 19, he correctly noted that the "antecedent referent of 'these' [commandments] is clearly the jot and tittle of the law mentioned in verse 18,"[38] even though the "jot and tittle" (neuter and feminine singular respectively) are not the grammatical antecedent of "these commandments" which is feminine plural. As Hodge noted, "παντα most naturally refers to the ιοτα η κεραια [the "jots and tittles"] of the law since the law is the context of verse 18. . . . ιοτα is neuter and κεραια is feminine, and since one word cannot be neuter and feminine, the neuter is quite appropriate."[39]

Next, Bahnsen deals with those who see "all things" as pointing to the beginning of New Covenant. He argues that some

> interpreters have wrung out this small phrase, attempting to extract more content from it than it was meant to communicate. Davies says that it refers to Jesus' death on the cross,[40] and this parallels the New English Bible's translation ". . . until all that must happen has happened," as well as Plumptre's application of this phrase to "the great facts of his messianic work."[41] . . . (All these variations only demonstrate the inevitable results of eisegesis—or the exegesis of one's *theological* scheme in the name of exegeting a Bible text; a verse like Matt 5:18, with its unparticularized παντα, is prey for such treatment.) Now such views might be appropriate pertaining to a verse like Matt 24:34 from the Olivet discourse . . . but they are unjustified in Matt

---

37. Bahnsen, *Theonomy*, 80; Bahnsen, *No Other Standard*, 280.
38. Bahnsen, *Theonomy*, 87.
39. Hodge, "Exegetical Response," 38.
40. Bahnsen, *Theonomy*, 80–81, quoting Davies, *The Setting of the Sermon on the Mount*, 334.
41. Bahnsen, *Theonomy*, 81, quoting Plumptre, *The Gospel According to St. Matthew, St. Mark and St. Luke*, vol. 6, 54.

5:18; the former has a definite referent and antecedent while the latter does not.[42]

Unfortunately this argument fails, since, as we have already seen, referents in Greek are not always grammatical antecedents, and the referent here in Matt 5:18 appears to be the stipulations of the Sinai Covenant.

Bahnsen also claims that *panta* "used without an article or preposition is to be taken in this absolutely general sense [of 'all things, everything'] (as in Matt. 11:27; John 1:3, 3:35, 21:17; 1 Cor. 2:10; 15:27, 28; Eph. 1:22a; Rev. 21:5) unless the context dictates some antecedent *whole* of which παντα constitutes the complete parts (e.g., Matt. 18:26; 22:4; Mark 4:34; Luke 1:3; Rom. 8:28; 2 Cor. 6:10; Gal. 4:1; Phil. 2:14; 1 Thess. 5:21; 2 Tim. 2:10; 1 John 2:27)."[43]

But this argument overlooks a significant consideration: the context in which *panta* is used does not have to explicitly dictate the antecedent whole to which the word is referring. For, as BAGD points out, *panta* often refers to the whole of a phrase or a concept that is implied from the context even though the parts of the phrase referred to do not agree with *panta* in either number or gender.[44] For example, "Matt 22:4 says, '... See, I have prepared my dinner [neuter, singular]; my oxen [masculine, plural] and fatted cattle [neuter, plural] are killed, and all things [παντα] are ready.' Matt 18:26 says, 'The servant therefore fell down before him, saying, "Master, have patience with me and I will pay you all"' [παντα]. παντα refers to all the money owed. The fact that παντα does not agree with anything else is inconsequential."[45]

Since *panta* does not require grammatical agreement with the concepts to which it is referring, Bahnsen's objection cannot be sustained, and thus *panta* may still be taken to refer to the "jots and tittles" of the Old Covenant itself. In addition, since Matt 5:18 features a context in which "the law or the prophets" is the "antecedent whole" and the "one smallest letter" and "one least stroke" (i.e., each single stipulation of the law) are the "complete parts" that would not disappear until the covenantal shift takes place, the context has both the antecedent whole and parts completely described by *panta*. Consequently, this is a verse

---

42. Bahnsen, *Theonomy*, 81.
43. Ibid., 83.
44. BAGD, 632.
45. Hodge, "Exegetical Response," 38–39.

in which *panta* need not take the absolutely general sense that Bahnsen believes to be necessary.

Bahnsen's final argument on this point is his belief that to "hold that 'all' refers to 'law and prophets' would create a trivial tautology (i.e., 'the law and the prophets will not become invalid until all the law and the prophets become invalid')."[46]

But Bahnsen has misunderstood the objection. His critics are not holding that "the law and the prophets will not become invalid until all the law and the prophets become invalid"; rather, they are saying that the least stroke of the law will not become invalid until their prophesied fulfillment is achieved in the winding up of the Sinai Covenant and the institution of the New. And such a statement is not a trivial tautology.

It is clear that *panta* may indeed have a more localized referent in Matt 5:18 than Bahnsen's "all things, everything." Even though "the law or the prophets" is not *panta*'s grammatical antecedent in this verse, it is clearly the referent to which *panta* refers. Since "the law or the prophets" (i.e., the Sinai covenant) form the antecedent whole of which the covenant stipulations constitute the component parts, Bahnsen's objections to the possibility that Christ is here referring to the details of the Old Covenant are insufficient. Consequently, his belief that *panta* must take the sense of the passing away of heaven and earth also fails. Since Bahnsen's final argument that making *panta* refer to "the law or the prophets" creates a trivial tautology has also been shown to be incorrect, the view that *panta* means everything involved in the inauguration of the messianic age remains acceptable despite Bahnsen's attempt to rule it out of court.

"come to pass"

With Bahnsen's next argument we turn to the meaning of *genetai* (come to pass). If *panta* refers to the end of the Old Covenant and the institution of the New, *genetai* will then mean that Christ is saying that not the least detail of the Old Covenant will disappear from that covenant until that Covenant's "time in office" is completed in the "coming to pass" of the New Covenant's institution.

Against this view, Bahnsen argues that making "all things" refer to the law founders since this "would place an unwarranted strain upon

---

46. Bahnsen, *Theonomy*, 83.

γενεται ('come to pass') and reforge it to mean πληροο."[47] Such a translation of *genetai* as "fulfilled" or "accomplished" he regards as "simply spurious [and] . . . deceptive [in that] a completely different word (πληροο) receives the translation of 'fulfill.'"[48] But we find in Matthew's Gospel a number of passages in which *genetai*, intended in the sense of "come to pass," is used in conjunction with *pleroosai*, and observing what is meant when these words appear together is highly significant for our understanding of Christ's intent here. In Matthew 1:22 the evangelist tells us that Joseph's dream "took place" or "was accomplished" (*genetai*) "to fulfill" (*pleroo*) a prophecy. Similarly, in 21:4, the procurement of the donkey and her colt "took place" (*genetai*) "to fulfill" (*pleroo*) another prophecy. We see this again in Matt 26:54, 56. In all these verses, the meanings of *pleroo* and *genetai* can be distinguished as follows: *pleroo* looks to the fulfillment of a prophecy, while *genetai* refers to specific events that have now come to pass or have been accomplished in order to achieve that prophetic fulfillment. Applying this distinction to Christ's words in Matt 5:17–18, we find that the events that will come to pass in verse 18 are the same events that necessitated Christ's coming to fulfill them in verse 17. Thus, we may well understand Christ as teaching in Matt 5:17–18 that his mission is not to destroy but to fulfill the Old Covenant and that not one jot or tittle will not disappear from that Covenant until that all things involved in that fulfillment come to pass.[49] In such a context, having "everything" refer to "the Mosaic covenant" places no strain whatsoever upon *genetai*, since *genetai*'s referent is the coming to pass of the events that bring about fulfillment of the Mosaic covenant in the institution of the New. Since the idea that making "all" refer to the law "would place an unwarranted strain upon γενεται and reforge it to mean πληροο" is demonstrably wrong, Bahnsen's claim that the "translation of . . . 'accomplished' is simply spurious [and] deceptive," is itself incorrect.

Thus, all of Bahnsen's arguments for rejecting the possibility that Christ intended "until all things come to pass" to refer to the end of the Old Covenant and the beginning of the New have failed. Once we recognize that "until all things come to pass" need not necessarily refer

47. Bahnsen, *Theonomy*, 83.

48. Ibid., 80.

49. The translators of the KJV noted this point and accordingly translated *genetai* in Matt 5:18 by "fulfilled."

to the end of the church age, Bahnsen's last argument against the possibility that "the law or the prophets" of verse 17 means the Sinai Covenant collapses.

We have now reached the point at which we can discuss the strongest difficulty facing the Theonomic thesis. The Jews did not think of the Mosaic law in terms of moral, ceremonial and civil subsets. They experienced it as the unified covenant under which they lived. When Jesus denies that he had come to destroy the Law or the Prophets, there is nothing in the context that suggests that he is referring to heretofore undefined subcategories of moral, civil, or ceremonial law rather than to the Mosaic covenant as a whole. Since Jesus made no distinction among the various sub-classifications of the law in his reply, we must take it as axiomatic that such distinctions were absent from the question he was addressing, absent from his own thought, and absent from that of his hearers. Indeed, Bahnsen himself noted that the term *the law* "comprises more than simply those aspects of the Mosaic legislation . . . which have permanent moral application and sanction; the class of commandments traditionally termed 'ceremonial' or 'ritual' is also within the scope of the term . . . Nothing in the text supports a restriction of this term's referent to the moral law."[50]

But when we combine Bahnsen's recognition that all the law was included within "the law or the prophets" with Christ's teaching that "not one jot or one tittle" of the law will be annulled until (as Bahnsen believes) the end of the church age, the Theonomic thesis encounters its insuperable difficulty. For the result of combining these propositions is the conclusion that no changes will be made to any aspect of any law until the end of the church age. But the Christian church has universally recognized that such changes did occur. Has the church been wrong for twenty centuries? Is Theonomy in error? Or is Bahnsen correct in his belief that there is a third alternative? Here, Bahnsen faces an immediate problem. It is obvious that the Christian church does not observe the ceremonial laws.

Bahnsen believed the answer to whether New Testament Christians are required to observe

> Older Testamental *ritual* . . . is yes and no. Yes Christians are still responsible to offer blood atonement for their sins and tend to the obligations of the temple, etc.; however, we must be

50. Bahnsen, *Theonomy*, 51.

> mindful of the fact that the *way* or *manner* in which Christians do these things under the New Covenant is *not* identical with the Older Testamental observation of the ritual and ceremony ... The Levitical priesthood, representing the Mosaic system of ceremonial redemption, could not bring perfection and so was *intended* to be superseded (Heb. 7:11 f., 28) ... when Jesus instituted a change in the priesthood ... the ceremonial principle was altered as well. This was inevitable because the ceremonial priests remained powerless to effect the perfect inward cleansing required. The former commandment with reference to ceremonial matters was set aside ... for the ceremony was imperfect ... The commandment which was annulled was "a commandment with respect to flesh." ... This law made nothing perfect, but Christ, who is a priest after the order of Melchizedek, does. Lest a contradiction with Matthew 5:17 f. be generated at this point, let us note that such a change in stipulation is *also* a confirmation of the Older Testamental laws implied in Psalm 110:1, 4.[51]

Unfortunately, Bahnsen does not lay out the complete structure of his argument here, and at least one of his critics has misunderstood his point. Bahnsen's thinking seems to run as follows: since the messianic prophecies, such as Ps 110:4, including the fulfillment of the ceremonial laws and their transformation by Christ, were already prophesied in the law that Christ confirmed in verse 17,[52] they are, therefore, not the kind of changes Christ prohibits when he announces, in verse 18, that no changes to the Law will take place before the end of the church age.

The problem with Bahnsen's argument is that the way Christ expresses himself in this clause of verse 18 precludes such an interpretation. While there is no doubt that the messianic prophecies were to be fulfilled after Christ preached this sermon, their fulfillment would entail some changes to the in-effect portions of the law.[53] Yet, in Matt 5:18, Christ does not discriminate between authorized changes prophesied by the law and unauthorized assaults on it: instead, he announces that not the least stipulation would disappear from the law so long as it is in force. This would seem to imply that the changes to the law that the Old Covenant prophesied would occur after "all things" have "come to

---

51. Ibid., 205–7.

52. Since Christ did not "confirm" the ethical stipulations of the law in Matt 5:17, but announced instead that He had come to fulfill the Old Covenant, Bahnsen's defense at this point is already suspect.

53. This was recognized by the writer to the Hebrews in Heb 7:12.

pass." The only way we could avoid this conclusion is if we could show that Christ's prohibition of changes to the law was intended as a general principle and not as an absolute truth. And the only way that such intent could be established is to demonstrate from clues within the immediate context that there is a real possibility that Christ meant his words to be understood in that way. To that search, we now turn.

We have already seen that Christ's use of "truly, I say unto you" argues against understanding his teaching in this verse as anything less than a statement of literal truth. But a Theonomist may reply that we must remain open to the possibility that Christ may have intended a categorical statement that admits of qualifications here: he certainly used such a statement later in this very sermon when, in Matt 5:33–37, he prohibited oaths. This latter teaching, while appearing to be equally absolute in the context of the sermon, was clearly intended not to be so understood, since God swears oaths,[54] Paul does likewise,[55] and even Christ himself would later testify under oath.[56]

Yet, there are a number of considerations that suggest that the two situations are not identical. For one thing, unlike verse 18, we do not find Christ using "Truly, I say to you" to preface his rebuke concerning swearing oaths. For another, when Christ uses a general statement to teach a principle admitting of exceptions rather than a categorical instruction admitting no exceptions, he almost invariably provides clues within the context of his statement that enable his hearers to understand that his statement does admit of qualifications.[57] When he forbade oaths,[58] Christ appeared to refer to a number of oaths that the people were then swearing. The oaths he cited were those that, in Pharisaic

---

54. E.g., Ps 110:4.

55. 2 Cor 1:23.

56. Matt 26:63, 64.

57. Christ made one major exception to his normal practice of providing clues to indicate he was not speaking literally when he spoke in John 6 about eating his flesh and drinking his blood—a teaching seemingly specifically designed to alienate the uncommitted among his followers. But this took place later in his ministry when Christ is no longer merely teaching the crowd, but has now moved on to challenging the uncommitted, something clearly apparent in the differing reactions of the crowds at the end of the two sermons. But, even here Christ's later explanation to his disciples does not contradict his earlier statement, instead it makes it clear that his earlier statement should be taken metaphorically.

58. Matt 5:33–37.

teaching, were regarded as less than fully binding. His audience, hearing these sample oaths, would have understood that Christ was not prohibiting all oaths; instead he was attacking the Pharisaic distinction between binding and non-binding oaths, and prohibiting only the latter.[59]

We ought, therefore, to expect that the context of Christ's teaching on his relationship to "the law or the prophets" would offer similar clues had Christ here intended to put forward "a categorical declaration, expecting it to be our operating assumption [that he would later] qualify . . . elsewhere."[60] But unlike his teaching on oaths, Christ's words in verses 17 to 20 offer no indications that this was his intent; instead, such indications as are present point in the opposite direction. When the Psalmist used the term *light* with reference to the law in Ps. 119, (the reference that Christ now transfers to his disciples by calling them the light of the world), that reference must have applied equally to the ceremonial provisions as much as its moral and civil stipulations.[61] Also, the fundamental charge to which Jesus was responding was the charge that he was breaching the covenant, a charge that involved all of the law, not just part of it. The most serious indication that a qualifiable categorical statement was not intended here, is that by using the words he did, Christ creates a situation in which neither he nor his apostles could deactivate any stipulations from the law before the end of the church age (which is Bahnsen's understanding of when "all things come to pass") without creating a full and formal contradiction with what Christ actually says here. When responding to charges against them, good speakers do not employ apparently absolute statements that will need to be refined later, for they know they will lose credibility when they make the necessary corrections.

In addition, when we remember that the additional purposes of this remark were to explain why he needed to come to complete the old covenant and why he was rebuking the Pharisees, we realize that Bahnsen's reading of this clause would contradict both purposes: if the Mosaic law was in any way amendable, Christ would not have needed to

---

59. See Carson, *Matthew*, 153.
60. Bahnsen, *Theonomy*, xxv.
61. In the context of Ps 119:105, 130, 140, the writer sees the word as the source of guidance for his life. This would of necessity include the ceremonial laws since it was by them that he was to approach God for the cleansing of his sins, and thus remain able to walk in fellowship with God.

come, and if the Mosaic law was amendable, the Pharisees could defend themselves against Christ's charge that they were destroying the Law by saying that their rulings were necessary resolutions to questions the Law did not answer. Yet another reason for believing that a general statement was not intended here is that Christ deliberately went out of his way to employ the strongest negation possible in Greek to establish the immutability of the law's least details. By so doing, he particularly emphasized the point that every letter or least stroke of the law would remain valid during the time that the law was to be in force.

The final argument against the possibility that Christ intended this statement to be understood only as a qualifiable general principle is the strongest of all; although the Jews knew from Jer 31:31–34 that God had plans to replace the Old Covenant, they did not realize that the new covenant necessarily implied at least some changes to the law. Instead, as we have seen Bahnsen document in detail, they mistakenly believed that all the law was eternal.

Bahnsen observed that the resemblance between Christ's teaching and the common Jewish understanding of the duration of the law is significant, but it is significant for a different reason than he has supposed. If we assume for a moment that Christ is here teaching the Theonomic thesis, he must have known that his words in this clause of verse 18, lacking any qualifications in the context such as redefinition of terms or mention of a broader model to be kept in mind, presented the same concept of the Law's eternal continuity as did contemporary Jewish teaching. Consequently, he must have known that his words could not possibly have been understood by his hearers in any other way than as a restatement of that teaching—that all the law was immutable "until heaven and earth disappear" or "until all things come to pass." Given that background, it is hard to see why Christ, if he intended to teach the Theonomic thesis, would not have qualified his statement in some way since he must have known how it would be received. Yet, instead of qualifying his statement to allow for the future changes implicit in the change from Old Covenant to New, Christ presents his teaching in terms that eliminate any possibility that he intended anything other than a prohibition of the slightest change to the Sinai Covenant law so long as that covenant was in force. Therefore, it is the better part of wisdom not to see this clause as anything less than a statement that so long as the law is in force, all the law is in force and not one of its least stipulations will disappear from it.

The consequence for Bahnsen's thesis is clear: if Christ intended to teach what Bahnsen thinks he intended, no changes to the civil, moral, or ceremonial laws may occur, unless the lawgiver wishes to contradict his statement in this clause.[62] Since Bahnsen's exegesis of these clauses of verse 18 contradicts his theology that at least the ceremonial laws do change in the New Covenant,[63] as well as his wish to assert that any judicial law may change if it can be shown to be amended by the lawgiver, Theonomists find themselves in a dilemma. They can either have Bahnsen's view that there are some changes to the laws that do occur in the New Covenant, or they may retain his exegesis of Matt 5:18, but they cannot have both. For Bahnsen's attempt to have his theological cake and eat his exegetical conclusions by promoting the

> thesis that Jesus . . . reiterates for all time the validity of the entire Mosaic law, not merely the "moral" law and that he does so in exhaustive detail . . . if correct, would necessarily either condemn Paul and the other apostles or destroy Theonomy. Paul not only relaxes one, but several of the Mosaic laws, and not merely the least, but several of the "major" laws, to wit, circumcision, the Jewish calendar, and the dietary laws.
>
> Bahnsen's only escape from such a conundrum is to argue that Paul does not actually break these laws but applies them differently to another covenantal context.[64]

But Bahnsen's proposed escape route meets a dead end when the writer of Hebrews, instead of calling the change of priesthood entailed by the New Covenant "a different application of the same law in another

---

62. It should be noted that the intent of Christ's statement (as Bahnsen understands it) does not rule out the right of the lawgiver to make future changes to the law, nor does it rule out his freedom to do so. But if Bahnsen's exegesis of Christ's statement is correct, it makes it impossible for the lawgiver to institute any changes to the law, including those prophesied in the Old Testament, without creating a full and formal contradiction with Christ's statement here (i.e., that no changes whatsoever will occur in the Mosaic law before the end of the church age). When such changes to the law are made later in the New Testament, the resultant spectacle of the lawgiver contradicting his statement in Matt 5:18 is a very strong attack on the lawgiver's credibility and trustworthiness.

63. Bahnsen, *Theonomy*, xxiv n. 9, cites pages 92, 211, 304, 306, 356, and 417 as passages where he sees New Testament changes to the Old Testament law.

64. Gordon, "Theonomy," 30.

When Will the Law Disappear? Matthew 5:18

covenantal context," explicitly recognized that it entailed a "change of law."[65] If a New Testament book recognizes, without condemnation, that a change of law has occurred, then the inescapable corollary is that whatever Christ meant by "until all things come to pass" must have occurred before that change of law took place. Since Christ's inauguration of the New Covenant took place before the letter to the Hebrews was written, and the end of the world did not, Christ must have been referring to the former event when he announced that the Law would not change until "all things come to pass."

WHAT CHRIST IS TEACHING IN VERSE 18

At the beginning of this chapter we saw that Bahnsen's view of Matt 5:18 would depend on whether at least three key premises could be established. Having now examined each of Bahnsen's attempts to show that his chosen premises are either the only possible meaning of the texts or are superior to all other relevant options, we can evaluate his argument as a whole.

Bahnsen believed that the third clause ("not one smallest letter nor one least stroke of the pen shall by any means disappear from the Law"), although referring to all the Mosaic law, is not as absolute as it seems to be. Yet, we have seen that there are no indications within the context of verse 18 that Christ intended to put forth a general statement admitting of subsequent qualifications here. Instead, the context provides a number of indications that Christ meant nothing less than a literal reading of his statement. These indications are: the charge to which Jesus was responding was a charge that involved all of the law, not just part of it; his use of the term *light* to refer to his disciples, a term that, when originally applied to the law, must have referred to the law as a whole; and, finally the reality that Christ was not likely to put forth a qualifiable general principle after emphasizing the truthfulness of his forthcoming answer with "Truly I say unto you," as good speakers do not employ inexact absolute statements which must be later qualified when responding to charges against them, since they will lose credibility when adducing the qualifications that formally contradict their earlier statements. In addition, since the purpose of this remark was to lay the foundation for his subsequent rebuke of Pharisaism, we realize that a hyperbolic reading of this clause does not close the door to the Pharisaic abuses of the law that Christ clearly intended to reject. Most decisive, however, is that Christ

---

65. Heb 7:12.

did not follow his normal practice where he intended his words to be qualified; this verse lacks any rhetorical device signaling that such qualification is his intent. Instead, by deliberately employing the strongest negation possible in Greek to establish the principle that the law was not to suffer any unauthorized changes whatsoever while it was in force, Christ went out of his way to establish the literal truthfulness of his statement that no legitimate amendment to any Mosaic stipulation would take place while the Old Covenant remained in place. Consequently, the first key premise supporting Bahnsen's view of verse 18 must be rejected.

While we can happily agree with Bahnsen that Christ intended "until heaven and earth disappear" as a reference to the end of the church age, Bahnsen's third premise that "until all things come to pass" also refers to the end of the church age, must be rejected. His claim that *panta* needs to be taken in the general sense of "all things, everything" has been shown to be incorrect in this context; he has failed to prove that *panta* cannot refer to all the detailed stipulations in both the law and prophets that were involved in Christ's fulfillment of the messianic prophecies, nor does such a referent create the trivial tautology that he believes it does. In addition, it is clear that *genetai* can well refer to the coming to pass of the events that brought about the end of the Old Covenant and the beginning of the New. Once again, Bahnsen lacks the necessary exegetical support needed to make his case.

In verse 17, Jesus had stated his mission with respect to the Old Covenant. Contra the erroneous belief of his enemies, Jesus is not calling for an immediate abandonment of the Sinaitic covenant. Instead, his purpose was not to destroy it but to supersede it by inaugurating the New Covenant, thus fulfilling the Old. In verse 18, Bahnsen's Theonomic claim that Christ here makes a general statement admitting of exceptions that the law continues in force until the end of the church age has been found to be untenable. Instead, Christ is making the following assertion: that until the end of the church age not one stipulation of the law will lose its authority until the covenantal shift takes place. By his use of two clauses, each beginning with "until" Christ prepares to lay out two differing applications of his teaching, each needed by a different group of his hearers. In verse 19, he begins to tell his followers what this teaching will mean for them, and in the following verse, after concluding the application to his disciples, he begins to apply his teaching to the Pharisees and those who would join them in rejecting him.

5

Christ Applies His Teaching
Matthew 5:19–20

BAHNSEN REGARDS VERSE NINETEEN as the clincher in his argument. He writes:

> The word "therefore" at the beginning of verse 19 can assist us in determining the meaning of what has just been said by demonstrating the practical consequences of that teaching ... Now *if* the Messianic advent of Jesus had the effect of ending the binding force of the Older Testament law, how could He go on to teach that the acknowledgment of, and obedience to the very minutiae of that law led to personal exaltation form God and that the opposite attitude led to debasement? Any orthodox view of Scripture and a consistent hermeneutic forces one to see that Matthew 5:17–18, in light of verse 19 represents Christ as confirming the entire Older Testament law.[1]

In a later article, he added:

> However you interpret "fulfill" and "until all things come about," you cannot—except at the cost of making Christ self-contradictory—interpret the Lord as teaching that it is acceptable to reject the validity or violate the obligation of any Old Testament commandment. Apart from New Testament qualifications upon that blanket affirmation, verse 19 condemns such an attitude. Consequently, verse 19 clinches the argument *in favor* of theonomic ethics, *even if* the treatment given to verses 17 and 18 should stand in need of some correction regarding details.[2]

---

1. Bahnsen, *Theonomy*, 86–87.
2. Bahnsen, "Exegesis," 5.

Once again, Bahnsen begs the question. If Christ has taught that "not one letter or one stroke of the pen shall by any means disappear from the law until" the inauguration of the New Covenant at the cross, verse nineteen does not clinch Bahnsen's argument. Instead, Christ is teaching his disciples to live under the Old Covenant until he inaugurates the New and warning them that should they either live or teach on the basis of the assumption that any changes to the Law take effect before that date, they will be least in the kingdom of heaven. This was a message that the disciples needed to hear; at the time that the Sermon on the Mount was preached, Christ's crucifixion and resurrection was at least a year in the future. In the interim many of his disciples were to be sent out as his messengers (Matt 10:1; Luke 10:1), and many more of his hearers would be telling their friends and neighbors about his teaching. Had any of these folks taught that since Messiah was present, the Old Covenant was no longer in force, it would not only have contradicted Christ's intent, but would have created both considerable premature excitement among nationalistic Jews unready to learn the nature of his Messiahship and equally unnecessary additional offense against his message among the Jews who were already opposing him. Once again, this is an alternative that Bahnsen does not consider.

With verse twenty, Christ concludes his message to his disciples by telling them that they needed a righteousness surpassing that of the Pharisees to enter the kingdom of heaven. This statement is an explicit warning that Christ saw the Pharisees as being outside the kingdom due to their not keeping the commandments. But this statement also has a second function. Because the Pharisees would reject Christ's completion of the Old Covenant and inauguration of the New, they would still be living under the old covenant. And against that background, Christ's statement fairly warns them that their emendations of the law have put them outside the kingdom of heaven.

SUMMARY

As we have examined Bahnsen's analysis of Matthew 5:17–20, it has became clear that the Theonomic view that Christ's purpose was to confirm the validity of the entire Mosaic law throughout the church age (except for any particular stipulations that the Lawgiver may amend) suffers from insufficient biblical support. Examining verse 17, we saw that none of Bahnsen's six reasons for holding that "the law or the prophets" referred to "the ethical stipulations of the law" were sufficient to establish that understanding; that *katalusai* need not mean "abolish" but was more likely intended to mean "destroy"; that the presence of *alla*, instead of forcing the meaning "confirm" on *pleroo*, must instead have its meaning determined by the otherwise determined meanings of *katalusai* and *pleroo*; and that "confirm" is an unsupportable translation for *pleroo*. Although Bahnsen was correct in holding that verse eighteen's "until heaven and earth disappear" has reference to the end of the church age, his attempt to make "until everything comes to pass" refer to that same event cannot be sustained. Finally, we have seen that Christ's assertion that neither the smallest letter nor the least stroke shall disappear from the law while it is in force is not in any way qualified in the text. Consequently, Bahnsen's attempt to justify the apostolic abrogation of Mosaic ceremonial stipulations, while not permitting the abrogation of the judicial laws, must be rejected as exegetically untenable. In addition, Bahnsen has employed a number of less likely or impossible translations or implications for key words, and he has failed to refute, and in some cases even discuss, alternative understandings of these words or phrases, even though most of these understandings were found in the standard reference works of which he was known to be aware. In addition, he misquoted a number of commentators, both directly and by implication, to make them seem to support his thesis when they did not do so; and he gave only superficial responses to significant objections. Finally, in a number of places Bahnsen refuted his own arguments—seemingly without realizing that he had done so.

Instead of accepting the Theonomic thesis, we have found that it is far more likely that Christ intended "the law or the prophets" to be a reference to the Sinaitic covenant that he had come to complete, rather than destroy, by instituting the prophesied New Covenant in its place. With verse eighteen, Christ makes it clear that the obligations of the law would continue unchanged until that change occurred. Applying this message to his disciples in verse nineteen, he warns them that they must do and teach the law until the inauguration of the New Covenant, and in verse 20 and those that follow, he warns the Pharisees and their followers that if they chose to reject his New Covenant, they would have to follow all the Mosaic law as originally given, and not as they had amended it, if they wanted to enter the kingdom of heaven.

Although the Christian Reconstruction debate has led many Christians to ask many of the right questions, Bahnsen's Theonomic thesis does not provide those questions with their biblical answers. Having investigated the strength of Theonomy's scriptural support, we have discovered that it is built on a foundation of sand.

6

Reformed History and Theonomy

Bahnsen and Theonomists who follow him have objected to the traditional Reformed understanding of Calvin and the WCF previously outlined in the first chapter of this book. We must therefore examine whether the traditional understanding of Calvin and the Westminster Divines is correct and respond to the points that Bahnsen and others have posed.

CALVIN AND HIS FOLLOWERS

Any discussion of Calvin's teaching on the civil laws of Moses must begin with the following passage from *Institutes of the Christian Religion*. Calvin wrote:

> 14. In states, the thing next in importance to the magistrates is laws, the strongest sinews of government, or, as Cicero calls them after Plato, the soul, without which, the office of the magistrate cannot exist; just as, on the other hand, laws have no vigor without the magistrate. Hence nothing could be said more truly than that the law is a dumb magistrate, the magistrate a living law. As I have undertaken to describe the laws by which Christian polity is to be governed, there is no reason to expect from me a long discussion on the best kind of laws. The subject is of vast extent, and belongs not to this place. I will only briefly observe, in passing, what the laws are which may be piously used with reference to God, and duly administered among men. This I would rather have passed in silence, were I not aware that many dangerous errors are here committed. For there are some who deny that any commonwealth is rightly framed which neglects the law of Moses, and is ruled by the common law of nations. How perilous and seditious these views are, let others see: for me it is enough

to demonstrate that they are stupid and false. We must attend to the well-known division which distributes the whole law of God, as promulgated by Moses, into the moral, the ceremonial, and the judicial law, and we must attend to each of these parts, in order to understand how far they do, or do not, pertain to us. Meanwhile, let no one be moved by the thought that the judicial and ceremonial laws relate to morals. For the ancients who adopted this division, though they were not unaware that the two latter classes had to do with morals, did not give them the name of moral, because they might be changed and abrogated without affecting morals. They give this name specially to the first class, without which, true holiness of life and an immutable rule of conduct cannot exist.

15. The moral law, then (to begin with it), being contained under two heads, the one of which simply enjoins us to worship God with pure faith and piety, the other to embrace men with sincere affection, is the true and eternal rule of righteousness prescribed to the men of all nations and of all times, who would frame their life agreeably to the will of God. For his eternal and immutable will is, that we are all to worship him, and mutually love one another. The ceremonial law of the Jews was a tutelage by which the Lord was pleased to exercise, as it were, the childhood of that people, until the fulness of the time should come when he was fully to manifest his wisdom to the world, and exhibit the reality of those things which were then adumbrated by figures (Gal. 3:24; 4:4). The judicial law, given them as a kind of polity, delivered certain forms of equity and justice, by which they might live together innocently and quietly. And as that exercise in ceremonies properly pertained to the doctrine of piety, inasmuch as it kept the Jewish Church in the worship and religion of God, yet was still distinguishable from piety itself, so the judicial form, though it looked only to the best method of preserving that charity which is enjoined by the eternal law of God, was still something distinct from the precept of love itself. Therefore, as ceremonies might be abrogated without at all interfering with piety, so also, when these judicial arrangements are removed, the duties and precepts of charity can still remain perpetual. But if it is true that each nation has been left at liberty to enact the laws which it judges to be beneficial, still these are always to be tested by the rule of charity, so that while they vary in form, they must proceed on the same principle. Those barbarous and savage laws, for instance, which conferred honor on thieves, allowed the promiscuous intercourse of the sexes, and other things even fouler and more absurd, I do not think entitled to be considered

as laws, since they are not only altogether abhorrent to justice, but to humanity and civilized life.

16. What I have said will become plain if we attend, as we ought, to two things connected with all laws, viz., the enactment of the law, and the equity on which the enactment is founded and rests. Equity, as it is natural, cannot but be the same in all, and therefore ought to be proposed by all laws, according to the nature of the thing enacted. As constitutions have some circumstances on which they partly depend, there is nothing to prevent their diversity, provided they all alike aim at equity as their end. Now, as it is evident that the law of God which we call moral, is nothing else than the testimony of natural law, and of that conscience which God has engraven on the minds of men, the whole of this equity of which we now speak is prescribed in it. Hence it alone ought to be the aim, the rule, and the end of all laws. Wherever laws are formed after this rule, directed to this aim, and restricted to this end, there is no reason why they should be disapproved by us, however much they may differ from the Jewish law, or from each other (August. de Civit. Dei, Lib. 19 c. 17). The law of God forbids to steal. The punishment appointed for theft in the civil polity of the Jews may be seen in Exodus 22. Very ancient laws of other nations punished theft by exacting the double of what was stolen, while subsequent laws made a distinction between theft manifest and not manifest. Other laws went the length of punishing with exile, or with branding, while others made the punishment capital. Among the Jews, the punishment of the false witness was to "do unto him as he had thought to have done with his brothers" (Deut. 19:19). In some countries, the punishment is infamy, in others, hanging; in others, crucifixion. All laws alike avenge murder with blood, but the kinds of death are different. In some countries, adultery was punished more severely, in others more leniently. Yet we see that amid this diversity they all tend to the same end. For they all with one mouth declare against those crimes which are condemned by the eternal law of God, viz., murder, theft, adultery, and false witness; though they agree not as to the mode of punishment. This is not necessary, nor even expedient. There may be a country which, if murder were not visited with fearful punishments, would instantly become a prey to robbery and slaughter. There may be an age requiring that the severity of punishments should be increased. If the state is in a troubled condition, those things from which disturbances usually arise must be corrected by new edicts. In time of war, civilization would disappear amid the noise of arms, were not men overawed by an unwonted severity of punishment. In steril-

ity, in pestilence, were not stricter discipline employed, all things would grow worse. One nation might be more prone to a particular vice, were it not most severely repressed. How malignant were it, and invidious of the public good, to be offended at this diversity, which is admirably adapted to retain the observance of the divine law. The allegation, that insult is offered to the law of God enacted by Moses, where it is abrogated and other new laws are preferred to it, is most absurd. Others are not preferred when they are more approved, not absolutely, but from regard to time and place, and the condition of the people, or when those things are abrogated which were never enacted for us. The Lord did not deliver it by the hand of Moses to be promulgated in all countries, and to be everywhere enforced; but having taken the Jewish nation under his special care, patronage, and guardianship, he was pleased to be specially its legislator, and as became a wise legislator, he had special regard to it in enacting laws.[1]

In this passage, Calvin plainly asserts that Mosaic laws need not always be instituted by magistrates in the New Covenant era. Instead, he followed the ancient distinction between the moral law (defined as being contained in "two heads, the one of which simply enjoins us to worship God with pure faith and piety, the other to embrace men with sincere affection") and the judicial laws ("certain forms of equity and justice, by which they [OT Israel] might live together innocently and quietly.") While the moral law "is the true and eternal rule of righteousness prescribed to the men of all nations and of all times, who would frame their life agreeably to the will of God" the civil laws are not necessarily applicable for all states at all times since ". . . it is true that each nation has been left at liberty to enact the laws which it judges to be beneficial, [yet] . . . these are always to be tested by the rule of charity, so that while they vary in form, they must proceed on the same principle" of charitable equity. If they do proceed on that principle, then "wherever laws are formed after this rule, directed to this aim, and restricted to this end, there is no reason why they should be disapproved by us, however much they may differ from the Jewish law, or from each other." In addition, Calvin plainly declares that judicial punishments need not always be the same as those originally given by Moses.

Although the Genevan reformer had great zeal in applying particular Old Testament civil stipulations to the local situation if he thought

---

1. Calvin, *Institutes,* book 4, chapter 20, sections 14–16.

that the national character and current stresses indicated a need for them, Calvin made his judgments on how to apply Mosaic judicials on a case-by-case basis, rather than anticipating the Theonomic assertion that the New Testament mandates a general adoption of all stipulations of the Mosaic civil code save for those stipulations that have been amended by the lawgiver. When Calvin observed that some circumstances (national character, current events) had changed from the biblical circumstance in which the civil law was given, he felt free to assume that the Mosaic civil laws were no longer the pattern to be followed.

Such a stance did not make Calvin an antinomian. For even when Calvin held that a particular Mosaic civil law was no longer the best expression of the moral law for contemporary situations, he believed that the relevant principles of the moral law, (by which he meant the Decalogue), remained valid. It was these moral laws that remain the test of whether or not a given nation's civil legislation, while differing from Mosaic civil law, remained in accordance with public righteousness.

Calvin's views present a major problem for Theonomic advocates. Some follow R. J. Rushdoony, the founding father of the Theonomic school, in arguing that Calvin is here giving way to his "classical humanism [and uttering] heretical nonsense."[2] Others believe that Calvin's remarks are not expressing "radical hostility to the Mosaic judicial laws"[3] since Calvin's remarks are an attack on Anabaptists, who not only advocated adopting "the Mosaic judicials [but] did so in a revolutionary manner [together with] . . . civil disobedience and revolution."[4] The major evidence adduced in favor of this view is that Calvin's colleague, Strasbourg reformer Martin Bucer (for whose exegesis Calvin had the greatest respect), taught, in contrast to the revolutionary Anabaptists, that the Mosaic civil laws should only be instituted by legitimate authority. For, while "in a Christian state, the Mosaic legislation has a binding force . . . Christians in a pagan state should submit to the powers that be until a time of reformation."[5]

However, the idea that Calvin could not possibly be disagreeing from Bucer's views when he wrote *Institutes* overlooks two key factors. The first problem is a chronological impossibility: Calvin published the

2. Rushdoony, *Institutes*, 9.
3. Jordan, "Calvinism."
4. Ibid.
5. Jordan, "Calvinism," commenting on Bucer's *De Regno Christi*.

first edition of the *Institutes* in 1536—two years before he met Bucer—whereas *De Regno Christi*, which outlines Bucer's political views, was not written and published until 1550.[6] Thus, when Calvin wrote *Institutes*, he had not yet met Bucer, and there is no evidence that he knew Bucer's views on the question.[7] In addition, since Calvin did not revise his assessment of the Mosaic judicial laws after spending two years working closely with Bucer, nor after *De Regno Christi* appeared,[8] we can be certain that Bucer's own opinion on the contemporary validity of the Mosaic judicials did not influence Calvin's views in *Institutes*.

In addition, although Bucer can sometimes sound Theonomic when discussing Mosaic penalties,[9] there is a real question as to whether he qualifies as a Theonomist in the Reconstructionist sense of the word. Although Bucer is closer to Reconstructionist Theonomy than is Calvin, he clearly does not follow Bahnsen's hermeneutic. For when he discusses a potential reformation of English civil laws in *De Regno*, he does not do so in terms of contemporary applicability of Mosaic case laws; instead, he frames his discussion in terms of the continuing applicability of the Decalogue.[10] Nor did he believe that all Mosaic laws necessarily applied in his day. Instead, he

> had a doctrine of natural law which enabled him to discriminate between what is valid and what is not. This criterion was the *ratio legis* or *ratio pietatis*, which for Bucer was synonymous with love for God and one's neighbour, the golden rule, or the *Liebesgebot*. It has a definitely Thomistic ring about it . . . Bucer distinguished positive law which is outdated by time and circumstances . . . from natural law . . . "And the judicial and ceremonial laws are not abolished where they inhere with the lex aeterna. In the ju-

---

6. The one book written by Bucer that Calvin did know of by 1536 was *Enarrationes perpetuaein sacra quatuor evangelia* (1530), which had no influence on Calvin's civil law discussion. See Ganoczy, *The Young Calvin*, 159.

7. Although Bucer wrote a commentary on Romans that was published in 1536, it is unlikely that Calvin was able to read it before *Institutes* was published since Calvin must have finished *Institutes* before May of that year, by which time we find him fleeing from the French authorities.

8. Calvin's last revision of the *Institutes* was published in 1559.

9. Bucer, *De Regno Christi*, 378, 383. It is difficult for English-speaking readers to grasp Bucer's exact position on the contemporary applicability of Mosaic civil law since the sole translation of *De Regno Christi* now available is an abridgement that omits at least one crucial passage necessary to a full understanding of Bucer's views.

10. Bucer, *De Regno Christi*, 359–61.

dicial laws are to be found principles of eternal validity . . . But even those laws which are not necessary for salvation, are fitting for Christians, that all things may be done [decently and in order]." The use of the *ratio pietatis* and Bucer's doctrine of "love the consummation of all justice" certainly moderated the force of his legalism . . . The ambivalence of his position is revealed in the four reasons he gave why Leviticus xviii does not prohibit a man to marry his brother's widow: 1. the patriarchs had done this; 2. Deuteronomy requires it; 3. Christians are not bound to Moses anyway; 4. the law of Moses may be abrogated in special cases. If the third reason is true, why trouble with the others?[11]

While Bucer and Calvin together assert that instituting large portions of the Mosaic judicial laws remains a desirable goal for Christian states, they differ from Bahnsen in that both assert that Christians are not bound to Moses anyway and the law of Moses may be abrogated in special cases: two premises Bahnsen denies in cases of laws unmodified by the Lawgiver. For both Bucer and Calvin, the decision of which Mosaic civil laws should be introduced when is a matter to be decided by Christian reason in particular cases, rather than by Bahnsen's premise that the general institution of the Old Testament civil laws is a universal new covenant duty for Christians. We must therefore conclude that Bucer's position is somewhat more nuanced than the Theonomic thesis.

An additional problem with the argument that Calvin was attacking only the violent Anabaptist methods of imposing Mosaic law is found in the fact that some of his contemporaries who advocated the replacement of the common law by Mosaic judicials joined Calvin in denying that violence was an acceptable means of achieving their goal. The most famous of these men was Andreas Carlstadt, who, although widely believed to have seconded Müntzer's view that imposing the Mosaic laws by force was justified, did not, in fact, do so.[12] But Carlstadt did advocate the contemporary validity of at least some Mosaic laws, and his reasoning anticipates a principle reason that inspired Bahnsen. Carlstadt wrote:

---

11. Avis, op. cit., 15, 16, commenting on a passage in *De Regno* that is not translated in the Pauk abridgment.

12. Carlstadt publicly rejected Müntzer's plea for a military alliance, wrote against his actions, and incited his congregation to write a public letter against Müntzer, as well. These letters may be found in Pater, *Karlstadt as the Father of the Baptist Movements*, 279–86.

> Several admirers of images will say, "The old law prohibits images, but the new one does not. We follow the new and not the old law."
>
> Dear brothers, may God preserve you from such heretical adage [sermon] and word and may you never say, "We do not follow the old law, nor do we accept it," since it belongs to non-Christians and breaks and diminishes the teaching of Christ. For Christ verifies his teaching through Moses and the prophets. He says that he did not come to break the law, but to fulfill it [Matt 5:17]. He also taught his disciples how he had to live and suffer that Scripture might be fulfilled. Christ did not trespass on the smallest letter in Moses' law. Neither did he add or subtract anything from Moses. In short, Christ did not set aside anything which pleased God in the old law. Christ stood by the old law both in intent and in content.[13]

While Carlstadt used Matt 5:17 here only to justify his applying many other Old Testament texts against idolatry to the situation presented by images in Christian churches, it is not impossible to infer from Carlstadt's comments that he would have argued for the continuity of all Mosaic civil laws on the same basis.[14] Luther seems to have understood him in this way: it was to counter this passage that Luther wrote his famous rejection of the Mosaic law as a rule for Christian living:

> Now then, let us get to the bottom of it all and say that these teachers of sin and Mosaic prophets are not to confuse us with Moses. We don't want to see or hear Moses. . . . We say further, that all such Mosaic teachers deny the gospel, banish Christ, and annul the whole New Testament . . . For Moses is given to the Jewish people alone, and does not concern us Gentiles and Christians. We have our gospel and New Testament. If they can prove from them that images must be put away, we will gladly follow them. If they, however, through Moses would make us Jews, we will not endure it.[15]

In addition, Carlstadt was not alone in his stand: around the same time we find others advocating the judicials by peaceful means. Melancthon opposed a different group of Anabaptists who pressed for

---

13. Carlstadt, "On the Removal of Images," in *The Essential Carlstadt*, 119.

14. Article 16 of the Apology to the Augsburg Confession claimed that Carlstadt was "insane in imposing upon us the judicial laws of Moses" (The Book of Concord).

15. Luther, "Against the Heavenly Prophets," in *Luther's Works*, 40:92.

the introduction of Mosaic law into the courts,[16] possibly "Wolfgang Stein and Jacob Strauss who pressed for the introduction of the Mosaic polity."[17] With these latter men, it is clear that they sought to advance their cause by means of reason, not threat of arms.

Against this background of strong differences between those who supported imposing Mosaic judicials by force, if necessary, and those who rejected the use of violence to do so, it is significant that Calvin does not content himself with merely rebuking the use of rebellious force to institute the civil laws.[18] Since Calvin directly assaults the necessity of instituting Mosaic civil laws and punishments into New Covenant states without limiting his attack to ungodly methods of achieving that goal, his attack must be seen as attempting to refute the nonviolent advocates of a solely Mosaic judicial system as well as the violent ones. Since we may presume that both Carlstadt and the others who shared his estimate of the Mosaic judicial laws—and his horror at Müntzer's methods of imposing them—would have accepted the qualification "except where amended by the Lawgiver," the principle that Calvin has rejected is essentially that of Bahnsen's Theonomy.

A final Theonomic response to Calvin's statement is to notice that, whatever his theoretical stance, once in action Calvin promoted the adoption of many Mosaic civil laws, and therefore he is best described as an inconsistent advocate of Theonomy. As Bahnsen wrote, "John Calvin, despite vacillating or equivocal statements earlier in his career, was one such [Theonomic] advocate."[19] This view is often accompanied with a claim that Calvin, in his Sermons on Deuteronomy (preached in 1555 and 1556), contradicted the already cited material in the *Institutes* that presumably constitutes the "vacillating or equivocal statements" Bahnsen mentioned.

There are, however, three reasons why this assessment cannot be accepted. First, Theonomists have yet to provide references to any of the Deuteronomy sermons in which Calvin repudiates his *Institutes*

---

16. As noted by Avis, "Moses and the Magistrate," 11.

17. Ibid., 19.

18. This was something Calvin had already repudiated in his preface to the *Institutes*, when he wrote: "But if any, under pretext of the gospel, excite tumults (none such have yet been detected in your realm) . . . then there are laws and legal punishments by which they may be punished up to the measure of their deserts" (Calvin, *Institutes*, 19).

19. Bahnsen, "The Theonomic Thesis in Confessional and Historical Perspective."

position. Second, Calvin regarded the *Institutes* as his systematic theology, and he insisted, as early as the Preface to the 1539 edition of the *Institutes*, that the commentaries he would later publish were to be read in its light, rather than vice versa:

> I have endeavored to give such a summary of religion in all its parts, and have digested it into such an order as may make it not difficult for any one, who is rightly acquainted with it, to ascertain both what he ought principally to look for in Scripture, and also to what head he ought to refer whatever is contained in it. Having thus, as it were, paved the way, I shall not feel it necessary, in any Commentaries on Scripture which I may afterwards publish, to enter into long discussions of doctrines or dilate on common places, and will, therefore, always compress them. In this way the pious reader will be saved much trouble and weariness, provided he comes furnished with a knowledge of the present work as an essential prerequisite.[20]

In light of this statement, we may not read Calvin's commentaries in a way that contradicts his statements in the *Institutes*, especially since Calvin continually revised *Institutes* to reflect the changes in his views to which his exegetical studies had brought him, and, in his final revision of the Institutes, published three years after preaching his Deuteronomy sermons, Calvin expressed no changes to his views concerning the contemporary applicability of the Mosaic judicials. If he had come to a Theonomic view of the place of the Old Testament laws in the New Covenant while preaching those sermons, he would have revised his views on the civil law in *Institutes* to bring them into line with the Theonomic views to which he had then (hypothetically) come. But Calvin let his earlier views stand, which strongly argues against the view that he had adopted a more Theonomic approach in the interim.

Finally, also in 1563, Calvin published his *Commentaries on the Four Last Books of Moses*. This latter volume clearly demonstrates that Calvin's "equivocal or vacillating statements" were not limited to "earlier in his career" but continued almost to its end, and that his position, even at this late date, was indeed not Theonomic, but turned upon a different hermeneutical principle. For example, Calvin argues that one Mosaic civil law commanding the destruction of idols "was a political precept

---

20. Calvin, *Institutes*, 21.

and only given temporarily to the ancient people."[21] Again, concerning the remission of debts prescribed in Deut 15:1–6, Calvin wrote that although "we are not bound by this law at present, and it would not even be expedient that it should be in use, still the object to which it tended ought still to be maintained, i.e., that we should not be too rigid in exacting our debts, especially if we have to do with the needy . . . The condition of the ancient people, as I have said, was different."[22]

We find the same distinction when Calvin writes of usury. When he writes: "It is abundantly clear that the ancient people were prohibited from usury, but we must needs confess that this was part of their political constitution. Hence it follows, that usury is not now unlawful, except insofar as it contravenes equity and brotherly union,"[23] he is clearly distinguishing "a temporary political element from a permanent moral obligation to brothers in Christ."[24]

In all these examples from the *Four Last Books*, Calvin takes positions that contradict the Theonomic premise. Instead of instituting all divinely unamended Mosaic judicial laws, Calvin believed that the civil laws did not need to be instituted as a whole in New Covenant–era states. While the fundamental moral principles of the former covenant (the Ten Commandments) were taken up by Christ or his apostles as moral norms for the New Covenant, Calvin argues, on the basis of Gal 3:24 and 4:4, that the Mosaic civil laws were given only until Christ came, and therefore the civil crimes and penalties of Moses' law—penalties originally given as stipulations to the Sinai covenant—need not always to be

---

21. Calvin, *Commentaries on the Four Last Books of Moses*, vol. 2, 399. Calvin is here commenting on Deut 7:20–26.

22. Ibid., vol. 3, 154. Theonomists may reply that neither this, nor the abovementioned mentioned law annulled by Calvin lie within the scope of the Mosaic judicial laws. Non-Theonomists however might not dismiss these instances so easily, especially if the Theonomists wish to legislate either flexibility in interest repayments or the criminalization of idolatry.

23. Ibid., vol. 3, 132. In the more than fifteen years since Godfrey's "Calvin and Theonomy" brought this passage from Calvin's *Four Last Books* into the debate, no Theonomist I am aware of has attempted to address the problem it poses for the attempt to co-opt Calvin as a Theonomist. For it shows, even to the end of his life, that Calvin's underlying hermeneutical principle was not the Theonomic thesis. Strevel's failure to question Godfrey's understanding of this passage in "Theonomic Precedent" nullifies his argument that Calvin had adopted a Theonomic hermeneutic in *Four Last Books*.

24. Godfrey, "Calvin and Theonomy," 307.

followed after that covenant ended.[25] For Calvin, the fundamental principles of the moral law remained valid in the New Testament era both as obligations for individual Christians, and the basis by which to judge the appropriateness of given civil laws. No law, no matter how different from the law given at Sinai, no matter how much its punishment differed from the Mosaic civil laws, could be justly disapproved of, as long as it aimed at the same goal of divine equity to which the Mosaic laws pointed.[26]

The crucial distinction between Calvinist and Theonomist arises from this fact, a distinction that even Bahnsen recognized when, in reply to the Calvin-Westminster critic John Frame (who wanted to minimize the distinction between the two camps), Bahnsen distinguished between Theonomists and non-Theonomists as follows: "There is an objective and precise difference: viz., all theonomists affirm (while non-theonomists deny) that we should presume that Old Testament criminal and penal commands for Israel as a nation (not specially revealed earlier) are a standard for all nations of the earth."[27]

Since Bahnsen, (thanks largely to his understanding of Matt 5:17–20), believed that every stipulation of the Mosaic Judicial laws applies today unless specifically amended by the Lawgiver, while Calvin saw that particular unamended Mosaic judicial statutes were clearly restricted to Israel and could be amended by today's lawmakers at need without divine authorization, provided equivalent equity remained despite the change, it is clear that the two men have different understandings of the critical word "standard." If we accept Bahnsen's definition, we must recognize that Bahnsen has defined the difference between Theonomists and non-Theonomists in a way that excludes Calvin from the Theonomic camp.

Calvin's decidedly un-Theonomic hermeneutic was reinforced by Bullinger, who wrote "The Apostle's of our Lord Jesus Christ did burden no man with the laws of Moses,"[28] since the attempt to institute all the judicial laws would be "more than half mad."[29]

Calvin's successor Beza reiterated Calvin's view when he wrote that although

---

25. Calvin, *Institutes*, book 4, chapter 20, section 15.
26. Ibid., sections 15 and 16.
27. Bahnsen, *No Other Standard,* 27, 28 n. 18.
28. Bullinger, *The Decades of Henry Bullinger*, vol. 1, 342.
29. Ibid.

we do not hold to the forms of the Mosaic polity, yet when such judicial laws prescribe equity in judgments, which is part of the Decalogue, we, not being under obligation to them insofar as they were prescribed by Moses to only one people, are nevertheless bound to observe them to the extent that they embrace that general equity which should everywhere be in force . . . The Lord commands that a deposit be returned, and that thieves be punished . . . Because it follows natural equity, and expounds that perpetual precept of the Decalogue, *Thou shalt not steal*, to this extent all are bound to fulfill them both. The thief is sentenced to make restitution for the theft, sometimes twice as much, sometimes four times as much . . . This penalty is purely political, and it binds the one nation of the Israelites, to whom alone it was adapted. Therefore it is permitted for the magistrate, in his exercise of sovereignty and for definite and good causes, to prescribe a more severe manner of punishment.[30]

Since Calvin's *Institutes* were the theological textbook in Oxford and Cambridge universities,[31] Calvin's approach had a lasting impact in England. Note how closely William Perkins (the most influential English theologian between Calvin and Westminster) follows in his steps: "Moral law . . . is contained in the Decalogue or ten commandments; and it is the very law of nature written in all men's hearts . . . in the creation of man: and therefore it binds the consciences of all men at all times . . . Judicial laws of Moses . . . were specially given by God, and directed to the Jews; who for this very cause were bound in conscience to keep them all . . . But touching other nations and specially Christian commonwealths in these days, the case is otherwise."[32]

It is clear that Perkins recognized that moral law was both the law of nature written on all men's hearts since creation, and limited to the Decalogue alone. But this did not mean, however, that Perkins saw all Mosaic civil laws as irrelevant for contemporary states. For he added that "judicial laws, so far as they have in them the general or common equity of the law of nature are moral; and therefore binding in conscience, as the moral law."[33]

---

30. Theodore Beza, *De Haereticis a civili Magistratu puniendis Libellus*, 222–23, quoted in Isbell, "Divine Law," lines 284–96.

31. Cremeans, *The Reception of Calvinist Thought in England*, 82.

32. William Perkins, "A Discourse of Conscience," vol. 1, 513, quoted in Isbell, "Divine Law," lines 306–13.

33 Perkins, "A Discourse," vol. 1, 514, quoted in Isbell, "Divine Law," lines 303–5.

For Perkins, a judicial law would only apply if it had within it the general equity of the Decalogue, which for Perkins was "the law of nature." This insight would prove highly influential as the Westminster Divines sought a way to apply the wisdom of the Mosaic judicials to contemporary states.

Perkins' successor at Cambridge's Great St. Mary's church was Paul Baynes, who not only reiterated Calvin's threefold division of the law into moral, judicial, and ceremonial, but also echoed the common Puritan identification of the "underlying principle" behind the civil laws with the law of nature. And in another echo of Calvin, Baynes also denied that all Mosaic civil stipulations are necessarily binding in New Covenant era states. For

> we are free from [the judicial laws] as ordinances political delivered; they bind us, 1, as the perpetual equity of God, agreeable to the law of nature and moral, is in them; 2, we are bound, not to the particular determination of punishment, but the general; with liberty both to intend and exchange the kind, and to mitigate or release the kind; freed from all particularities and circumstance, bound only to the substance, or somewhat proportionable.[34]

Just before his death in 1640, the highly respected minister John Ball wrote *A Treatise of the Covenant of Grace*, a book that provides a valuable glimpse of English Covenant Theology on the eve of the Westminster Assembly. Although the book was not published until five years later, it was known in manuscript to the five Westminster Divines who wrote its Preface.[35] Although Ball did not discuss the question of whether or not the Mosaic judicials continue, he, like Calvin and Perkins, limited the Moral Law to the Ten Commandments: "The Law was written in tables of stone, yet so as it was engraven in the tables of the heart, though not in the plenty and abundance that afterward; for under the Old Testament God would have both letter and Spirit, but more letter and less Spirit."[36]

---

34. Baynes, *An Entire Commentary upon the Whole Epistle of St. Paul to the Ephesians*, 161.

35. The later works of two of these men, Daniel Cawdrey and Anthony Burgess, are critical for our determining how the Divines understood the Mosaic judicial laws' contemporary application.

36. Ball, *A Treatise of the Covenant of Grace*, 165. Ball's earlier comment—"The obedience that God required at his [Adam's] hands was partly natural, to be regulated according to the Law engraven in his heart by the finger of God himself, consisting in the true unfeigned and perfect love of God, and of his neighbour for the Lord's sake"

THE WESTMINSTER CONFESSION OF FAITH

Rousas Rushdoony, the founder of modern Theonomy believed modern Theonomy differed from the Westminster Confession on one point. He believed that "one of the errors of the [Westminster] Confession" [was holding in 19:4], without any confirmation from Scripture . . . that the 'judicial laws' of the Bible 'expired' with the Old Testament,"[37] a view he believed "makes the Confession is guilty of nonsense."[38]

Most Theonomists, however, follow Bahnsen, who took a different tack. Against the view that understands 19:4 as "saying that the penal sanctions and case laws of the Old Testament no longer bind people and thus the Civil Magistrate is freed from the obligation to enforce public justice by executing those criminals specified in God's law,"[39] Bahnsen argued that this was *not* the Westminster position. Instead, he believed that in "the Westminster outlook civil magistrates have not been given autonomy in their various tasks, but are obligated to observe *all* the commandments of God (23.3), even those which elaborate and illustrate the Decalogue."[40]

When *Theonomy in Christian Ethics* was first published, Bahnsen was criticized as holding that the Confession's use of "general equity means, essentially, that everything in the Mosaic judicial law that *can* be applied today *must* be applied today, [and that] the responsibility of the magistrate to the entire moral law implies a theonomic position."[41] Since the majority of Reformed scholars then held that the Divines chose the Calvin-Westminster view of how the civil laws are meant to apply in the new Covenant, Bahnsen's understanding was highly controversial.[42] When Sinclair Ferguson wrote "An Assembly of Theonomists," which critiqued his view, Bahnsen felt obliged to reply.

The key passage of the Confession, section 4 of chapter 19, states: "To them [the people of Israel] also he gave sundry judicial laws which

(Ball, *Treatise*, 10)—does not contradict this claim since, at that point, Ball is summarizing the Decalogue.

37. Rushdoony, *Institutes*, 551. Rushdoony did not notice that the Divines adduced Gen 49:10 with 1 Pet 2:13, 14 to buttress this point.

38. Ibid.

39. Bahnsen, *Theonomy*, 516–17.

40. Ibid., 517.

41. Ferguson, "Assembly," 323. Ferguson footnotes *Theonomy*, 353–63.

42. Gentry has documented the early extent of the debate in "Theonomy and Confession," 161–65.

expired together with the state of that people, not obliging any other now further than the general equity thereof may require."

Ferguson claimed that "the logic of the Confession is clear. The moral law is central and permanent... The statement on the judicial law appears to be less sharply but no less carefully worded... it maintains that the judicial laws 'expired' (i.e., their envisioned period of validity has come to an end). These laws are not now obligatory for other states beyond the requirements of general equity."[43]

Ferguson understands the Westminster Divines as saying that while exhaustive enforcement of the Mosaic civil laws is no longer required, the moral purposes (general equity) that underlie those civil laws remain binding today.[44] When the underlying general equity of a given civil law remains binding today then the institution of the corresponding Mosaic civil law or punishment is justified since the case laws "still have some value as illustrations of the way in which the principle of general equity should be applied; and to that principle of general equity the legal systems of all nations are bound."[45]

Ferguson also recognized that while "there may be similarities in the practical outworking of these two principles (e.g., a Theonomist and a nontheonomist may, on their different principles, reach the same conclusion about the appropriate response to a particular act—which almost certainly explains how it is that theonomists mistakenly assume that the response of the Puritans to specific crimes proves they were also theonomists). But whatever similarities may arise because of the Confession's qualifying clause, it is absurd to suggest that the [different hermeneutical] principles [of Confessional Calvinism and Theonomy] ... are identical."[46]

Ferguson took the trouble to repeat this point later. "It may be that the Confession's teaching on the Mosaic judicials extends as far as to include certain applications of the law ... sought by theonomists: [but] ... to argue that its teaching bears an exclusively theonomic interpreta-

---

43. Ferguson, "Assembly," 321–22.

44. These distinctions were also adopted by the Baptists and Congregationalists. See sections 19:4 of Houghton, ed., *A Faith to Confess*, and "The Savoy Declaration of Faith and Order."

45. Ferguson, "Assembly," 326.

46. Ibid., 327.

tion is to read its intention backward and confuse a legitimate specific application with the fundamental governing principle."[47]

Seen in this light, Bahnsen's claim that "Ferguson . . . had to acknowledge that section 19.4 in the Confession is indeed consistent with the theonomic position,"[48] is a serious misreading of Ferguson's paper. For Bahnsen has somehow missed Ferguson's entire point, which was that even though on some points the Divines anticipate Theonomic results, the two sides arrive at their conclusions by significantly different roads.

Bahnsen adduced three main arguments for his view that the Westminster Confession implies a Theonomic hermeneutic. They are: the syntax of the Confession, the views of individual Divines, and the concept of general equity.

The Syntax of the Confession

Bahnsen began his rebuttal to Ferguson with a sketch of the political history leading up to the English Civil War and the setting up of the Westminster Assembly and the Solemn League and Covenant. Unfortunately, Bahnsen fails to mention some far more significant religious and theological influences that were also current. As Ferguson notes,

> the Reformation's doctrine of the priesthood of all believers was accompanied by a perhaps less clearly articulated but no less real appreciation of the prophethood of all believers . . . [Some feared that Evangelical theology, by] asserting the freedom of individuals to read and interpret Scripture for themselves, would bring with it theological and spiritual anarchy [leading to] the wholesale disintegration of society. . . . On the one hand, the Reformation principle drove people back to the authority and relevance of the Old Testament for society; on the other hand, it led to inevitable and acute tension over the question of tolerance and its limits . . .

---

47. Ferguson, "Assembly," 329. Despite Ferguson's comments that the debate turns on the differing hermeneutics by which the two sides reached their conclusions, every published Theonomic response to Ferguson that I have seen (except for Strevel) echoes Bahnsen's erroneous assumption that Puritan advocacy of particular Mosaic crimes or punishments necessarily entails that the Puritans were Theonomists. As long as Theonomists continue to miss the significance of Ferguson's distinction, they will be letting one of the most cogent arguments against the view that the Westminster Confession is Theonomic stand by default.

48. Bahnsen, "Westminster Assembly."

E. F. Kevan's standard work "The Grace of Law," contains a twelve-page list of the books relevant to this subject written within some sixty or seventy years of the Westminster Assembly.[49]

This background is highly significant. For Ferguson goes on to note that section 19:4 of the Confession affirms two things of the Mosaic civil laws. First,

> they have "expired with . . . the state of that people." They have come to the end of their appointed term, somewhat as the copyright on a book does after a specified period of time. 2) They must be viewed as "not obliging any other [sc. people] now further than the general equity thereof may require." The "now" here is eschatological. It points us to the work of Christ in death, resurrection, ascension, and Pentecost as marking the transition from one epoch to another in God's redemptive purposes; "now" in the present epoch, peoples are not under obligation to the judicial law given through Moses beyond the requirement of general equity.[50]

Then Ferguson goes on to outline the essential difference between the Calvin-Wesminster view and Theonomy as far as the Confession is concerned. He claims that a

> *prima facie* reading of these words suggests that the fundamental affirmation of the Confession is that the Mosaic judicial laws have expired. This position is further qualified lest any reader draw the mistaken implication that the Mosaic judicial system is completely irrelevant to the Christian epoch. But this qualification does not negate the basic thrust of the section that these "sundry judicial laws" have now "expired." Certainly this is the interpretation the average twentieth-century reader naturally places on the wording. Just as the copyright on this book will expire after a certain period of time . . . so the Mosaic case laws have "expired." Yet they still have some value as illustrations of the way in which the principle of general equity should be applied, and to that principle of general equity the legal systems of all nations are bound.
>
> The theonomist may respond . . . that such a *prima facie* reading is likely to be an uninstructed one and may even contain

---

49. Ferguson, "Assembly," 317–18. For a shorter list of works written within a few years of the Assembly see Coldwell, *Chronology*.

50. Ferguson, "Assembly," 321.

an emotional bias against a biblical view of the judicial law and indeed of God himself.

[While] some reactions to theonomic thinking reveal a flawed view of both God and Scripture . . . this is not, in itself, an adequate justification for a theonomic reading of the Confession. For the problem with the theonomic reading is that the particular way the Divines have expressed their opinion is not the *natural way* of expressing a *theonomic* view. It is certainly not the way contemporary theonomists express their position. For the Confession, the governing principle is that the judicial laws have expired (whatever else may be said to clarify their relevance), whereas, for theonomists the governing principle is that the Mosaic judicials have not expired but are still in force. Christ has confirmed them and they are still perpetually binding.[51]

Then, after an excusus reviewing the longstanding Protestant discussion of the role of the civil laws, Ferguson concludes:

it is difficult to the point of impossibility—in *this* context in which the question of the continuation of the Mosaic judicials had been long and heatedly discussed—to believe that the Westminster Divines would attempt to express a theonomic viewpoint by the wording we actually find in the Confession. At this point the *prima facie* reading of the text not only has the virtue of common sense in its favor; it also has the weightier consideration that a theonomic interpretation is psychologically improbable, given the substantial Puritan awareness of the issues at stake. Had they intended to state a view identical to contemporary theonomy, it would have been natural to stress first of all the continuing obligation of the judicial laws, and then give ancillary recognition, that inevitably their application must be "contextualized" appropriately to the society in which they are to be applied.

This consideration places in jeopardy the claim that the Confession is theonomic as . . . Bahnsen contends . . . [Although it] may be that the Confession's teaching on the Mosaic judicials extends as far as to include certain applications of the Mosaic law consistent with those sought by theonomists: but to argue that its teaching bears an exclusively theonomic interpretation is to read its intention backward and confuse a legitimate specific application with the fundamental governing principle.[52]

---

51. Ferguson, "Assembly," 326–27.
52. Ferguson, "Assembly" 328–29.

That the syntax of section 19:4 is not the natural way to express a Theonomic viewpoint is one of Ferguson's three main arguments against the view that the Westminster Divines were an assembly of Theonomists. Sadly, Bahnsen did not address this point in his reply.

Individual Divines and Their Views

As we have seen, Theonomists believe that since Christ taught in Matt 5:17–18 that all divinely unamended Mosaic laws continue to be valid to the end of the church age, the legitimately biblical meaning of general equity cannot require anything less than that all Mosaic civil laws and punishments to be instituted in the church age unless such laws have been amended by the Lawgiver. Had the Westminster Divines anticipated and employed Bahnsen's hermeneutic, it is certain that they would never have allowed for any changes to the Old Testament civil laws unless they could make the case that such changes were so authorized. But an examination of the work of some key Divines and Commissioners demonstrates that while some anticipated Bahnsen's position, the Assembly as a whole did not adopt this Theonomic hermeneutic.[53]

Among the Westminster Divines, Herbert Palmer and Daniel Cawdrey most closely anticipated Bahnsen's Theonomic views at a number of points. In his sermon of August 13, 1644, Palmer argued that "whatsoever law Law of God, or command of His, we find recorded in the Law-book in either of the volumes of God's statutes, the New Testament or the Old Testament, remains obligatory to us, unless we can prove it to be expired, or repealed. So it is with the statute law of this nation, or of any nation."[54]

Bahnsen makes a special point of noting that he is only repeating the views of George Gillespie (who, Ferguson agrees, was one of the most influential members of the Assembly): "What did section 19.4 mean for the Puritans in historical context? Nearly all students recognize that the leading theologian and most persuasive authority at the Westminster Assembly was the Scottish commissioner, George Gillespie. In 1644, while at the Assembly, he published in London a tract entitled 'Wholesome Severity Reconciled with Christian Liberty.' The preemi-

---

53. For thorough documentation of the views held by many of these men at the time of the Assembly, see Coldwell, "The Westminster Assembly & The Judicial Law, Chronology," 3–55.

54. Cited in Gentry, *Theonomy and Confession*, 181.

nent Westminster divine could hardly have been clearer or more to the point."⁵⁵

Bahnsen then provides a number of quotes that, he believes, demonstrate that Gillespie was a Theonomist. Unfortunately, Bahnsen failed to discuss a significant statement by Gillespie (which Ferguson had quoted) that demonstrates that even though Gillespie's views were close to Theonomy, he was no Theonomist. For a little later in the same treatise from which Bahnsen has quoted, Gillespie, in the midst of arguing for state enforcement of Mosaic penalties for religious heretics, writes that certain kinds of toleration are acceptable, of which

> the fifth and last is that kind of toleration whereby the Magistrate when it is in the power of his hand to punish and extirpate, yet having to do with such of whom there is good hope either of reducing them by convincing their judgments, or of uniting them to the Church by a safe accommodation of differences, he grants them a *supersedeas* [forbearance]; or though there be no such ground of hope concerning them, yet while he might crush them with the foot of power, in Christian piety and moderation, he forbears so far as may not be destructive to the peace and right government of the Church, using his coercive power with such a mixture of mercy as creates no mischief to the rest of the Church. I speak not only of bearing with those who are weak in faith (Rom. 15:1), but of sparing even those who have perverted the faith, so far as the word of God and rules of Christian moderation would have severity tempered with mercy: that is (as has been said) so far as is not destructive to the Church's peace, nor shakes the foundations of the established form of church government, and no further.⁵⁶

According to Gillespie, a magistrate who may lawfully punish and extirpate, may lawfully grant forbearance in cases in which he hopes to win the offenders back to orthodoxy, or refrain from executing the proper Mosaic punishment since it will bring great danger to the

---

55. Bahnsen, "Westminster Assembly."

56. Gillespie, "Wholesome Severity Reconciled with Christian Liberty," lines 754–65. In view of the use that Theonomists have made of this book, some have recently questioned whether Gillespie was its author. Although published anonymously, the work has been almost universally accepted as having been written by Gillespie since his cousin, Patrick Simson, who lived in his household and at times acted as his secretary, claimed that Gillespie was the author. For the full case for Gillespie's authorship, see Coldwell, "Whose Severity?" in *The Anonymous Writings of George Gillespie*.

church's peace. Such exemptions are nowhere provided for in the Mosaic civil laws, and Gillespie's stance would effectively abrogate the Mosaic penalties in those cases in which the magistrate exercises forbearance and does not inflict the Mosaic judicial remedy. Moreover, Gillespie sees no need to justify his variance from his (hypothetical) Theonomic norm. If the hermeneutic he used to justify contemporary use of the Mosaic law was that of modern Theonomy, Gillespie could never have justified his claim that such forbearances were legitimate. It is unfortunate that Bahnsen did not discuss this statement by Gillespie because it clearly excludes the Scottish Divine from the Theonomic camp. The conclusion is evident: although Gillespie was probably the most thoroughgoing advocate for the continuity of the Old Testament civil laws among the Scottish Commissioners, he "does not simply adopt the viewpoint that the Mosaic penology can be applied without reference to general equity and Christian moderation and mercy."[57]

Other significant men are known to have taken positions even further removed from Theonomy. Even Gillespie's close theological ally and fellow Scottish commissioner Samuel Rutherford rejected Bahnsen's Theonomic premise when he specifically affirmed, in connection with Sabbath offenses, that while "some moral transgressions Moses punished with death, as Sabbath breaking, it followeth not therefore that the godly Prince may now punish it with death."[58] Although Rutherford clearly speaks of the Sabbath commandment as moral in nature, not ceremonial, and thus valid in the present age, he demurs from the application of the Mosaic punishment for that offense. It is no longer proper for the Magistrate to punish Sabbath breakers with the death penalty. Rutherford explained why he reached this decision when he continued, "It follows not therefore, such transgressors are made free, through Christ, of all bodily punishment, as *Libertines* inferre, for though the temporariness of the punishment be only in the measure of the punishment, yet not in the punishment it selfe."[59]

Rutherford's denial that biblical measure of punishments are not always necessary was no accident. He repeated his view elsewhere. "*Judicial* laws may be *judicial* and *Mosaical*, and so not obligatory to us, according to the degree and quality of punishment . . . No man but sees

---

57. Ferguson, "Assembly," 342–43.

58. Rutherford, *Free Disputation*, 190, quoted in Ferguson, "Assembly," 340.

59. Rutherford, *Free Disputation*, 190, 191, quoted in Ferguson, "Assembly" 341.

the punishment of theft is of common moral equity, and obligeth all nations, but the manner or degree of punishment is more positive: as to punish theft by restoring four oxen for the stealing of one ox, doth not so oblige all nations, but some other bodily punishment, as whipping, may be used against thieves."[60]

Since the New Testament nowhere contains a statement that the punishment for theft has changed, nor any statement from which one could by necessary consequence infer the changes that Rutherford permits, it is clear that Rutherford stood outside the Theonomic camp as far as the Mosaic penalties are concerned. It is equally clear that he was no Theonomist as far as Mosaic crimes were concerned. At the very time when the Assembly was considering the meaning of "the description of 'ceremonial and judicial' law," Rutherford not only argued that that New Covenant states had the right not to follow Mosaic punishments: he went further and argued and denied the proposition that all Divinely unamended Mosaic civil crimes should continue to be such in New Covenant states.

> But sure Erastus erreth, who will have all such to be killed by the Magistrate under the New Testament, because they were killed in the Old; . . . Why, but then the whole judicial law of God shall oblige us Christians as Carolostadius [Carlstadt] and others teach? I humbly conceive that the putting of some to death in the Old Testament, as it was a punishment to them, so was it a mysterious teaching of us, how God hated such and such sins, and mysteries of that kind are gone with other shadows. *But we read not* (saith Erastus) *where Christ hath changed those laws in the New Testament.* It is true, Christ hath not said in particular, *I abolish the debarring of the leper seven days, and he that is thus and thus unclean shall be separated till the evening*; nor hath he said particularly of every carnal ordinance and judicial law, it is abolished.
>
> But we conceive, the whole bulk of the judicial law, as judicial, and as it concerned the Republic of the Jews only, is abolished, though the moral equity of all those be not abolished; also some punishments were merely symbolical, to teach the detestation of such a vice, as the boring with an awl the ear of him that loved his master, and desired still to serve him, and the making of him his perpetual servant. I should think the punishing with death the man that gathered sticks on the Sabbath was such; and in

---

60. Rutherford, *Free Disputation*, 298–99.

> all these, the punishing of a sin against the Moral Law by the magistrate, is moral and perpetual; but the punishing of every sin against the Moral Law, *tali modo*, so and so, with death, with spitting on the face: I much doubt if these punishments in particular, and in their positive determination to the people of the Jews, be moral and perpetual: As he that would marry a captive woman of another religion, is to cause her first pare her nails, and wash herself, and give her a month, or less time to lament the death of her parents, which was a judicial, not a ceremonial law; that this should be perpetual, because Christ in particular hath not abolished it, to me seems most unjust; for as Paul saith, *He that is circumcised becomes debtor to the whole law, sure to all the ceremonies of Moses his law.*[61]

Rutherford's argument makes it clear that he followed Calvin, who clearly believed that every nation could amend Mosaic civil stipulations without authorization and set its own equitable punishments rather than being obliged to institute all divinely unamended Mosaic judicial laws and punishments.[62] By abandoning Mosaic civil laws if there is no reason for their continuance, Rutherford also removes himself from the Theonomic camp altogether. But Rutherford goes further still: in his next sentence, commenting on the view that all Old Testament civil laws and punishments must be applied today because Christ has not abolished them, (which is an almost perfect anticipation of Bahnsen's hermeneutic), Rutherford rejects that thesis as an example of the heresy we call salvation by works: "So I argue, *a peri*, from the like, He that will keep one judicial law, because judicial and given by Moses, becometh debtor to keep the whole judicial law, under pain of God's eternal wrath."[63]

---

61. Rutherford, *Divine Right of Church Government*, 493–94. Failure to consider this passage in Rutherford has often led Theonomists and their allies (e.g., Foulner, p. 6) to seriously misunderstand Rutherford's position.

62. Calvin, *Institutes*, book 4, chapter 20, section 16.

63. Rutherford, *Divine Right of Church Government*, 494. If Rutherford not only rejected the Theonomic view that judicial laws must be perpetual because Christ has not abolished them, but also defined the consequence of that view as obliging the heresy of "works salvation," the question may be asked: Is Bahnsen's Theonomy also heretical? The answer is no. For Rutherford has overlooked a key premise. Circumcision was not just one Mosaic stipulation among many and equal to the others, but was distinct among them in that it alone was the sign of entry into the Old Covenant now superseded by the New. Gentiles seeking circumcision, therefore, were implicitly rejecting Christ's New Covenant in favor of the Old (and that the Galatians were observing days and months and seasons and years, as mentioned in Gal 4:10, would have been *prima*

Thus, Bahnsen misrepresents both Gillespie and Rutherford when he claims that "Ferguson then fallaciously proceeds to portray Rutherford's subordinate disagreement with Gillespie about the manner or severity of certain of the civil penalties as an anti-theonomic dispute, rather than as an intramural debate among theonomists about what the Biblical evidence specifically requires."[64] Rather, it is Bahnsen who incorrectly identifies them as Theonomists despite Gillespie introducing a non-Mosaic flexibility into Mosaic punishments and Rutherford specifically renouncing both Theonomic distinctives. Since the dispute took place between a clear non-Theonomist (Rutherford) and someone closer to Theonomy but still not a Theonomist (Gillespie), Ferguson's account of the matter is accurate, whereas Bahnsen's is not.

Gillespie and Rutherford were not the only Scottish Commissioners who would have rejected Bahnsen's Theonomy. Their colleague Robert Baillie would have done so as well. In 1646, Baillie wrote,

> I grant the New English polishers of Brownism do not express their Tenets in terms so hugely gross; yet see how near they come to them in substance, when they tell us that no Magistrate may make any laws about the Bodies, Lands, Goods, Liberties of the Subject, which are not according to the Laws and Rules of Scripture, Scripture being given to men for a perfect rule, as well in matters of Civil justice, as of devotion and holiness; and if so, then they must make it as unlawful and contrary to the Scriptures perfection, for any man to make Laws in matters of Righteousness and of the state, as in matters of Holiness and of the Church . . . Eighthly, what men besides them have made so bold with Kings and Parliaments, as not only to break in pieces their old Laws, and to divest them of all power to make new ones; but also under the Pretext of a divine right, to put upon their necks that unsupportable yoke of the Judicial Law of the Jews, for peace and for war, without any power to dispense either in addition or subtraction. I grant this principle of Barrow is limited

---

facie evidence for Paul that they had done just that). Committing oneself to keep the entire Old Covenant is a damnable rejection of Christ. But when a Gentile applies particular Old Testament civil covenant stipulations within the New Covenant due to incorrect belief that they have been carried over by Christ and instituted in the New Covenant, it cannot be shown either by Scripture or by necessary consequence deductions from Scripture that such individuals are necessarily taking on *all* the obligations of the Old Covenant. Therefore Bahnsen's Theonomy, although erroneous, is certainly not heretical.

64. Bahnsen, "Westminster Assembly."

> by Mr. Cotton to such Judicials as do contain in them a moral equity; but this moral equity is extended by him to so many particulars, as Williams confesses the whole Judicial Law to be brought back again thereby, no less than by the plain, simple, and unlimited Tenet of the rigidest Brownists.[65]

Although Gillespie, Rutherford, and Baillie formed a majority of the Scottish Commissioners, and their opinions must therefore be recognized as powerful influences on the Assembly, they are not the most significant witnesses to how the Divines understood the question of the contemporary validity of the Mosaic civil laws. The most authoritative witnesses to the Assembly's collective mind on this issue are the writings of the men who drafted section 19:4. It is, therefore, especially unfortunate that Bahnsen did not interact with critical statements written by two of these men.

Anthony Burgess plainly rejected the Theonomic hermeneutic when, preaching about eighteen months before the Assembly adopted section 19:4, he affirmed that "the manner of the punishment belonging to God's judicial law, that may be altered,"[66] and William Gouge, preaching to his weekly lecture in his London church around the time of the Assembly, provides a detailed explanation of how such a change can be possible.[67]

> Besides the ceremonial law, the Jews had a judicial law, proper and peculiar to that polity. This law concerned especially their

---

65. Baillie, *A Dissuasive From the Errors of the Times*, 127, 128. Baillie is referring to John Cotton's book, *Moses His Judicials*, often incorrectly believed to be the standard view of how the contemporary Puritans of New England applied the Mosaic judicial laws in their situation. In fact, Cotton's book was never made law in the colony (as was shown by Logan, "New England Puritans and the State," 372–75). While in fairness to Bahnsen and those who follow his lead, one must note their claim that they are only applying those judicial laws today that contain a moral equity, it must be equally noted that anchoring the justification for Theonomic ethics in Bahnsen's reading of Matt 5:17–19 brings every Mosaic judicial within that compass until and unless any judicial law can be shown to be amended by the Lawgiver either explicitly or as a good and necessary consequence of a statement by the Lawgiver addressing other matters. Such an approach effectively extends the category of laws with moral equity to such an extent, that Theonomists, as much as Cotton or the Brownists, cause the whole Judicial Law to be brought back again thereby.

66. Burgess, *The Magistrate's Commission from Heaven*, 8, cited in Ferguson, "Assembly," 337.

67. Although Gouge had not been an original member of the Third Committee, he was added to it in January 1645 specifically to help with the topic of God's law. See Van Dixhoorn, "Reforming the Reformation," 245.

civil estate. Many branches of that law appertained to the Jewish priesthood; as, the particular laws about the cities of refuge, whither such as slew any unawares fled, and there abode till the death of the high priest, Num 35:25. And laws about lepers, which the priest was to judge, Lev 14:3. And sundry other cases which the priest was to judge of. Deut 17:9. So also the laws of distinguishing tribes, Num 36:7; of reserving inheritances to special tribes and families, of selling them to the next of kin, Ruth 4:4; of raising seed to a brother that died without issue, Gen 38:8, 9; of all manner of freedoms at the year of jubilee, Lev 25:13, etc.

There were other branches of the judicial law which rested upon common equity, and were means of keeping the moral law: as putting to death idolaters and such as enticed others thereunto; and witches, and willful murderers, and other notorious malefactors: So likewise laws against incest and incestuous marriages; laws of reverencing and obeying superiors and governors: and of dealing justly in borrowing, restoring, buying, selling, and all manner of contracts, Exod 22:20; Deut 13:9; Exod 20:18; Num 35:30; Lev 20:11, etc., 19:32, 35.

The former sort were abolished together with the priesthood. The latter sort remain as good directions to order even Christian politics accordingly.

1. By these kinds of laws the wisdom of God was manifested in observing what was fit for the particular kind and condition of people; and in giving them answerable laws, and yet not tying all nations and states thereunto.

2. That liberty which God affordeth to others to have laws most agreeable to their own country, so as they be not contrary to equity and piety, bindeth them more obediently to submit themselves to their own wholesome laws, and to keep peace, unity, and amity among themselves.[68]

Gouge recognized that some Jewish judicial laws expired with the Jewish state, yet other judicial laws do not expire because they rest on common equity. Yet these laws do not tie "all nations and states thereunto." With these words, Gouge also denies Bahnsen's Theonomy.

---

68. Gouge, *A Learned and Very Useful Commentary*, second part, 171. This commentary consists of lectures originally given before the Assembly and later published.

The Concept of General Equity

The Confession is clear: The "sundry judicial laws" expired with the state of Israel and do not oblige any [other people] now "further than the general equity thereof may require." This raises two questions: What is general equity, and how far may it require?

Bahnsen believes that when "the Westminster theologians spoke of the 'general equity of' the judicial laws, they referred to the underlying moral principle which is illustrated by the particular cases mentioned in the judicial laws. Thus in Confessional context we find that they offered as a proof text the example of 1 Cor 9:8–10—which applies the illustration of the muzzled ox (via the underlying principle) to the case of the unpaid pastor."[69]

Sinclair Ferguson agrees that the referent of general equity is the moral principle illustrated by the particular cases. He argues that the Divines agreed with Paul Baynes' remark that the judicial laws "bind us as the perpetual equity of God agreeable to the law of nature and moral, is in them."[70]

Ferguson also expands on the history of the term *equity* in English law. He notes that "equity is a technical [term] when used in relation to the law, as it is here by the Divines, and has a lengthy pedigree stretching back to . . . Plato and Aristotle [who] discussed the idea of *epieikia*, and Roman law incorporated the principle of *aequitas*. The principle of equity thus passed into the Anglo-Saxon, early Norman and English systems of justice [where] it became an important element in the legal system itself . . . in the Confession [the expression "general equity" is] a *terminus technicas*, a well-defined concept in English jurisprudence."[71]

This technical sense of equity had entered and remained in English law because the common law courts were limited in their scope. They worked entirely on precedent:

> If no statute law clearly applied the judge was required to make his decision according to the nearest applicable law. Little discretion was permitted to the common law judge. Obviously this frequently led to injustice—especially if the law was not intended to be used for such cases. So if a man believed himself to have been wronged, he could appeal to the Court of Chancery where the

---

69. Bahnsen, "Westminster Assembly."
70. Baynes, *An Entire Commentary*, 162, cited in Ferguson, "Assembly," 333.
71. Ferguson, "Assembly," 330.

Chancellor would decide his case. The chancellor was not bound by the common law. He was bound merely by equity—a system of principles of justice that enabled him to decide a case when the law did not directly apply.[72]

As Ferguson recognized, courts of chancery were necessary because "implicit in the idea of equity is the recognition that the creation of a series of laws does not in and of itself guarantee that justice will be appropriately administered. It involves the recognition that laws must be applied existentially, since the application of 'the letter of the law' may in fact distort the real purpose of the law and ignore the individuality and particularity of circumstances. The legal principal of equity, therefore, meant . . . answering the question, How would the lawgiver apply his law in this situation?"[73]

To the contemporary courts, "equity" meant "the recourse to general principles of justice (the *naturalis aequitas* of Roman jurists) to correct or supplement the provisions of the law. *Equity of a statute*: the construction of a statute according to its reason and spirit, so as to make it apply to cases for which it does not expressly provide."[74]

As we have seen in our review of Calvin and his followers, both lawyers and ministers in sixteenth or seventeenth century England understood the *naturalis aequitas* of the Romans to be the Ten Commandments. From these general principles of justice, the English Chancellors could fashion remedies for injustices created by misapplying precedents created by the lower courts.

Bahnsen seems not to have been aware of the technical meaning of *equity* within English law and believed that Ferguson "exegetically confuses the notion of an 'equity found in the law' with the logically distinct and philosophically different notion of 'the equity of the law.'"[75] However, Bahnsen did not define which of these "equities" is the one that he thinks Ferguson advocated, nor how it differs from the one that he believed the Divines discussed. Nor does he supply any supporting evidence, such as a statement wherein the term *general equity* is defined differently by a Divine during the Assembly. A more serious problem with this answer to Ferguson is that Bahnsen overlooked the fact that

72. Troxel and Wallace, "Men in Combat," 309.
73. Ferguson, "Assembly," 330.
74. Oxford English Dictionary, online edition.
75. Bahnsen, "Westminster Assembly."

both he and Ferguson picked the same text to identify how general equity works in practice, i.e., 1 Cor 9:8-10, and explained how it is applied in very similar terms.[76] It is hard to claim that one does not understand a concept when you pick the same Scripture to illustrate it as he does—and do so in almost identical terms.

Westminster Divine William Gouge provides a critical witness to the contemporary use of the phrase *general equity*. In his commentary on Hebrews, Gouge writes,

> This was it, which is here said to be according to the law: and that the judicial, ceremonial and moral law. 1. By the judicial law the Levites had not their portion in Canaan for their inheritance, as other tribes had: therefore in lieu thereof, by the said law they had the tenth of the rest of the people. 2. The holy services which they performed to the Lord for the people were ceremonial. Therefore the recompense given, was by a like law. 3. The general equity that they who communicate unto us spiritual matters should partake of our temporals: and that they who are set apart wholly to attend God's service should live upon that service, is moral.[77]

Gouge uses the term *general equity* when justifying his application of a ceremonial law to a different situation for which it was not originally intended. For him, the term meant an eternal and morally valid principle, which, although it underlay a ceremonial law, was not restricted to that ceremonial or judicial law itself. In this case the principle involved is "the labourer is worthy of his hire," which in turn is an application of the Decalogue commandment, "Thou shalt not steal." Unless the term *general equity* can be shown to be used otherwise by another Divine who was a member of the committee that wrote section 19:4, we must believe that the Divines understood general equity as Gouge used it here—that is a moral principle that is an application of one of the ten commandments.

Sherman Isbell has correctly summarized the matter:

---

76 Ferguson, "Assembly," 330. See also Bahnsen, *By This Standard*, 130. In 1 Cor 9:8-10, the Corinthian Christians needed to know how their pastors were to be supported. On this point the Old Testament appeared to be silent: the Mosaic law did not specifically provide for the maintenance of religious teachers who were neither priests nor Levites. Paul's answer takes general moral principles, "thou shalt not steal" and "the labourer is worthy of his hire," originally applied to the oxen, and applies them to the contemporary situation.

77. Gouge, *Hebrews*, second part, 149.

The Confession uses the term *general equity* to identify the element in the judicial laws which is of enduring obligation. The meaning of this term is evident from the chapter in which it appears. There is an equity or righteousness which on four other occasions in this chapter is said to still oblige, amidst all the changes in redemptive history. That equity is the moral law, which 1) was first given at creation, 2) was afterwards delivered in the ten commandments, 3) is distinguished from the ceremonial and judicial laws as such, 4) is always backed by the authority of the Creator, and 5) is strengthened by Christ in the Gospel: "God gave to Adam a law, . . . by which He bound him and all his posterity to personal, entire, exact, and perpetual obedience . . . This law, after his fall, continued to be a perfect rule of righteousness . . . Beside this law, commonly called moral, [are the ceremonial and judicial laws] . . . The moral law doth for ever bind all . . . to the obedience thereof; and that, not only in regard of the matter contained in it, but also in respect of the authority of God the Creator, who gave it: neither doth Christ, in the Gospel, any way dissolve, but much strengthen this obligation."[78]

Isbell continues:

Confirmation that "general equity" signifies the moral law is furnished by an examination of the earlier Reformed and contemporary Puritan literature which forms the background and context for the writing of the Confession. These writers regarded equity as identifiable by reference to well-known standards. In the classical Reformed tradition, equity is the righteousness of the moral law, which is 1) embodied in a natural law binding upon all men as creatures under the authority of the Creator, and 2) common to moral teaching found in the Scriptures as a whole. We shall see that Calvin and the Puritans did not allow the judicial laws to define equity. Conformity to the moral law was the standard against which these writers reviewed the judicial laws and isolated the elements of perpetual equity in them.[79]

The Westminster Divines, then, understood "general equity may require" to mean righteously applying the eternal moral law provision or provisions underlying a specific Mosiac civil law to a situation for which that civil law was not directly intended. That the Divines used the term

---

78. Isbell, *Divine Law*, lines 211–24. Isbell then demonstrated that key Reformation and Westminster era theologians used general equity in this sense.

79. Isbell, "Divine Law," lines 225–34.

general equity to label the continuing element in the civil laws confirms that they believed that the Mosaic laws were not directly or automatically applicable to the English situation. And by making contemporary application of the Mosaic judicials turn on the question of whether or not "general equity may require," the Divines required those advocating such an institution to prove the contemporary applicability of the stipulation in question.

It appears that the Divines meant us to reason in something like the following way: "Thou shalt not steal" justifies all civil laws and punishments dealing with theft. If theft is as wrong today as it was in ancient Israel, then general equity requires that theft be criminalized and punished either as it was in Israel or in a fashion in which the criminal receives an equally just degree of punishment. If the biblical punishment for theft (i.e., restitution and fine, plus optional flogging) remains the most equitable punishment for that crime in today's different circumstances, then the same punishment, or one of equivalent equity, should be in our law books today.

We have seen that both Bahnsen and Ferguson would define general equity as the moral principle illustrated by case laws. We must next consider whether there is a difference in the extent to which each side will apply it.

The question between Calvinist and Theonomist is not whether Christians are required to use the concept of general equity as a tool to apply the fundamental principles of God's law to contemporary situations unknown in Moses' day. Both groups affirm that premise. The question between them is whether or not general equity requires Christians to work towards enshrining all Mosaic civil laws together with their punishments (with the usual exception on which both sides agree—when specifically changed by the lawgiver) into the law codes of modern states. As Ferguson points out, to Theonomists, the words *general equity* mean something rather different than the term's technical meaning in English law. Instead, he asserts, Theonomists believe that general equity means that "where the Mosaic judicial law *can* be applied, it *must* be applied just as it was in the Old Testament. For all practical purposes this means that the second statement of Confession XIX, iv is taken to be determinative of the meaning of the first statement. The effect is that in the view of theonomists 'general equity' means essentially that the *Mosaic law has actually expired minimally: it remains obligatory and must be applied maximally.*"[80]

Bahnsen replied that Ferguson "overstates and thus misconstrues the Theonomic view of 'general equity.'"[81] But if Bahnsen's exegesis of Matt 5:17–18 is correct, Theonomists are inevitably committed to applying all unamended Mosaic judicial stipulations at least as they were applied in the Old Testament, which is Ferguson's point.

The Meaning of "Moral Law" and the Extent of General Equity

At this point, we must examine another point of difference between the two sides: how did the Divines understand the term "moral law" as used in chapter 19? We have seen that Perkins and Bayes, for example, narrowed the meaning of this term to the Decalogue. Yet, in addition to this definition of the term "moral law," some English theologians from the Reformation to Westminster also used the word "moral" in different ways when talking about the Mosaic law. As Anthony Burgess notes, the multiple meanings of the term created confusion: "And here it must be acknowledged, that the different use of the word Moral hath bred many perplexities; yea, in whatsoever controversy it has been used it hath caused mistakes."[82]

One of these different uses of the word "Moral" involved the question of whether or not a particular Mosaic Law was just in itself. About ten months before the debate over the civil and judicial laws took place in the Assembly, Westminster Divines, Herbert Palmer and Daniel Cawdrey wrote that the term Moral Law should not be limited to the Decalogue. Instead, they believed that the term could be expanded to include other judicial stipulations that were eternally binding. For ". . . there may . . . be found some laws which are but positive;[83] and not natural which yet after they were once given, did (and do) concern all men in all ages to observe, both under the Old Testament and under the New, and so we think deserve the term of Moral Laws. We therefore so understand the word, as to imply any Law of God expressed in Scripture,

---

80. Ferguson, "Assembly," 330.
81. Bahnsen, "Westminster Assembly," line 46.
82. Burgess, *Vindiciae Legis*, 148.
83. Positive law refers to "law actually and specifically enacted or adopted by proper authority for the government of . . . society . . . jurisprudence enforced by a sovereign political authority" (Black's Law Dictionary, s.v. "positive law").

whether it can be proved Natural, or not; which from the time it was given to the end of the world, binds all succeeding generation of their posterity to whom it was given."[84]

Although Bahnsen does not mention Palmer and Cawdrey's work, he also does not follow the customary distinctions between the moral, civil, and ceremonial subcategories of the Mosaic that had been customary since Calvin. Instead, he argued that while the Decalogue is included in the moral law, the latter cannot be limited to the commandments alone. Ultimately, Bahnsen divides the entire Mosaic law into two main classes, Moral and Restorative, and he specifically defines the term *moral law* so as to include the Mosaic civil stipulations. Bahnsen defines the term as follows:

> Moral Law (reflecting God's absolute righteousness and judgment, but not showing the means of salvation *per se* for sinners)
>
> A. It guides life into the paths of righteousness
>
>   1. by defining holiness and sin
>
>   2. by restraining evil (through penal sanctions, etc.)
>
> B. It drives us to Christ and gracious restoration (since we are condemned as sinners therein).[85]

To emphasize the point, Bahnsen also claimed that, for the Divines, "the substance of the judicial laws was just as binding as the Ten Commandments. The judicial laws served to give definition to the Ten Commandments; to invalidate the former would therefore be to invalidate (or alter) the [latter]. That is why we read that, according to the Westminster standards, the Decalogue is not the full extent of the moral law, but rather the 'summary' of the moral law ([Westminster] Larger Catechism [WLC] #98).[86] We are bound to the whole moral law and not simply its summary expression."[87]

---

84. Cawdrey and Palmer, *Sabbatum Redivivum*, 3.

85. Bahnsen, *Theonomy*, 212.

86. "Where is the moral law summarily comprehended? Answer: The moral law is summarily comprehended in the Ten Commandments" (Westminster Larger Catechism Question 98).

87. Bahnsen, "Westminster Assembly." When this article was printed, a rare error occurred at the end of the second sentence when the word "former" (which cannot possibly be Bahnsen's intent) replaced the word which, given the context, Bahnsen must have intended, i.e., "latter."

If the Divines meant to define the term *moral law* so as to include the Mosaic civil stipulations as well as the Decalogue, then it is contra-Confessional to argue against the contemporary validity of any Mosaic judicial law applied to an identical situation in a modern state. But, contra Bahnsen, there are several reasons why we can be certain that the Divines intended to define the term "moral law" as referring to the Ten Commandments and nothing more, rather than following Cawdrey and Palmer in expanding the number of Mosaic stipulations identified by the term.[88]

First, the Confession explicitly defines the moral law as the commandments when, in WCF 19 it plainly states that "God gave to Adam a law . . . [which] after his fall . . . was delivered by God upon Mount Sinai in ten commandments . . . Besides this law, commonly called moral . . ."[89]

One of the authors of these words, Anthony Burgess, had previously echoed Calvin's limiting of the moral law to the Decalogue when he wrote that "the moral law had the great preheminency, being twice written by God himself in tables of stone. Now the whole body of these laws is . . . divided into moral, ceremonial and judicial. . . . The word moral [is here used] as to denote that which is perpetual and always obliging . . . as opposite to that which is binding but for a time."[90]

In addition, any claim that the moral law is more than the Decalogue fails to consider the answer to WLC 92, which specifically identifies the moral law as the "rule of obedience revealed to Adam in a state of innocence, and to all mankind in him, besides a special command not to eat of the tree of the knowledge of good and evil." By understanding the moral law as given to Adam in the garden, the Divines made a distinction in section 19:4 between the moral law and the civil laws later given to Israel "as a body politic."[91]

---

88. Although Cawdrey had been added to the committee that "perfected" the Confession in early September 1646, he moved no changes to the language of chapter 19 in the two weeks before the chapter was approved on the 25th. See Van Dixhoorn, "Reforming the Reformation," vol. 6, 345–46. Presumably, he was satisfied that the last clause of 19:4 was sufficiently strong to identify Mosaic laws that remain applicable in the New Covenant era.

89. Westminster Confession, 19:2, 3a.

90. Burgess, *Vindiciae Legis*, 147–48. The sermons in this work were preached within six months of the Assembly's discussion of these matters.

91. WCF 19:4.

Finally, WLC #98 and its answer do not state that the Decalogue is an incomplete summary of the moral law requiring supplementation from elsewhere in the Scriptures. Instead, the answer to this question claims that the moral law is "summarily comprehended in the Ten Commandments," something quite different. The Oxford English Dictionary (OED) gives the following contemporary meanings for *summarily*. Available meanings were: "in a summary or compendious manner; chiefly of statement, in few words, compendiously, briefly."[92] The OED also shows that *compendious* then meant: "containing the substance within small compass, concise, succinct, summary; comprehensive though brief; *esp.* of literary works; also of their authors."[93] Finally, *comprehended* in such a context meant either "understood" or "included," as in "education comprehends the training of many kinds of ability; from the Latin *comprehendere*"[94] (a meaning well known to the Divines, all of whom had received their university instruction in Latin).[95] The OED gives the following contemporary definitions for *comprehend*, none of which allows for a partial inclusion of the item or subject that is comprehended.

> To grasp with the mind, conceive fully or adequately, understand, "take in." (App. the earliest sense in English.); ... To lay hold of all the points of (any thing) and include them within the compass of a description or expression; to embrace or describe summarily; summarize; sum up; ... To include or comprise in a treatise or discourse: now more usually said of the book, etc. ... To include in the same category; To enclose or include in or within limits; To enclose or have within it; to contain; to lie around.[96]

Since *summarily* and *comprehended* both assumed that the concept summarized was comprehensively contained within a small compass, when the WLC teaches that the moral law is "summarily comprehended in the ten commandments," it is teaching that anything not in the Ten Commandments is not included in the moral law as the Divines defined the term.

---

92. Oxford English Dictionary (OED), 2nd ed., s.v. "summarily."
93. OED, s.v. "compendious."
94. *New Lexicon Webster's Dictionary of the English Language*, s.v. "comprehend."
95 Isbell, "Divine Law," lines 413–15.
96. OED, s.v. "comprehend."

It is noteworthy that Cawdrey and Palmer not only anticipated Bahnsen in extending the term *moral law* to encompass more than the Ten Commandments, they also anticipated his point that only an amendment of particular laws by the Lawgiver would be sufficient to justify any claim that a Mosaic statute was not applicable in New Covenant–era states.

> And so we suppose we may upon just reason infer, that the *silence of the New Testament concerning a law, expressly and clearly delivered in the Old Testament, is a confirmation rather than an abrogation of it, or an intimation that it is expired*: judicious divines giving this for a reason of the silence of the New Testament in diverse points, which are most vehemently urged in the old, as against incestuous marriages fore noted (and that others are but slightly and as it were occasionally mentioned, as laws about tithes and usury, etc.) because they are so clearly and importunately pressed in the Old. And therefore till we see better reasons to the contrary, than any we have yet met with in all our disputers' books, we must needs hold, that all the laws *of the Old Testament are perpetuated to this day, if there be nothing against them in the New Testament* by way of *repealing them, or at least in reason,* which might plead for an *expiration.* And if any one think, that by this assertion, sundry of the laws which are usually counted judicial will prove to be in force still; we answer, that perhaps it may prove so indeed . . . So we are afraid, that many Divines, (not to say some churches and States nowadays) have been a little too bold in rejecting sundry laws as being merely judicial which upon further advisement might perhaps be found moral and perpetual.[97]

Despite these arguments, which prefigure Bahnsen's own in considerable detail, the Divines were clearly not convinced of this proto-Theonomic view. Instead of determining whether Mosaic stipulations continued to be valid based on whether or not they were abrogated in the New Testament, the Divines turned the question on the different ground of whether general equity still required that particular laws needed to be enforced.

Why did the Divines not follow Cawdrey and Palmer's suggestion? We cannot be certain, but two considerations are apparent. First, as we have seen, the Divines were not united on the question of which Mosaic

---

97. Cawdrey and Palmer, *Sabbatum Redivivum*, 22–23.

judicials continued, and Cawdrey and Palmer's suggestion would not have commended itself to the Assembly, divided as it was. Second, the Divines knew that the Mosaic judicial laws were not given to all men and nations. Instead, they were given as covenant stipulations to Israel, a nation in a specific covenant relationship to God not shared by any other nation—a relationship that had ended when the institution of the New Covenant rendered the Mosaic covenant obsolete. They also knew that the New Covenant, unlike the Mosaic one, was not made between God and a community or state, but between God and individuals.[98] Although the Divines recognized that many Mosaic civil laws were universally applicable, they also had to consider the possibility that some Mosaic civil statutes might have derived their validity from Israel's covenant relationship to God rather than being a universally applicable application of general equity of the moral law to civil ethics.

By writing section 19:4 in the way they did, the Divines provided a workable method of determining the contemporary validity of Mosaic civil stipulations upon which all could agree without dividing over questions of which laws did or did not remain valid, and they also made it possible for Christians freely to consult the wisdom of the Mosaic civil laws, and apply only those provisions still required by general equity to their changed covenantal and national circumstances.[99] Using the idea of general equity to test all laws seems to have been an acceptable compromise to Cawdrey and Palmer since they are not recorded as intervening in the debate on the question.

---

[98]. Although God promises He will make the new covenant with "the house of Israel and the house of Judah" (Jer 31:27), it is clear from Rom 9:29 that this covenant's benefits are accessible only by elect individuals rather than the nation as a political entity.

[99]. When the Westminster Confession was written, only rulers had the responsibility for the laws they passed. While subjects could protest, they were not responsible for instituting and enforcing the laws. In the intervening years, a significant change has occurred: current democratic political theory assigns final sovereignty to the voters who elect governments, not governments themselves. Although the Confession was not addressed to our contemporary situation, by stating that any of God's laws that are not covenant specific to Israel still apply "now," it provides, in principle, the guidance God's people need today to help us exercise our responsibility to institute and reform civil governments in ways that glorify God.

Points Bahnsen Did Not Answer

It is unfortunate that Bahnsen did not respond to some significant considerations that Ferguson has brought to our attention. We shall now examine the points Bahnsen effectively conceded by his lack of response.

The first of these is Ferguson's observation that the Divines were not of one mind regarding how far the Mosaic laws and punishments still applied. According to Ferguson, the Divines held a range of views on the question.[100] We have seen that Cawdrey and Palmer anticipated Bahnsen's Theonomy in considerable detail; Gillespie was close to but not identical to Bahnsen; and, moving further away, we find Baillie, Rutherford, and the rest of the Divines ending with Independents such as Goodwin, who specifically denied that the civil laws were automatically applicable today, writing that "to us Christians it is not the judicial and ceremonial, but the moral law which is obligatory."[101]

It is certain that this diversity of views affected the drafting of the Confession: the basic intent of the Divines seems to have been to put forward a Confession that propounded a clear statement of doctrine upon which as many as possible generic Calvinists could agree and from which as few as possible would be excluded. That the Divines were aiming for such an inclusivist Confession is clearly shown at other points in their discussions. In another "of the most controversial . . . debates . . . Gillespie defused the discussion with the remark, 'When that word is left out, is it not a truth, and *so every one may enjoy his own sense*."[102]

Ferguson correctly points out the significance of Gillespie's remark. If even Gillespie, "one of the most acute and rigorous theologians in the Jerusalem chamber, was suggesting wording that would be faithful to Scripture and yet provide liberty for each to read the text in the light of his own [differing] understanding of the biblical teaching,"[103] then we cannot conclude that the Confession attempted to enforce one particular view of each of the minor points on which the Divines disagreed. Since it is known that the Divines held a diversity of views concerning the continuance of the Mosaic civil laws, the most likely interpretation of section 19:4 is that it, too, is a self-conscious consensus statement happily

---

100. Ferguson, "Assembly," 339–46.

101. Goodwin, *The Works of Thomas Goodwin*, vol. 11, 26, quoted in Ferguson, "Assembly," 344.

102. Ferguson, "Assembly," 346.

103. Ibid.

designed to accommodate a measure of differing views. Therefore, "the view that the Confession is committed specifically to a theonomic understanding of the Mosaic judicial law code and penology is not viable."[104]

What Did the Divines Mean by 19:4?

Rutherford wrote: "*Judiciall* Lawes may be *judiciall* and *Mosaicall*, and so not obligatory to us, according to the degree and quality of punishment."[105] Ferguson correctly observes that these words,

> more than any others, provide the clue to the nuance of meaning intended [by the Divines in 19:4] . . . Rutherford believes: 1) Some judicial laws were distinctly Mosaical in form. 2) The Mosaic punishment for breaching such judicial laws is not obligatory now. 3) Nevertheless, there is a constant principle that breaches of them may properly be punished.
>
> This, presumably, is what Rutherford understood the Confession to mean when it spoke of the judicial laws not obliging now beyond the demands of general equity. Equity required punishment: the Mosaic law required fixed punishment for a temporary age. That punishment is no longer mandatory.[106]

Testing the Divines' View: The Proof Texts

The Confession gives a number of proof texts for section 19:4, which are intended to provide confirmation from Scripture for the Confession's teaching. Under 19:4, we find the following: Exod 21—22:29; Gen 49:10 with 1 Pet 2:13–14; Matt 5:17 with 38, 39; and 1 Cor 9:8–10. Note that in two cases the word "with" appears in the footnotes together with the references. It is clear that the Exodus passage is used to confirm that "God gave sundry judicial laws" and that Gen 9:10 and 1 Pet 2:13, 14, taken together, are meant to show their expiry. For "the scepter shall not depart from Judah, nor the ruler's staff from between his feet, until Shiloh comes, and to him shall be the obedience of the peoples." After Shiloh (Christ) came, the peoples are commanded to "submit yourselves for the Lord's sake to the king . . . or governors." So it is not at all surprising that Anthony Burgess understood those Scriptures as entailing a systematic

---

104. Ibid., 345.
105. Rutherford, *Free Disputation*, 298, cited in Ferguson, "Assembly," 341.
106. Ferguson, "Assembly," 341–42.

repeal of the Mosaic judicial laws, since "the Judicial laws, because they were given to Israel as a politic body, that polity ceasing, which was the principal, the accessory falls with it."[107] For, as Burgess continues:

> *Abrogation* is then properly, when a Law is totally taken away. And this Abrogation arises sometimes from the express constitution at first, which did limit and prescribe the time of the laws [sic] continuance: sometimes by an express revoking and repealing of it by that authority which made it: sometimes by adding to that repeal an express law commanding the contrary. Now it may be easily proved, that the Ceremonial, and Judicial laws they are abrogated by express repeal. The Judicial Law 1 *Pet* 2:13, where they are commanded to *be subject to every ordinance of man:* and this was long foretold *Gen 49:10. The Law-giver shall be taken from Judah.*[108]

Ferguson sums up Burgess' argument: "The abrogation of the state of the people implies abrogation of the accessory to it, namely the particular legal system."[109] One would therefore expect that the remaining Scriptures—Matt 5:17 with 38, 39 and 1 Cor 9:8–10—were intended by the Divines to show just what they meant by general equity. Bahnsen argues that since the proof texts include "Matthew 5:17, (Christ's statement that he did not come to abrogate the law)" means that general equity "cannot be understood as abrogating . . . the death penalty for blasphemers, and so forth."[110] But, as Ferguson notes, Bahnsen is assuming that "the Westminster Divines would exegete the text in the same way he does. This however begs the question. Bahnsen does not refer to the fact that the Divines also cite Matthew 5:38–39 *alongside* verse 17."[111]

Ferguson then outlines the problem thus created. While it

> may well be a correct understanding of the passage, but it clearly does nothing to explain why the Divines cited Matthew 5:38–39 as the proof for their proposition that the Mosaic judicial laws have "expired" and do not bind "further than the general equity thereof may require." Although it is not always possible to be

---

107. Burgess, *Vindiciae Legis*, 168b. NB this edition of *Vindicae Legis* has an error in its pagination resulting in two page 168's; the second of which is found 6 pages after the first.

108. Ibid., 211–12.

109. Ferguson, "Assembly," 334.

110. Bahnsen, *Theonomy*, 517.

111. Ferguson, "Assembly," 336.

dogmatic about why the Divines combine proof texts as they do, it seems that in this instance they viewed turning the other cheek as the *telos* [goal or end] of the lex talionis. For them, therefore, *pleroosai* does not seem to have meant "to confirm" but "to show the ultimate purpose of," and, in this instance, also implies "to abrogate." In the thinking of the Divines, this combination of proof texts indicates that the lex talionis is abrogated by the law of forgiveness . . .

[It] is interesting to notice that Anthony Burgess adopted the view that the law was given to the people at the time of Moses because of the corrupt state in which they had left Egypt: the law was intended to restrain the kind of impiety that broke loose in the golden calf incident. Recognizing that some of his contemporaries held that in the Sermon on the Mount Christ had abolished capital punishment, Burgess argues that the *lex talionis* was given to restrain private vengeance in the first place (and thus is fulfilled by turning the other cheek). In rejecting the abolitionist view of Matt 5:38–39, Burgess holds that capital punishment may still be inflicted. But in doing so he appeals back, beyond the Mosaic law to the Noahic provisions in Genesis 9:6 as providing the perpetual reason for capital punishment for murder . . . Here Burgess' approach (which may well form the basis for the Confession's logic) differs from that of theonomy.[112]

Burgess' approach was not an isolated view among the Westminster Divines. In his St. Andrews University lectures, given fifteen years after the Assembly and later published as *Examen Arminianismi*, Samuel Rutherford also anchored the contemporary validity of capital punishment in God's word to Noah rather than in the Mosaic stipulations. Responding to the question of *"whether it should be permissible for the Magistrate to cause profligate people and murderers to receive capital punishment?"* Rutherford affirms "that it is entirely lawful . . . 1. Because Gen 9:6 The one who sheds the blood of man will have his own blood shed of by man."[113]

Bahnsen's next argument was a claim that 1 Cor 9:9–10 shows that "case law of the Old Testament . . . was still authoritative and binding after Christ's advent."[114]

---

112. Ferguson, "Assembly," 336–37, citing Burgess, *Vindiciae Legis*, 188–89.

113. Rutherford, quoted in Richard, "Samuel Rutherford: *Examen Arminianismi*," 270, 271.

114. Bahnsen, *Theonomy*, 517.

To this, Ferguson responds that while

> the text is adduced by the Divines to indicate application of the case law *to the Christian community* . . . it is by no means clear that this particular citation demonstrates in what sense this particular case law is to be applied *in the state*. It is doubtful if the Divines' citation here will bear the weight of Bahnsen's claims that they viewed it as "Paul's utilization of the case law of the Old Testament in a way that shows it was still authoritative and binding after Christ's advent."[115] It is altogether more likely that the Divines understood this text as an illustration of their statement that the judicial laws are not binding now "further than the general equity thereof doth require." They viewed 1 Corinthians 9:8–10 as an illustration of how general equity works; the notion that it demonstrates the binding nature of Mosaic case law was not in view.[116]

Ferguson should not be understood as arguing that the Confession forbids the application of any and all of the Mosaic penalties, nor does the Confession advocate such a view. But it is clear from section 19:4 that a Mosaic punishment may not automatically be imposed simply because it is Mosaic. We may only conclude that a Mosaic punishment remains appropriate now if we can demonstrate that the general equity under that law still applies in the same way today. If that general equity can be shown to apply, then that Mosaic punishment may be justly imposed.

Two Final Points

Theonomists may argue that Ferguson left two additional significant supporting arguments for a Theonomic view of the Confession untreated, and that therefore the Confession must be regarded as Theonomic in outlook after all.

First, Theonomists may observe that since "God's revealed standing laws are a reflection of His immutable moral character,"[117] any attempt to change God's laws is an attack on God's character. But this assertion is incorrect. Laws are not righteous solely because they show God's character; they are righteous because they are the holy God's decreed response to particular situations that besmirch his holiness. If a material element

---

115. Ibid.
116. Ferguson, "Assembly," 335.
117. Bahnsen, *Theonomy*, xxvi.

in the situation changes, the righteous response or range of righteous responses to that situation may be different—without affecting God's character in the least.

Bahnsen draws his last argument from chapter 23 of the Confession, which argues that the magistrate must enforce both tables of the law. Theonomists make much of Kline's point that Theonomy seems to be taught in this chapter, but they neglect to notice that Kline's argument renders the Divines guilty of "blatant self-contradiction" since 19:4 says that the sundry judicial laws are "not obliging any other now, further than the general equity thereof may require." Thus Theonomists need to consider the very real possibility that Kline is mistaken.[118]

Although Ferguson does not deal with this issue, it presents no real problem for the Calvin-Westminster position. One may simply argue that the Divines believed that the magistrate's authority to enforce Mosaic judgments of first table offenses arises not from the Theonomic hermeneutic, but from a belief that general equity still requires that the magistrate apply those particular laws. If the magistrate's duty to enforce the tables of the law arises only from general equity and not a continuation in detail of the Mosaic civil laws, then the Confession is both non-Theonomic and internally consistent.

CONCLUSION

Having worked through Bahnsen's attempt to rebut Ferguson's article, we have seen that in each case his attempts have fallen short. Ferguson's summary of his argument, therefore, may well serve the same purpose here. Bahnsen has failed to disprove Ferguson's points "(1) that a theonomic interpretation is not the most natural reading of the syntax; (2) that a *thoroughgoing* theonomic interpretation of the principle of general equity is not characteristic of the Puritan tradition; and (3) that the theonomic interpretation of the principle of general equity is not identical with that adopted by the Puritan writers."[119] And so we may, with Ferguson,

> conclude that the Confession clearly does not expound, nor does it proscribe a theonomic viewpoint. It may be that some members

---

118. This point has been cogently made by Duncan, "The Westminster Confession of Faith," lines 7–42.

119. Ferguson, "Assembly," 334.

of the Assembly were prepared to stretch the meaning of "general equity" as far as contemporary theonomists do . . . however, I know of no evidence . . . that any individual commissioner to the Assembly believed that Sabbath-breakers and rebellious children should be put to death *on the authority of the Mosaic law*. Rutherford specifically repudiates such a position, as we have seen. The strongest position a theonomist could adopt *on the basis of the Confession* would be that it did not *a priori* reject the application of the Mosaic judicial punishment for crimes considered *seriatim* [i.e., on a case-by-case basis]. But theoretical theonomy as such is not the teaching of the Westminster Confession of Faith.[120] [Therefore] . . . we must conclude that the Westminster Confession of Faith cannot be appealed to as an expression of theonomy in its contemporary form. Further, it would be erroneous to argue that one cannot subscribe to the Confession of Faith unless one is a theonomist. Nor can it be argued that not to subscribe to theonomy is to reject the Westminster Confession of Faith's teaching on the law of God.[121]

LATER REFORMED OPINION

As we have reviewed the writings of Calvin and his followers as well as section 19:4 of the Westminster confession, we have discovered that Bahnsen's Theonomy differs from the latter at two key points. While Bahnsen claims that all of the divinely unamended Mosaic judicial stipulations are included in the moral law, Calvin, his most influential followers, and the WCF assert that the moral law identifies only the Decalogue. While Theonomy claims that only with divine authorization may specific Mosaic stipulations may be amended or discarded and that all others must be applied today, Calvin and the WCF recognize that the only Mosaic stipulations needing to be instituted in contemporary states are those that remain equitable despite the change in covenants.

Theonomists have sometimes asserted that Theonomy is nothing more than the traditional Reformed justification of the contemporary applicability of the Old Testament law in the New Covenant era. We have already seen that this is incorrect as far as the early Reformers and Westminster Divines are concerned. But now we must consider the writings of later theologians who have also commented on the matter.

120. Ibid., 348.
121. Ibid., 346.

We begin with David Dickson, who, in 1684, wrote what is believed to be the first commentary on the Confession. He wrote:

> *Did the Lord by Moses give to the Jews as a Body Politic sundry judicial lawes, which expired together with their state?*
>
> Yes.
>
> *Do they oblige any other now, further than the general Equity thereof may require?*
>
> No. Exod 21 from the first to the last Verse. Exod 22:1 to verse 29. Gen 49:10. 1 Cor 9:8, 9, 10. 1 Pet 2:13, 14. Matt 5:17, 38, 39.
>
> Well then, do not some err, *though otherwise orthodox* who maintain, "*That the whole Judicial Law of the Jews, is yet alive and binding on all of us who are Christian Gentiles?*"
>
> Yes.
>
> *By what reason are they confuted?*
>
> (1), Because the Judicial Law was delivered by Moses to the Israelites as a Body Politick; Exod 21 . . .
>
> (2), Because, this Law, in many things which are of particular Right, was accommodated to the Commonwealth of the Jews and not to other nations also; Exod 22:3. Exod 21:2.
>
> Lev 25:2, 3. Deut 24:1, 2, 3. 25:5, 6, 7.
>
> (3) Because, in other things, which are not of particular Right, it is neither from the Law of Nature obliging by Reason; neither is it pressed upon Believers under the Gospel, to be observed.
>
> (4) Because, Believers are appointed under the Gospel to obey the civil Laws, and Commands of those under whose governments they live, provided they be just, and that for Conscience sake; Rom 13:1, 1 Pet 2: 13, 14; Tit 3:1.[122]

With his assertion that if a Mosaic judicial is neither obliging by reason from the law of nature, nor pressed upon believers in the gospel, then it does not apply today, Dickson contradicts Bahnsen's Theonomic hermeneutic.

The next major figure to consider is Herman Witsius. Writing in 1693, he echoes the WCF's threefold distinction, noting that among

> several kinds of laws given [Israel] . . . there are principally three mentioned by divines. The moral or the Decalogue, the ceremo-

---

122. Dickson, *Truth's Victory*, 144–45.

nial, and the political or forensic . . . The law of the Decalogue was given [Israel]; which, as to its substance, is one and the same with the law of nature, and binds men as such . . . As a peculiar people who had a polity or government suitable to their genius and disposition in the land of Canaan. A republic constituted not so much according to those forms which philosophers have delineated, but which was, in a peculiar manner, a theocracy . . . God himself holding the reins of government therein, Judg 8:23. Under that view God prescribed them political laws.[123]

Witsius notes that the Mosaic judicial laws were prescribed by God for a peculiar form of government now no longer in existence. In the same work, Witsius repeats his identification of the Decalogue with the law of nature: "The Decalogue contains the sum of the law of nature, and as to its substance is one and the same therewith, so far is it of perpetual and universal obligation. And thus far all Divines are agreed, Socinians not excepted."[124]

Finally, Witsius also limits the referent of "the law" in Matt 5:17 to the Ten Commandments when he writes, "But that Christ speaks of the law of the Decalogue, we gather from what follows where he explains the precepts of that law."[125]

Another key figure is the English covenant theologian John Brown of Haddington, who in 1796 limited the applicability of the Judicials to the Jews: "The judicial law directed the civil managements of the Israelites under God, as their principal governor, with respect to their encampments, marches, wars, inheritances, marriages, punishments, rulers etc . . . and is reducible to the correspondent precepts of the moral [law] and never bound any but the Jews, in their national establishment, further than moral equity requires."[126]

Brown also claimed that the moral law is the Decalogue alone since the "whole moral law, which regulates our love to God and men, and all the actings of it, is contained in the ten commandments."[127] In addition, Brown also specifically identifies the commandments with the law of nature: "The ten commandments, above explained, may be viewed

123. Witsius, *Economy of the Covenants*, vol. 2, 162.
124. Ibid., 175.
125. Ibid., 178.
126. Brown, *Compendious View*, 431.
127. Ibid., 435.

... as a Law of Nature antecedent to and disengaged from any covenant-transaction between God and us ... God, as a Creator and absolute Sovereign imposed it ... upon man's heart in his creation ... included in the instamped image of God the lawgiver. Gen 1:26, 27; Eccl 7:29."[128]

Next, we turn to Robert Shaw, who in his commentary on the Confession wrote that the "*Judicial* law ... as far as the Jewish polity was peculiar, has also been entirely abolished; but as far as it contains any statutes founded in the law of nature common to all nations, it is still obligatory."[129]

In the late 1800s, Princeton theologian Charles Hodge wrote his *Systematic Theology*, which remained a major Reformed textbook well into the late twentieth century. Although he does not explicitly name the Decalogue as the moral law, Hodge does say that

> the question whether the Decalogue is a perfect rule of duty is, in one sense, to be answered in the affirmative. (1.) Because it enjoins love to God and man, which, our Saviour teaches, includes every other duty. (2.) Because our Lord held it up as a perfect code, when he said to the young man in the Gospel, "This do and thou shalt live." (3.) Every specific command elsewhere recorded may be referred to some one of its several commands. So that perfect obedience to the Decalogue in its spirit, would be perfect obedience to the law.[130]

But when Hodge discussed the continuity of the judicials, he made it clear that he was no Theonomist:

> A third class of laws have their foundation in certain temporary relations of men, or conditions of society, and are enforced by the authority of God. To this class belong many of the judicial or civil laws of the ancient theocracy; laws regulating the distribution of property, the duties of husbands and wives, the punishment of crimes, etc. These laws were the application of general principles of justice and right to the peculiar circumstances of the Hebrew people. Such enactments bind only those who are in the circumstances contemplated, and cease to be obligatory when those circumstances change. It is always and everywhere right that crime should be punished, but the kind or degree of punishment may vary with the varying condition of society. It

---

128. Ibid., 475.
129. Shaw, *Exposition of the Confession of Faith*, 225.
130. Hodge, *Systematic Theology*, vol. 3, 271.

is always right that the poor should be supported, but one mode of discharging that duty may be proper in one age and country, and another preferable in other times and places. All those laws, therefore, in the Old Testament, which had their foundation in the peculiar circumstances of the Hebrews, ceased to be binding when the old dispensation passed away.

It is often difficult to determine to which of the last two classes certain laws of the Old Testament belong; and therefore, to decide whether they are still obligatory or not. Deplorable evils have flowed from mistakes as to this point. The theories of the union of Church and State, of the right of the magistrate to interfere authoritatively in matters of religion, and of the duty of persecution, so far as Scriptural authority is concerned, rest on the transfer of laws founded on the temporary relations of the Hebrews to the altered relations of Christians. Because the Hebrew kings were the guardians of both tables of the Law, and were required to suppress idolatry and all false religion, it was inferred that such is still the duty of the Christian magistrate. Because Samuel hewed Agag to pieces, it was inferred to be right to deal in like manner with heretics. No one can read the history of the Church without being impressed with the dreadful evils which have flowed from this mistake. On the other hand, there are some of the judicial laws of the Old Testament which were really founded on the permanent relations of men, and therefore, were intended to be of perpetual obligation, which many have repudiated as peculiar to the old dispensation. Such are some of the laws relating to marriage, and to the infliction of capital punishment for the crime of murder. If it be asked, How are we to determine whether any judicial law of the Old Testament is still in force? the answer is first, When the continued authority of such law is recognized in the New Testament. That for Christians is decisive. And secondly, If the reason or ground for a given law is permanent, the law itself is permanent.[131]

The final witness to whom we turn is John Murray, who disclaimed Bahnsen's position when he wrote that "it would not be contrary to the analogy of our Lord's teaching elsewhere to regard Him as here abrogating the regulatory penal provisions of the Mosaic economy (which could not be regulatory in the New Testament age)."[132]

---

131. Hodge, *Systematic Theology*, vol. 3, 267–68. Bahnsen agrees that Hodge was no Theonomist when he claims that Hodge "left his customary cogency here and used some of the most infelicitous reasoning imaginable in moral philosophy or scriptural exegesis (of which he offers none)" (Bahnsen, *Theonomy*, 304 n. 1).

132. Murray, *Principles of Conduct*, 174.

Given that Murray denied that the penal provisions of the Mosaic economy were regulatory in the New Testament age, it is clear that he did not advocate Bahnsen's Theonomy.

We have now reviewed the positions taken by the major Reformed theologians who followed in the wake of the Westminster Divines. Their combined statements make it certain that they employ a hermeneutic different from Bahnsen's, and that the latter's approach has never been a significant Reformed justification for the continuity of the Mosaic judicial stipulations in the present age.

7

Theonomy and Legal Practice: One Practical Problem

Some critics of Theonomy have argued that Jesus' treatment of the woman caught in adultery proves that Jesus did not teach "the abiding validity of the law in exhaustive detail" with respect to the Old Testament civil laws. Their argument works like this: the law provided that she should be stoned, but Jesus "got her off" in a way that would be illegitimate if Theonomy were scriptural.

In responding to these critics, Bahnsen put forth a very significant misunderstanding of an important Mosaic judicial principle. Although his error at this point is not directly relevant to the Theonomic thesis, it must not be allowed to obscure the true meaning and real value of this principle.

Bahnsen's argument works like this: even though he believed that the story of the woman taken in adultery was not authentic, he also believed that even if

> this passage be accounted as part of the infallible autograph of John's gospel, rather than weakening the present thesis, it strongly confirms it! Christ demands that the very *details* of the Mosaic Law be followed in John 8:7. The Pharisees . . . came to test Jesus but, as elsewhere *they* failed to know the law. God requires, in conviction for capital crimes that the witnesses who bring the accusation against a person be innocent of that very same crime (Deut. 19:15); furthermore, the law specified that in the event of capital punishment the accusers had to cast the first stones (Deut. 17:7). Christ was merely enforcing the precise demands of God's holy law in John 8:7; the one who was without sin should cast the first stone.[1]

---

1. Bahnsen, *Theonomy*, 228, 229.

Bahnsen's claim that Deut 19:15 teaches that "God requires, in conviction for capital crimes that the witnesses who bring the accusation against a person be innocent of that very same crime" is incorrect. That verse is best translated: "A single witness shall not rise up against a man on account of any iniquity or any sin which he has committed; on the evidence of two or three witnesses shall a matter be confirmed." For Bahnsen's reading of the text to be correct, the Hebrew word translated "single" in the first clause needed to be the Hebrew word for "a" to achieve the reading "a witness." In addition, the verb for "committed" must be reflexive (i.e., the word "he" in the phrase "he has committed" must be "he himself" referring to the witness, not the accused). But in the Hebrew text of this passage, the word translated "single" not the word "a," it is the word for the number "one"[2] and the verb "committed" is not reflexive. Thus the text is not legislating against a criminal giving testimony in the case of a later instance of the same crime that the witness had earlier committed; instead, Deut 19:15 is a twofold prohibition of single witness testimony being accepted as conclusive in criminal trials.[3]

If God's intent for the verse was to prohibit an uncaught criminal from giving testimony in a subsequent crime, either the first clause would have been "a witness shall not rise up against a man on account of any iniquity or sin which he himself has committed" or the second would have been "no criminal's testimony shall be valid in a later trial for the same type of crime of which he was convicted."

Bahnsen should have realized that the purpose of Deut 19:15 is not about prohibiting the testimony of an uncaught criminal testifying regarding a crime similar to one he had previously committed, for Deut 19:15 is nothing more than an application of the principle first given to Israel in Num 35:30, where Moses commands: "If anyone kills a person, the murderer shall be put to death on the testimony of witnesses, but no person shall be put to death on the testimony of one witness."

New Testament allusions to Deut 19:15 also rule out Bahnsen's interpretation. In John 8:13, the Pharisees attempt to cast doubt on the veracity of Jesus' testimony concerning himself by saying, "You are bearing witness of yourself, your witness is not true"—i.e., his testimony was invalid because it was unsupported. That this is an allusion to Deut 19:15

---

2. Halladay, *A Concise Hebrew and Aramaic Lexicon of the Old Testament*, 9.

3. The very next verse goes into the question of how God required the Hebrew judges to resolve questions of conflicting testimony.

and the principle drawn from it that only confirmed testimony could be accepted as valid is shown by Jesus' retort, "Even in your law it has been written that the testimony of two men is true. I . . . bear witness of myself and My Father who sent Me bears witness of Me."[4] If Bahnsen's interpretation of Deut 19:15 was the correct understanding of the law, the Pharisees could never have used an allusion to it in an attempt to muzzle Jesus since he had never been convicted of false witness.[5] Moreover, if Bahnsen's understanding of Deut 19:15 was correct, Jesus would not have replied with the fact that the Father was his second witness, but with the fact that he had never been convicted of false witness.

This Mosaic judicial principle was later taken up by Paul and applied within the Church when he prohibited receiving a charge against an elder on the basis of single witness testimony (1 Tim 5:19).

If we ask whether this principle should be applied in today's world, the biblically unjust and wrongful murder convictions of Donald Marshall, David Milgaard, and Steven Truscott in Canadian courts, together with their later reversals, provide all the answer we need. The original trials in these cases were significantly affected by the judges and juries giving undue weight to single witness testimony at key points. When the present author read the reports of the reversals in these cases, he noted the initial trials' deviations from Mosaic practice.

Since the parties in single witness disputes are witness and accused, and the situations that give rise to them are unaffected by the change in covenants, there is every reason to believe that "general equity may require" magistrates to prohibit single witness testimony from determining the outcome of criminal trials. Yet if Bahnsen's misunderstanding of this text becomes more widely followed, we may lose sight of this point, and our courts may lose a tremendous bulwark against injustice.[6]

---

4. John 8:13–17.

5. John 8:46.

6. The present writer once encountered an articulate and educated Theonomist who would not accept that a Theonomist might have *biblical* grounds, of which single witness testimony was one, for protesting the carrying out of death sentences in particular cases. That conversation demonstrated that Theonomic overestimation of Bahnsen's work could lead to such serious legal and theological errors that systematic refutation was essential.

Bibliography

Alford, Henry. *The Greek Testament: With a Critically Revised Text, a Digest of Various Readings, Marginal References to Verbal and Idiomatic Usage, Prolegomena, and a Critical and Exegetical Commentary.* Vol. 1. Ed. and rev. by Everett F. Harrison. Chicago: Moody, 1958.

The Apocrypha, Revised Standard Version. Online: http://etext.virginia.edu/rsv.browse.html.

Avis, P. D. L. "Moses and the Magistrate: A Study in the Rise of Protestant Legalism." *Journal of Ecclesiastical History* 26 (1975), 149–72.

Bahnsen, David. "The Life of Greg L. Bahnsen." In *The Standard Bearer: A Festschrift for Greg L. Bahnsen*, edited by Steven M. Schlissel, 9–27. Nacogdoches, TX: Covenant Media Foundation, 2002.

Bahnsen, Greg L. *By This Standard: The Authority of God's Law Today.* Tyler, TX: Institute for Christian Economics, 1985.

———. "Cross-Examination: A Biblical Standard for Civil Law." No pages. Online: http://www.cmfnow.com/articles/pe176.htm.

———. "The Exegesis of Matthew 5:17–19." No pages. Online: http://www.cmfnow.com/articles/pb055.htm.

———. "Forward." In *The Debate over Christian Reconstruction*, edited by Gary DeMar et al. Atlanta: American Vision, 1988.

———. "God's Law and Gospel Prosperity: A Reply to the Editor of the Presbyterian Journal." Online: http://www.cmfnow.com/articles/pe041.htm.

———. "Interview with Dr. Greg Bahnsen." *Contra Mundum* 2. Online: http://www.cmfnow.com/articles/pe125.htm.

———. *No Other Standard: Theonomy and Its Critics.* Tyler, TX: Institute for Christian Economics, 1991.

———. "Response to Wayne G. Strickland." In *The Law, the Gospel, and the Modern Christian*, edited by Willem A. VanGemeren. Grand Rapids: Eerdmans, 1993.

———. "The Theonomic Position." In *God and Politics: Four Views on the Reformation of Civil Government*, edited by Gary Scott Smith. Phillipsburg, NJ: Presbyterian & Reformed, 1989.

———. "The Theonomic Thesis in Confessional and Historical Perspective." 1980. No pages. Online: http://www.cmfnow.com/articles/pe144.htm.

———. *Theonomy in Christian Ethics.* 3rd ed. Nacogdoches, TX: Covenant Media Foundation, 2002.

———. "The Westminster Assembly and the Equity of the Judicial Law." No pages. Online: http://www.cmfnow.com/articles/pe170.htm.

———. "What is 'Theonomy?'" No pages. Online: http://www.cmfnow.com/articles/pe180.htm.

Bibliography

Bahnsen, Greg, and Kenneth L. Gentry. *House Divided: The Break-Up of Dispensational Theology.* Tyler, TX: Institute for Christian Economics, 1989.

Baillie, Robert. *A Dissuasive From the Errors of the Times.* London: 1646.

Ball, John. *A Treatise on the Covenant of Grace.* London: 1645.

Banks, Robert J. *Jesus and the Law in the Synoptic Tradition.* Cambridge: Cambridge University Press, 1975.

Barker, William S., and W. Robert Godfrey, editors. *Theonomy: A Reformed Critique.* Grand Rapids: Academie, 1990.

Baynes, Paul. *An entire commentary upon the whole Epistle of St. Paul to the Ephesians.* Edinburgh: James Nichol, 1866.

Bauer, W., W. F. Arndt, and F. W. Gingrich. *A Greek-English Lexicon of the New Testament and Other Early Christian Literature.* Chicago: University of Chicago, 1959.

Black, Henry Campbell. *Black's Law Dictionary.* 2nd ed. St. Paul: West Publishing Co., 1910.

Blass, Friedrich, Albert Debrunner, and Robert Walter Funk. *A Greek Grammar of the New Testament and Other Early Christian Literature.* Chicago: University of Chicago 1961.

The Book of Concord. No pages. Online: http://www.bookofconcord.org/augsburg defense/15_politicalorder.html.

Broadus, John A. *Commentary on the Gospel of Matthew.* Philadelphia: The American Baptist Publication Society, 1886.

Brown, Colin, editor. *New International Dictionary of New Testament Theology.* Grand Rapids: Zondervan, 1975.

Brown, Francis, S. R. Driver, and Charles A. Briggs, editors. *A Hebrew and English Lexicon of the Old Testament.* Oxford: Clarendon, 1972.

Brown, Harold O. J. *Heresies: The Image of Christ in the Mirror of Heresy and Orthodoxy from the Apostles to the Present.* Garden City, NY: Doubleday, 1984.

Brown, John. *Compendious View of Natural and Revealed Religion in Seven Books.* Edinburgh: Murray & Cochrane, 1796.

Bruce, A. B. *The Synoptic Gospels.* Edited by W. Robertson Nicoll. The Expositor's Greek Testament 1. New York: George H. Doran, n.d.

Bruce, F. F. *The Epistle to the Galatians: A Commentary on the Greek Text.* The New International Greek Testament Commentary. Grand Rapids: Eerdmans, 1982.

Bucer, Martin. *De Regno Christi.* Translated and edited by Wilhelm Pauck. In *Melancthon and Bucer.* Library of Christian Classics 19. London: SCM, 1969.

Bullinger, Heinrich. *The Decades of Henry Bullinger.* Translated by H. I. Edited by Thomas Hardgin. 4 vols. Cambridge: Cambridge University Press, 1849–52.

Burgess, Anthony. *The Magistrate's Commission From Heaven.* London: 1644.

———. *Vindiciae Legis, or a vindication of the morall law and the covenants, from the errors of Papists, Arminians, Socinians, and more especially Antinomians in XXX lectures preached at Laurence-Jury London.* London: 1647.

Calvin, John. *Commentaries on the Four Last Books of Moses.* Translated by Charles William Bingham. Grand Rapids: Baker, 1979.

———. *Commentary on Corinthians,* vol. 2. Online: http://www.ccel.org/ccel/calvin/calcom40.pdf.

———. *Commentary on Isaiah.* Translated by Rev. William Pringle. No pages. Online: http://www.ccel.org/c/calvin/comment2/is55-66.htm.

―――. *A Harmony of the Gospels: Matthew, Mark, and Luke*, vol. 1. Translated by A. W. Morrison. Grand Rapids: Eerdmans, 1975.

―――. *Institutes of the Christian Religion*. Translated by Henry Beveridge. Grand Rapids: Eerdmans, 1989.

―――. *Institutes of the Christian Religion*. 1539 edition. No pages. Online: http://www.ccel.org/ccel/calvin/institutes.ii.ix.html.

Carson, D. A. *Matthew: Chapters 1 through 12*. The Expositor's Bible Commentary. Grand Rapids: Zondervan, 1995.

―――. *The Sermon on the Mount: An Evangelical Exposition of Matthew 5-7*. Grand Rapids: Baker, 1978.

Cawdrey, Daniel, and Herbert Palmer. *Sabbatum Redivivum: Or the Christian Sabbath Vindicated*, London: 1645.

Coldwell, Chris. "The Westminster Assembly & the Judicial Law: A Chronological Compilation and Analysis. Part One: Chronology." In *The Confessional Presbyterian* 5 (2009) 3-55.

―――. "Whose Severity? Was George Gillespie the Author of Wholesome Severity Reconciled with Christian Liberty?" In *The Anonymous Writings of George Gillespie*. Dallas: Naphtali, 2001.

Cremeans, Charles Davis. *The Reception of Calvinist Thought in England*. Chicago: University of Illinois Press, 1949.

Davies, W. D. *The Setting of the Sermon on the Mount*. Cambridge: Cambridge University Press, 1964.

Davis, D. Clair. "A Challenge to Theonomy." In *Theonomy: A Reformed Critique*, edited by William S. Barker and W. Robert Godfrey. Grand Rapids: Academie, 1990.

Dickson, David, and George Sinclair. *Truth's Victory over Error or, the true principles of the Christian religion, stated and vindicated*. Edinburgh: John Reid, 1684.

Duncan, J. Ligon. "The Westminster Confession of Faith: A Theonomic Document?" No pages. Online: http://www.providencepca.com/essays/theonomy.html.

Edersheim, Alfred. *The Life and Times of Jesus the Messiah*. Grand Rapids: Eerdmans, 1971.

Fairbairn, P. *The Revelation of the Law in Scripture*. Grand Rapids: Zondervan, 1957.

Fee, Gordon D. *The First Epistle to the Corinthians*. New International Commentary on the New Testament. Grand Rapids: Eerdmans, 1987.

―――. *New Testament Exegesis: A Handbook for Students and Pastors*. 3rd ed. Louisville: Westminster, 2002.

Fee, Gordon D., and Douglas Stuart. *How to Read the Bible for All Its Worth*. Grand Rapids: Academie, 1982.

Ferguson, Sinclair. "An Assembly of Theonomists?" In *Theonomy: A Reformed Critique*, edited by William S. Barker and W. Robert Godfrey, 315-49. Grand Rapids: Academie, 1990.

Foulner, Martin A. *Theonomy and the Westminster Confession: An Annotated Sourcebook*. Edinburgh: Marpret, 1997.

Fowler, Paul B. *God's Law Free from Legalism: Critique of Theonomy in Christian Ethics*. Jackson, MS: Reformed Theological Seminary, 1985.

Fox, Everett. *The Five Books of Moses: A New Translation with Introductions, Commentary, and Notes*. The Schocken Bible 1. New York: Schocken, 1995.

Frame, John. "Machen's Warrior Children." No pages. Online: http://www.frame-poythress.org/frame_articles/2003Machen.htm.

Free Church of Scotland. "Theonomy and the Confession of Faith." No pages. Online: http://www.freechurch.org/pq1.html.

Friberg, Timothy, and Barbara Friberg. *Analytical New Testament: Greek Text Analysis*. Grand Rapids: Baker, 1981.

Ganoczy, Alexandre. *The Young Calvin*. Translated by David Foxgrover and Wade Provo. Philadelphia: Westminster, 1987.

Gentry, Kenneth L. *Covenantal Theonomy*. Nacogdoches, TX: Covenant Media Foundation, 2005.

―――. "Civil Sanctions in the New Testament." In Gary North, ed. *Theonomy: An Informed Response*, 135–63. Tyler, TX: I.C.E., 1991.

Gillespie, George. "Wholesome Severity Reconciled with Christian Liberty." 1645. No pages. Online: http://www.naphtali.com/articles/george-gillespie/wholesome-severity.

Godfrey, W. Robert. "Calvin and Theonomy." In *Theonomy: A Reformed Critique*, edited by William S. Barker and W. Robert Godfrey, 299–312. Grand Rapids: Academie, 1990.

Goodwin, Thomas. *The Works of Thomas Goodwin*, vol. 11. Edinburgh: Nichol, 1861.

Gordon, T. David. "Critique of Theonomy: A Taxonomy." *Westminster Theological Journal* 56 (1994) 23–43.

Gouge, William. *A Learned and Very Useful Commentary on the Whole Epistle to the Hebrews*. London: 1655.

Guelich, Robert A. *The Sermon on the Mount: A Foundation for Understanding*. Waco, TX: Word, 1982.

Halladay, William L. *A Concise Hebrew and Aramaic Lexicon of the Old Testament*. Leiden: Brill, 1971.

Harris, R. Laird. "Theonomy in Christian Ethics: A Review of Greg L. Bahnsen's Book." *Presbyterion: Covenant Seminary Review* 5 (1979) 1–15.

Hatch, E., and H. A. Redpath, editors. *A Concordance to the LXX and Other Greek Versions of the Old Testament*. 2 vols. Graz: Akademische Druck-u. Verlagsanstadt, 1954.

Hawkins, R. A. "Covenant Relations in the Sermon on the Mount." *Restoration Quarterly* 12 (1969) 1–9.

Hebrew Union College, Jewish Institute of Religion. "Comprehensive Aramaic Lexicon." No pages. Online: http://cal1.cn.huc.edu/aramaic_language.html.

Hendriksen, William. *Exposition of the Gospel according to Matthew*. New Testament Commentary. Grand Rapids: Baker, 1973.

Henry, Matthew. *Commentary on the Whole Bible, Genesis to Revelation*. Edited by Leslie F. Church. Grand Rapids: Zondervan, 1961.

Hodge, Charles. *Systematic Theology*, vol. 3. Grand Rapids: Eerdmans, 1940.

Hodge, Steven R. "An Exegetical Response to Bahnsen's Use of Matt. 5:17–19 in *Theonomy in Christian Ethics*." MTh thesis, Capital Bible Seminary, 1990.

Houghton, S. M., editor. *A Faith to Confess: The Baptist Confession of Faith of 1689*. Liverpool: Carey, 1975.

House, H. Wayne, and Thomas Ice. *Dominion Theology: Blessing or Curse?* Portland: Multnomah, 1988.

Institute for Christian Economics. No pages. Online: http://freebooks.entrewave.com/freebooks.

Isbell, Sherman. "The Divine Law of Political Israel Expired." No pages. Online: www.westminsterconfession.org/a-godly-society/the-divine-law-of-political-israel-expired-general-equity.php.

Jamieson, Robert, A. R. Fausset, and David Brown. *Commentary, Practical and Explanatory, on the Whole Bible*. Grand Rapids: Zondervan, 1976.

Jordan, James. "Calvinism and 'The Judicial Law of Moses'" (1978) No pages. Online: http://www.reformed.org/ethics/index.html?mainframe=/ethics/Jordan_judicial_laws_Moses.html.

Karlstadt, Andreas Rudolff-Bodenstein von. *The Essential Carlstadt: Fifteen Tracts*. Translated and edited by E. J. Furcha. Waterloo, ON: Herald, 1995.

Kevan, Ernest F. *The Moral Law; (God's Law)*. Jenkintown, PA: Sovereign Grace, 1963.

Kittel, Gerhardt, and Gerhard Fredrich, editors. *Theological Dictionary of the New Testament*. Translated by Geoffrey W. Bromiley. Grand Rapids: Eerdmans, 1960.

Kline, Meredith G. "Comments on an Old-New Error." Online: http://www.meredithkline.com/klines-works/articles-and-essays/comments-on-an-old-new-error/.

———. *The Structure of Biblical Authority*. Grand Rapids: Eerdmans, 1972.

Koehler, Ludwig, and Walter Baumgartner, editors. *The Hebrew and Aramaic Lexicon of the Old Testament*, vols. 2, 3, 4. Leiden: Brill, 1994–2000.

Lee, F. Nigel. "Are the Mosaic Laws for Today?" No pages. Online: http://www.dr-fnlee.org/docs4/atmlft/atmlft.pdf.

Liddell, Henry George, and Robert Scott. *A Greek-English Lexicon*. Revised by Henry Stuart Jones. Oxford: Clarendon, 1968.

Lloyd-Jones, D. Martyn. *Studies in the Sermon on the Mount*, vol. 1. Grand Rapids: Eerdmans, 1959.

Logan, Samuel T. "New England Puritans and the State," In *Theonomy: A Reformed Critique*, edited by William S. Barker and W. Robert Godfrey, 372–75. Grand Rapids: Academie, 1990.

Long, Gary D. *Biblical Law and Ethics: Absolute and Covenantal*. Perspectives: Studies in Baptist Thought. Rochester, NY: Backus, 1981.

Longenecker, Richard. *Galatians*. Word Biblical Commentary. Dallas: Word, 1990.

Luce, A. A. *Teach Yourself Logic*. London: English University Press, 1958.

Ljungman, Henrik. *Das Gesetz Erfullen, Matt5,17 ff und 3,15 untersucht*. Lund: Gleerup, 1954.

Luther, Martin. "Against the Heavenly Prophets." In *Luther's Works*, vol. 40. Translated by Bernhard Ehrling, edited by Conrad Bergendhoff, 79–225. Philadelphia: Fortress, 1958.

Meyer, H. A. W. *Critical and Exegetical Hand-book to the Gospel of Mathew*. Translated by Peter Christie. Rev. and ed. by Frederick Crosbie and William Stewart. Meyer's Commentary on the New Testament. New York: Funk & Wagnalls, 1890.

Moo, Douglas J. "'Law,' 'Works of Law,' and 'Legalism' in Paul." *Westminster Theological Journal* 45 (1983) 73–100.

Moule, C. F. D. "Fulfillment Words in the New Testament: Use and Abuse." *New Testament Studies* 14 (1968) 293–320.

Murray, John. *Principles of Conduct: Aspects of Biblical Ethics*. Grand Rapids: Eerdmans, 1978.

North, Gary. *Hierarchy and Dominion*. Harrisonburg, VA: Dominion Educational Ministries, 2004.

———. *The Sinai Strategy*. Tyler, TX: Institute for Christian Economics, 1986.

———. editor. *Theonomy: An Informed Response*. Tyler, TX: Institute for Christian Economics, 1991.

North, Gary, and Gary DeMar. *Christian Reconstruction: What It Is, What It Isn't*. Tyler, TX: Institute for Christian Economics, 1991.

Olson, Walter. "Invitation to a Stoning: Getting Cozy with Theocrats." No pages. Online: http://www.indegayforum.org/articles/olson16.html.

Oss, Douglas A. "The Influence of Hermeneutical Frameworks on the Theonomy Debate." *Westminster Theological Journal* 51 (1989) 227–58.

Pater, Calvin Augustine. *Karlstadt as the Father of the Baptist Movements: The Emergence of Lay Protestantism*. Toronto: University of Toronto Press, 1984.

Plumptre, E. H. *The Gospel According to St. Matthew, St. Mark and St. Luke*. Edited by Charles John Ellicot. A Bible Commentary for Bible Students. London: Cassel, [192-?].

Poythress, Vern S. "Effects of Interpretive Frameworks on the Application of Old Testament Law." In *Theonomy: A Reformed Critique*, edited by William S. Barker and W. Robert Godfrey, 103–23. Grand Rapids: Academie, 1990.

———. *The Shadow of Christ in the Law of Moses*. Brentwood, TN: Wolgemuth & Hyatt, 1991.

Richard, Guy M. "*In Translatiōne*: Samuel Rutherford: *Examen Arminianismi*, Chapter 19: Of the Civil Magistrate." *Confessional Presbyterian* 4 (2008) 270.

Ridderbos, Herman N. *Matthew*. The Bible Student's Commentary. Grand Rapids: Zondervan, 1987.

———. *When the Time Had Fully Come*. Grand Rapids: Eerdmans, 1957.

Robertson, A. T. *A Grammar of the Greek New Testament in Light of Historical Research*. Edited by George Doran. New York: Hodder & Stoughton, 1919.

Robinson, John A. T. *Redating the New Testament*. London: SCM, 1976.

Ross, Philip S. *From the Finger of God: The Biblical and Theological Basis for the Threefold Division of the Law*. Fearn: Christian Focus, 2010.

Rushdoony, R. J. *Institutes of Biblical Law*. Nutley, NJ: Craig, 1973.

———. *Law and Society: Institutes of Biblical Law*, vol. 2. Vallecito, CA: Ross House, 1982.

Rutherford, Samuel. *Divine Right of Church Government*. London: 1646

———. *A Free Disputation Against Pretended Liberty of Conscience*. London: 1649.

The Savoy Declaration of Faith and Order 1658. No pages. Online: http://www.reformed.org/documents/Savoy_Declaration.

Sawyer, Jack. "Moses and the Magistrate." MTh diss., Westminster Theological Seminary, 1986.

Shaw, Robert. *An Exposition of the Confession of Faith of the Westminster Assembly of Divines*. Philadelphia: Presbyterian Board of Publication, 1846.

Strevel, Christopher B. "Theonomic Precedent in the Theology of John Calvin." In *The Standard Bearer: A Festschrift for Greg L. Bahnsen*, edited by Steven M. Schlissel, 319–68. Nacogdoches, TX: 2004.

Troxel, A. Craig, and Peter J. Wallace. "Men in Combat over the Civil Law: General Equity in WCF 19:4." *Westminster Theological Journal* 64 (2002), 307–18.

Van Dixhoorn, Chad. "Reforming the Reformation: Theological Debate at the Westminster Assembly, 1643–1652." PhD diss., University of Cambridge, 2004.

Van Til, Cornelius. *Christian Theistic Ethics*. Philadelphia: Westminster Theological Seminary, 1958.

Vos, Geerhardus. *Biblical Theology*. Grand Rapids: Eerdmans, 1975.
Wenham, David. "Jesus and the Law." *Themelios* 4 (1979) 92–96.
Winzer, Matthew. "The Westminster Assembly & the Judicial Law: A Chronological Compilation and Analysis. Part Two: Analysis." *The Confessional Presbyterian* 5 (2009) 56–88.
Witsius, Herman. *The Economy of the Covenants between God and Man: Comprehending a Complete Body of Divinity*. Utrecht: 1693. Reprint, Escondido, CA: den Dulk Christian Foundation, 1990.
Young, Edward J. *The Book of Isaiah*, vol. 3. Grand Rapids: Eerdmans, 1972.

General Index

Adam, 11, 32, 146, 163, 167
alla (but), 42–43, 57, 60–62, 68–69, 88, 96, 103, 131
Antiochus Epipanes, 40–41, 47, 54
apo (from), 111, 112
Arian controversy, 70

bebiaoo (establish), 75
Brownism, 157

covenant theology, 146

English Civil War, 149
exegesis, 15,

general equity, 2, 6, 12–14, 23–24, 26, 28, 31–32, 56, 145–50, 152, 154, 160–65, 169–70, 172–73, 175–78, 185, 192
genetai (come to pass), 119–23

hermeneutics, 5–6

istemi (confirm), 75, 84, 88

kataluo (destroy/annul), 41–42, 59, 87
King James Version, 59–60

"the law or the prophets," 44–58, 110–11

mala, 70–71, 74–75, 88, 102
Moral Law/Decalogue/Ten Commandments, 4, 8–9, 10–14, 26, 30–32, 56, 63–64, 76, 121, 134, 136–38, 143–49, 151, 156, 159, 161–63, 165–71,177–80
Mosaic civil laws/Mosaic judicial laws, 1–3, 5, 7–13, 18, 21, 23–26, 29, 31–35, 64, 137, 139–41, 143–46, 148, 150, 152, 154, 156, 158, 164, 170–71, 173, 176, 179
Mosaic Covenant/Old Covenant/ Sinaitic Covenant, 2, 5, 9–11, 17, 19–20, 22, 24–25, 30, 32, 35, 47–48, 51, 53–60, 82, 87, 98, 101, 103, 110, 111, 118–22, 124, 125, 128, 131, 156–57, 170
Moses and the Magistrate, 8, 141, 187, 192

Old Covenant
Old London Confession, 2
on me (never, certainly not), 109
Oxford English Dictionary, 161, 168

panta (all things, everything), 116–19
parelthe (disappear) 109–10
pleroo (fill/fulfill/complete), 43, 57, 59–60, 62, 64–83, 85, 88–89, 91–93, 95–97, 99–103, 120, 131
    as proposed translation (confirm), 43, 60, 62, 64–86, 88, 92–94

Savoy Declaration of Faith, 2, 148, 192
Septuagint/LXX, 66, 72–73, 75–77, 78, 84, 91, 95, 190
Sojourners (magazine), 2
Solemn League and Covenant, 149

Tea Party, 3
Theonomy, 1–7, 9, 11, 28–29, 31–37, 39, 189–90, 183, 185, 187, 192
  and later Reformed Opinion, 177, 179, 181–82
  and Matthew, 5, 44, 46, 48–51, 53–56, 58, 60–68, 71–73, 76–80, 84–85, 89–90, 92–93, 98–103, 105–6, 108–10, 113–21, 124, 126, 129, 132
  and the Westminster Confession of Faith, 12–25, 27 133, 135, 137–39, 141, 143, 145, 147–57, 159, 161, 163, 165–67, 169, 171, 173–77

Theonomy debate, 1, 3–4, 7, 15, 31, 34, 192
Theonomy in Christian Ethics, 1, 3, 7, 15, 18, 29, 147, 187, 189–90

Westminster Confession of Faith (WCF), 1–3, 7, 10–13, 18, 133, 147, 167, 176–78, 189, 192
Westminster Divines, 2, 7, 9–12, 14, 23–24, 133, 146, 148, 151–52, 163, 165, 173–74, 177, 182

Names Index

Avis, P. D. L., 8, 139, 141, 187

Bahnsen, David, 36, 187
Bahnsen, Greg, 2–9, 12–24, 26–29,
    31–37, 39, 41–53, 56–110,
    112–22, 124–33, 138–39,
    141, 144, 147, 149, 151–54,
    156–62, 164–67, 169, 171,
    173–78, 181–85, 187–88,
    190, 192
Baillie, Robert, 157–58, 171, 188
Ball, John 10, 35, 146–47, 188
Banks, Robert J., 96, 188
Barker, William S., 6, 188–92
Baynes, Paul, 146, 160, 188
Bauer, W., W. F. Arndt, and F. W.
    Gingrich (BAGD), 33, 50,
    57–59, 61, 65–67, 72, 76–77,
    79, 81–84, 89, 103, 109–10,
    116, 118, 188
Bereshith, Rabbi, 112
Beza, Theodore, 144–45
Black, Henry Campbell, 165, 188
Blass, Friedrich, Albert Debrunner,
    and Robert Walter Funk
    (BDF), 49, 105, 188
Briggs, Charles A., 74, 188
Broadus, John A., 105, 188
Brown, Francis, 74, 188
Brown, Harold O. J., 70, 188
Brown, John, 179, 188
Bruce, A. B., 102, 188
Bruce, F. F., 59, 188
Bucer, Martin, 137–39, 188
Bullinger, Heinreich, 144, 188

Burgess, Anthony, 146, 158, 165,
    167, 172–74, 188

Calvin, John, 1–3, 5–9, 12–14, 16,
    23–24, 27, 29, 62–64, 133,
    136–39, 141–47, 150, 156,
    161, 163, 166–67, 176–77,
    188, 190, 192
Carlstadt, Andreas, 139–41, 155,
    191
Carson, D. A., 37, 62, 71, 83, 105–6,
    108, 124, 188
Cawdrey, Daniel, 146, 152, 165–67,
    169–71, 189
Coldwell, Chris, 152–53, 162, 189

Dalman, Gustav, 71, 82
DeMar, Gary, 4, 32, 187, 192
Driver, S. R., 74, 188
Duncan, J. Ligon, 176, 189

Fee, Gordon D., 50, 55, 189
Ferguson, Sinclair, 6, 10, 147–54,
    157–58, 160–62, 164–65,
    171–76, 189
Foulner, Martin, 156, 189
Fowler, Paul B., 29, 67–70, 189
Frame, John, 6, 144, 189

Gentry, Kenneth L., 6, 8, 19, 21,
    46, 53–56, 67, 103, 147, 152,
    188, 190
Gillespie, George, 14, 152–54,
    157–58, 171, 189, 190
Godfrey, W. Robert, 6, 143, 188–92
Goodwin, Thomas, 171, 190

Names Index

Gordon, T. David, 34, 51, 53, 55–56, 67, 103, 108, 126, 190
Gouge, William, 158–59, 162, 190
Guelich, Robert A., 51, 98, 190

Hatch, E., 75, 91, 190
Hawkins, R. A., 60, 190
Hendriksen, William, 89–90, 190
Hodge, Charles, 180–81, 190
Hodge, Steven R., 44, 49, 51–52, 60, 62, 76–80, 84–85, 91–92, 99, 104, 117–18, 190
House H. Wayne, 29, 72, 190

Ice, Thomas, 29, 72, 190
Isbell, Sherman, 145, 162–63, 168

Josephus, 112

Karlstadt, Andreas, Rudolff Bodelstein von. *See* Carlstadt, Andreas
Kevan, Ernest F., 99, 150, 191
Kline, Meredith G., 1–3, 176, 191
Koehler, 74, 84, 191

Lee, F. Nigel, 39, 191
Ljungman, Henrik, 71, 82, 191

Marshall, Donald, 185
Meyer, H. A. W., 46, 49, 191
Milgaard, David, 185
Moule, C. F. D. 71–72, 98, 191
Müntzer, Thomas, 139, 141
Murray, John, 62–64, 181–82, 191

North, Gary, 3–4, 7, 32, 190–92

Olson, Walter, 3, 27, 192
Oss, Douglas A., 192

Palmer, Herbert, 152, 165–67, 169–71, 189
Philo, 113
Poythress, Vern S., 5, 69, 76–83, 85–86, 88, 92–95, 192

Redpath, H. A., 75, 91, 190
Ridderbos, Herman N., 62, 65, 84–85, 192
Ross, Philip S., 8, 66, 74, 192
Rushdoony, Rousas J., 7, 21, 24–26, 111, 137, 147, 192
Rutherford, Samuel, 14, 154–58, 171–72, 174, 177, 192

Shaw, Robert, 180, 192
Shepherd, Norman, 4–5
Spurgeon, Charles, 62
Strevel, Christopher B., 6, 29, 143, 149, 192

Tillich, Paul, 1
Troxel, A. Craig, 161, 192
Truscott, Steven, 185

Van Dixhoorn, Chad, 158, 167, 192
Van Til, Cornelius, 1, 192

Wallace, Peter J., 161, 192
Wenham, David, 96–97, 193
Windisch, Hans, 62
Winzer, Matthew, 23, 193
Witsius, Herman, 178–79, 193

Scripture Index

OLD TESTAMENT

Genesis
15:6	78
25:24	66, 102
49:10	9, 29, 147, 172, 178

Exodus
20:4	102, 159

Leviticus
18:5	45

Numbers
7:88	77
30:14	75
35:30	159, 184

Deuteronomy
5	4
18:15	90, 102
19:15	31, 184–85
22:22	25
23:20	25
27:26	75

Judges
17	77

Ruth
4:7	75

1 Samuel
20:3	77

1 Kings
1:14	73–77, 81

2 Chronicles
13:9	77

Psalms
2:10–12	32
119:105	130, 40, 124
110:1	4, 122

Proverbs
30:6	27

Ecclesiastes
9:3	95

Song of Solomon
5:14	77

Isaiah
51:4–8	40

Jeremiah
31, 48, 98, 102, 113, 125, 170

Hosea
4:14	25

~

APOCRYPHA

Tobit
1:6	112

Sirach

45	77
48:1	40

2 Maccabees

2:19–22	41

4 Maccabees

12:14	77

NEW TESTAMENT

Matthew

1:22	91, 120
3:7	37
4:4	30
3:15	99–100
5:3–12	47
5:17	6, 15–16, 19–22, 28–29, 34–37, 42–104, 106–7, 109, 120, 122, 129–30, 140, 152, 158, 165, 172–73, 178–79, 187
5:17–18	29–30
5:17–19	21, 35, 158, 187, 190
5:17–20	35, 37
5:18	22, 29, 105–28
5:19–20	27, 64, 129–32
5:21–48	111
5:33–37	123
6:24	49
6:44	31
7:12	44–45, 53
7:23	31
7:28	37
10:1	130
10:11	14, 37, 50
10:34	60–62
11:4	46
11:13	53, 102–3
12:3	30
19:1–6	25
22:40	45, 53
26:54	120
26:56	89
28:19	31

Mark

1:44	30
2:25–28	30
3:35	31
12:31	32

Luke

1:6	30
1:32	32
3:5	95
5:27–32	37
6:1–5	37
6:5–11	37
10:1	130
16:16	44, 53
16:17	109–10
16:29	31, 44
22:20	102
24:44	44, 97

John

1:21	102
2:13–25	37
6:53	107
6:63	107
6:66	37
7:19	23, 30
8:1–11	34
8:7	183
8:13	40, 185
8:13–17	185
8:46	185
14:27	61

Acts

3:22	102
7:53	32
13:15	44
23:1–5	32

Romans

1:32	8
2:25	27, 59
3:21	44
6:12–19	30
7:6	34
7:12	10
13:1–7	28, 32
13:8	100
14	25
15:23	79

1 Corinthians

5:1–12	34
7:19	30
9:7–10	31
9:9–11	31
14:34	31

2 Corinthians

1:23	123
5:1	58
5:21	99
6:4	31
7:21	30

Galatians

2:9	10
2:18	58, 59, 87
2:21	45
3:15	101
3:19	102
5:13–18	30
5:13–26	34
5:18	34

Ephesians

5:11	30
5:17	30

1 Timothy

1:9–11	32
5:19	31, 185
6:11	30
6:14	30

2 Timothy

2:19	30
3:16	5, 10, 30

Hebrews

1:8	9, 32
7:12	29, 58–59, 122, 127
8:13	8
10:26–29	31

James

2:8–10	31
2:11	59
2:14–26	78
2:21	78
2:23	78–79
3:18	31
4:11	31

1 John

2:17	31
2:27	118
3:4	30

2 John

6	31

1 Peter

1:1	10
2:13	9, 29, 147, 172–73, 178
2:17	31
4:17	31

2 Peter

2:21	30
3:10	114

Revelation

3:2	79–80

www.ingramcontent.com/pod-product-compliance
Lightning Source LLC
Chambersburg PA
CBHW060608230426

43670CB00011B/2027